© Carlisle Press 2015 All Rights Reserved

All rights reserved. No portion of this book may be reproduced by any means, electronic or mechanical, including photocopying, recording, or by any information storage retrieval system, without written permission of the copyright owner, except for the inclusion of brief quotations for a review.

ISBN: 978-1-933753-37-9

Disclaimer: *This book is not a medical reference. The author and publishers cannot be held responsible for any harmful reactions to the suggestions, recommendations, hints, recipes, tips, or anything contained herein. The author of this book does not profess to be an expert or professional. This book is not intended to take the place of professional medical advice from your doctor or qualified persons. Always consult your physician with medical questions and research carefully before using herbs in any form.*

Design by Rosetta Mullet and Marlene Hershberger
Printed in the USA by Carlisle Printing of Walnut Creek

2673 Township Road 421
Sugarcreek, Ohio 44681

Carlisle Press
WALNUT CREEK

phone | 800.852.4482

Dedication

To David and Aric Schlabach

Mom, you nurtured my earliest herb garden dreams. You generously allowed me to fill the spaces between the retaining walls with sage and cilantro when petunias might have been prettier! Dad, you set up the greenhouse when my herb growing grew beyond the hobby stage. I'm grateful to have inherited both of your green thumbs.

Gracia's Herbs

Acknowledgments

Thanks to all my gardening friends, and especially, readers of "Gracia's Garden" in *Keepers at Home*. Your friendly feedback and enthusiasm for herbs motivated me to grow more plants and write more pieces. Thank you, Sharon, for urging me to compile the articles as a book. Now you no longer need your photocopies in a binder! Thank you, Susan and daughters. You've expanded the possibilities to help many others discover the wonderful world of herbs.

Contents

SECTION I   Planning Your Herb Garden 3
   Visit My Garden! 4
   Herbs for All Uses. 9
   Plotting Your Garden 16
   Starting Herbs by Seed. 21
   It's Planting Time 24
   Herbs Everywhere. 29
   Grow a Crop of Herb Gardeners. 34

SECTION II   Getting to Know Herbs .39
   Anise Hyssop 40
   Basil. 43
   Borage 47
   Calendula 50
   Catnip 54
   Chamomile 58
   Chives. 62
   Comfrey. 67
   Coriander or Cilantro 72
   Dill 76
   Echinacea 81
   Fennel. 85
   Garlic 88
   Horseradish 99
   Lavender. 103

Lemony Herbs 110
Lovage 117
Mint 121
Oregano 127
Parsley 130
Rosemary 135
Sage 138
Savory 143
Scented Geraniums 146
Sweet Bay 152
Sweet Marjoram 156
Thyme 158

SECTION III   **Harvesting Time** 163
Prime for Picking 164
Home-Dried Herbs 169
Putting Weeds to Work 175
Capturing the Fun of Fragrance 182

SECTION IV   **Herbs in the Kitchen** 191
Cooking with Herbs 192
Herbal Mixes 196
Herbs in the Bakery 200
Herbal Vinegars 207
Tomatoes + Herbs = Delicious 211
Beyond Lettuce 215
Please Eat the Petals 219
A Dash of Warmth 224

SECTION V   **A Season for Herbs** 229
Herbal Harbingers of Spring 230
A Summer Agenda 233
Fall Transitions 236
Winter Herbs 238

Resources 241
For Further Reading 244
Index 245

My doctrine shall drop as the rain, my speech shall distil as the dew, as the small rain upon the tender herb, and as the showers upon the grass.

DEUTERONOMY 32:2

SECTION 1

PLANNING YOUR
Herb Garden

Sweet basil
Thyme

"'Planning is half the fun', the old adage goes. And that goes for herb gardens, too. How thrilling—a dream, a plan, a reality! Perhaps you plan a garden dedicated to herbs, or you want a smaller herb border, or simply a space in the vegetable garden for herbs. I share some of my own experiences to help make those decisions easier."

—*Gracia*

Visit My Garden!

"I'd like to grow some herbs," a friend began wistfully, "but I don't know how to use them!" Really, herb gardening is not some mystical science for a few who know how. Herbs are either annuals or perennials, and are not more difficult to grow than the tomatoes in your garden or irises in your rock garden. In fact, most herbs do not require as much care as tomatoes or irises.

Many herbs do have popular uses for cooking or for medicine. But there's no need to let your unfamiliarity with these uses deter you from planting your dream herb garden. These skills can be developed once you're familiar with your plants, their growing habits, taste, and texture.

Once you've planted some herbs, the first benefit you'll receive is enjoying them outdoors, in the herb garden, admiring the plant's color, shape, fragrance, or blossoms. That's fairly effortless, isn't it?!

YOU'RE INVITED

Would you like to join me for a walk through my herb garden? Just a minute. Before we begin, I'll grab my gathering basket and plant shears. We'll gather some goods for tea afterwards. Here we go! Are you ready to exercise your senses, enjoying as we go?

A FEAST FOR THE EYES

As we near the herb garden, here's a good overall view. What a variety of colors, sizes, and shapes! Did you expect all herbs to be the same bland green? Certainly not!

You'll notice the garden has a sort of nine-patch layout. Teas are in one square, kitchen herbs in another, everlastings, fragrants, and medicinals in others with paths in between each. Thick layers of bark or leaf mulch keep the paths weed-free (or nearly so).

The tall plants—lovage, dill, fennel, and anise hyssop—stand out and seem to greet us eye to eye. Most of the plants are around knee height, filling their spot contentedly. Mint, lavender, basil, and tarragon are among these middle-sized herbs. The short, but important, creeping plants such as thyme, oregano, and marjoram spill over into the empty spots left by the taller plants. These variations in size help create an interesting, balanced look.

HERBAL RAINBOW

A rainbow of vibrant colors splashed throughout the garden enthralls us! Do you see the glowing red of bee balm? Evidently, we're not the only ones to notice it, for a hummingbird flits busily from one tubular flower to the next. We'll wait until it is done, then I'll pop a few flowers into the basket to give our tea a pinkish hue.

Warm shades of orange and yellow are seen in the calendulas bordering the medicinal block. Tall tansy's bright yellow, button-like flowers command a closer look.

Green flowers are rare, but the flower stalks of rue do have a yellowish-green tinge, as do dill's newly opening umbels. It's

VISIT MY GARDEN!

impossible to walk past dill without plucking a leaf to nibble!

The blue flowers capture our hearts! Five-petaled flax shyly lifts its soft, sapphire-blue petals to the sun. The unique star-shaped blossoms of borage add a cheery splash of azure. Did you know they're edible? Snip, snip. Try one! It tastes like a cucumber, doesn't it?!

A tall plant with abundant purple column flowers beckons us next. It's anise hyssop, a tasty tea plant with a licorice-like flavor. A bunch goes into the basket. Obviously, it's a popular plant. Bees buzz around it and—oh!—there's even a beautiful swallowtail butterfly. Strolling in the herb garden gives us renewed appreciation for God's creation, doesn't it?

Shades of lavender and pink adorn echinacea, chives, and sage. Striking clary sage, big and bold, thrusts its flower spikes skyward. Ah, the humming-bird is there now!

After absorbing all these colors, let's relax our eyes a bit by focusing on feverfew's cheery white blossoms. Chamomile nearby also boasts a multitude of flowers, white with a sunny yellow center.

Now, are we done checking out the colors? Not quite. Do you see plants with colorful *leaves?* Purple sage and bronze fennel have purplish hues, and golden oregano is a chartreuse mass. Opal basil, however, surpasses them all with deep reddish-purple foliage. Isn't it attractive?

Take a glance over the entire garden. Scattered throughout are plants with speckled or striped leaves of two or more colors. I love variegated plants! Most herbs have variegated forms—lemon thyme is green and white, as is pine-apple mint. 'Doone Valley' thyme and ginger mint are dark green spattered with yellow. Golden sage is mottled with two shades of green and 'Tricolor' sage has a green background streaked with pink and white. The variegated plants are surely eye-catching, aren't they?

JUST PLAIN GREEN?

Many herb plants are just plain green, but that doesn't mean they're just plain boring! When looking observantly, you'll notice that

L-R: Silver thyme, rosemary, sweet basil, common oregano

there are many shades of green in different textures. From catnip's woolly grayish green to dill's feathery dark green and sage's pebbly dusty green, each green plant is fascinating in itself, adding variation and depth.

Among the green plants, lemon balm and flat leaf parsley both have such naturally well-balanced shapes and lush foliage. Can you see why I like them? Lift a leaf carefully on the parsley. If you're lucky, you might see a black swallowtail caterpillar munching away.

FRAGRANT DELIGHTS

Now our noses detect a delightful whiff of—what is it?—lavender! When the plant is sun-warmed, it releases its scent without even being touched! Planting lavender along a heat-absorbing body such as a stone walk, retaining wall, or brick house is ideal.

We pause a while, savoring the enchanting fragrance. Do you notice the different kinds of lavender? English lavender, the common favorite, is loaded with blossoms. The named varieties, 'Lady', 'Munstead', and 'Hidcote' are slightly more compact with blue, blue flowers. 'Provence' is not the showiest (it has very pale flowers), but it is by far the most fragrant.

Although we could enjoy lavender for awhile longer, let's move on to the scented geraniums around the old stone wall. Like the common bedding geraniums, these are annuals unless brought indoors in winter. The flowers, as you can see, are pretty pinks or lavenders, but tiny. The fragrance is huge though! Rub a leaf to experience the perfumes: rose, coconut, lemon, spice, citronella, apple, and more!

Next is rosemary, another aromatic jewel. Each leaf is so richly infused with the fragrant oils that it feels slightly sticky when handled. Its clean, piney scent lingers on our fingers as we admire the shapely plants. They respond well to trimming and can be trained to tree-like or pyramidal figures. Can you tell that this is another of my favorites?

TASTE BUD TANTALIZERS

Here we are at the kitchen herbs, surrounded by plants that cannot be fully discovered unless tasted! Don't be afraid to pluck and nibble!

Let's start with "lemony" herbs—lemon balm, lemon thyme, and lemon basil. Mmm, genuine citrus flavor. A handful of lemon balm goes into the basket for our upcoming teatime.

Besides lemon basil, do you see the many other basils? What a variety! Tall, bushy, ruffly, smooth, green, opal—all are basils, but not all are the same! Their flavors range from the sweet of sweet basil to the spicy of 'Siam Queen'.

Oh, try this bit of French tarragon. Its sweet licorice flavor has a cooling effect on your tongue. Do you feel the slightly tingling sensation? Unusual, isn't it?

Pineapple sage is next. This warm-climate sage is treated like an annual here in Zone 6. I like these fruity leaves, hinting of Hawaii. Well, here's our friend hummingbird once more, probing the bright red flowers!

Now, close your eyes for a taste test with herbs that have copycat flavors! Here we go on number one! "Cucumber!" Right! It's actually salad burnet! Like borage, it tastes just like a fresh cuke, but has smooth leaves suitable for salads.

Second test. "Hmm, tastes like celery." Good! It's lovage.

Now, a harder one. It's a mint, but can you detect its distinctive variation? "Tastes like a peppermint patty, I think." Very good! It's chocolate mint!

Talking of tea, let's amble over to the mint beds. Did you expect to see so many?! Among them are citrusy lime, orange and grapefruit mints, fruity apple and pineapple mints, intriguing banana mint with a creamy, tropical twist, spicy ginger mint, and the favorite peppermint and spearmint. Did you think some of these would end up in the basket to round out our tea "collection?" No, we'll pick the most flavorful—Swiss mint! One nibble and you'll immediately understand why I prefer this one—genuine, robust mintiness with a clarity of sweetness.

Well, we've covered most of the herb garden and it's time to relax with a cup of tea. Do you choose Swiss mint with a touch of lemon or a touch of licorice? Of course, we'll sweeten it with a fresh leaf or two from the potted stevia on the patio, and tint it a rosy pink with bee balm petals. They're neutral in taste.

Hopefully, you can drop in again sometime! In the meantime, may you enjoy your very own herbs! Thanks for coming!

Herbs for All Uses

Having a well-rounded herb garden is within the reach of any interested gardener. A well-rounded selection of plants lends itself to a wide variety of uses: flavoring foods, brewing teas, stocking a safe medicine cabinet, and simply providing enjoyment for the senses.

Growing herbs and flowers (and vegetables, too) is not only enjoyable to the main gardener, but also benefits others. Children, especially, can learn by observing the process of planting, growing, and harvesting. Herbs provide opportunity for creativity and experimenting, with minimal cost. They also inspire fascination and thankfulness for God's plant world.

This collection of three dozen herbs is categorized by uses into groups of six. Depending on gardening space and your personal interests and needs, you might want to grow one, or several, or all categories. If you plan to expand your gardening area, plan the layout accordingly to accommodate future additions.

Key

	Tall	24 inches or taller	A	Annual
	Medium	10 to 24 inches	P	Perennial
	Creeper	Up to 10 inches	B	Biennial

Kitchen Herbs I

Basil	A	Medium
Chives	P	Medium
Dill	A	Tall
Oregano, Greek	P	Creeper
Parsley	B	Medium
Thyme	P	Creeper

Sweet basil

This group contains the basic, must-have kitchen herbs. The annuals can be planted in the garden; the perennials can have their designated place too. Or, have an herb bed close to your kitchen door for quick access when you need some herbs while cooking.

It's handy to have lots of fresh **basil** all summer long for flavoring tomato dishes and for use in canning. Basil adds zest to tomato soups, pizza sauce, salsa, and ketchup. Sweet basil remains the standby for cooking.

Chives, the ever faithful onion-flavored perennial, is easily divided. Its lovely, purple globe-like flowers can be dried. Hang a bunch somewhere in the kitchen for a touch of summer color.

Gracia's Herbs

Dill, whose name brings images of pickles, dips, stuffed eggs, and vinegars. 'Mammoth' dill is widely grown, but 'Dukat' is a variety that deserves more recognition. It has higher oil content, which means richer dill flavor! I highly recommend 'Dukat' for pickles.

Greek oregano is tasty in cooking and pretty in the herb garden, with fuzzy dark-green leaves and a slightly rambling, happy-go-lucky habit. Regular oregano is nearly tasteless in comparison to Greek oregano.

Parsley is another kitchen essential, with its major role in flavoring many foods from potatoes to noodles, and soups to tomato sauces. Curly parsley is often used fresh as a garnish. Nearly all of the curly parsley served in restaurants is thrown away, which is a shame because it is so high in zinc and other minerals. Flat leaf, or Italian, parsley is my favorite for cooking.

Our last herb in this group is **thyme,** charming in form with woody stems and perky upright sprigs. It creeps along, attracting bees with its tiny flowers in summer. It has an intense flavor all its own.

Kitchen Herbs II

Caraway	B	
Fennel	A	
Lovage	P	
Marjoram	P	
Rosemary	P	
Sage	P	

Rosemary

To complement the basic kitchen herbs and round out a more complete range of flavors, consider this group of herbs.

Caraway is grown for its flavorful seeds, often added to whole-grain breads, especially rye. My family likes them sprinkled on pizza. Being a biennial, the seeds will be produced in the plant's second year.

Fennel looks like dill, being tall with similar foliage, but it doesn't taste like dill! Instead, it has a sweet anise flavor. Both the leaves and seeds can be eaten.

Lovage, in the celery family, is a versatile herb. It has more leaves than stalks, looking like a bushy celery plant. The leaves can be used fresh or dried to add celery flavor to soups, dressing, and other main dishes. When chopped and used in foods, the stalks make a good celery substitute.

A low-growing, creeping herb is **marjoram.** It's a good filler for bare corners in the herb garden. Being a rather slow grower, it won't spread out of control. My favorite marjoram is the variegated variety, whose green and white leaves add a splash of interest. In taste, marjoram is similar to oregano.

Rosemary is known for its minty, pine flavor, good fresh or dried. **Sage** and sausage make a popular pair.

Kitchen Herbs III		
Anise	B	
Borage	A	
Nigella	A	
Salad Burnet	P	
Summer Savory	A	
Tarragon, French	P	

Nigella seeds

Here's a group that offers some advantages, both in taste and in growing. These plants' flavors range from licorice to cucumber to black pepper. Their plant shapes, leaves, and flowers are quite varied too.

Anise is a biennial, producing seed in its second year. These licorice-flavored seeds are harvested for use in cooking. They're best used ground or crushed.

Borage and **salad burnet** both share an unusual cucumber flavor. However, the similarity stops there. Borage is a tall, gangly plant with fuzzy leaves. Its edible, brilliant blue flowers are fun to toss into salads or float on top of drinks, being in a perfect star shape! Salad burnet has smooth, soft leaves which can be clipped and used with other salad greens.

Nigella, also known as love-in-a-mist, is a plant which makes one take a second look. Its light, feathery foliage surrounds blue flowers atop future seedpods. After bloom, the seedpods become dry and papery. Open the pod to find many little black seeds, which can be used atop bread loaves or biscuits.

Summer savory, with its peppery flavor, is often used to flavor meats, beans, and other main dishes. I've also dried entire plants when in bloom (attractive with dark foliage and pink flowers) and used them in arrangements. Another licorice-flavored plant, **tarragon,** is a pretty plant with smooth, slender green leaves and a mounded shape. The leaves are loaded with rich licorice flavor.

Teas		
Anise Hyssop	P	
Catnip	P	
Chamomile	A	
Lemon Balm	P	
Mint, Spearmint	P	
Peppermint	P	
Pennyroyal	A	

Mint, rosemary

Here's a collection of teas, both for enjoyment and tonic, with a wide range of flavors. All are easy to grow!

Anise hyssop rates high on my favorites list. For one thing, it takes almost no care, and it's an attractive plant, too. Its anise-like flavor makes it versatile in tea blends. Bees love its purple flowers.

Catnip, woolly and gray green, is a mint that soothes the stomach. The tea's "green" flavor is improved by adding honey. For a fruity, apple-pineapple tea, **chamomile** is the pick. It's an annual but liberally self-sows. Cheery, daisy-type flowers brighten the tea patch. **Lemon balm,** also known as melissa, brings in a citrus twist to this group.

Of course the mints, **peppermint** and **spearmint,** are the all-time favorites. **Pennyroyal,** an annual, possesses an intense, minty flavor. Its dense, bushy form makes it an excellent border plant.

HERBS FOR ALL USES |13|

Medicinals	
Aloe Vera	Houseplant
Calendula	A
Comfrey	P
Echinacea	P
Garlic	A
Goldenseal	P

Echinacea

If growing your own medicine cabinet appeals to you rather than resorting to a lot of chemical and drug remedies, this list is a good choice. Many of the other herbs covered in this article have similar qualities, but the plants grouped here are known primarily for their medicinal use. Of course, detailed medicinal analysis lies beyond the scope of this writing, so this is a mere introduction.

Aloe vera, the popular houseplant, has succulent leaves filled with a "wonder gel" that soothes burns. This plant needs very little care. **Calendula** is a colorful member of the marigold family, with flowers in shades of orange and yellow. The petals are used to make salves and tinctures, and are edible for a good source of carotenoids. **Comfrey,** sometimes called black root, also has properties useful for external use. This large plant spreads rapidly by underground runners, so situate accordingly.

For a plant combining looks and medicinal use, **echinacea** ranks high. Known as purple coneflower, it attracts butterflies and makes a good cut flower. All parts of the plant can be used for relieving symptoms of cold or cough. **Garlic,** the world's best natural antibiotic, is easy to grow, like its cousin the onion. **Goldenseal's** root is used as a topical antiseptic and immunity booster. It can be dried and ground. Being a woodland plant, goldenseal needs shade to grow.

Scent/Enjoyment		
Clary Sage	P	
Flax	P	
Hyssop	P	
Lavender	P	
Sweet Annie	A	
Sweet Woodruff	P	

Flax

The plants in this group are grown for their pleasant scents and lovely flowers or foliage. They're the kind of plants that are enjoyed by touching, sniffing, or gazing while strolling through the herb garden.

Clary sage is a bold, dominating plant with large, pebbly, gray-green leaves. In summer, tall flower stalks lined with pinkish flowers attract hummingbirds, butterflies, and bees. Unlike most sages, this is not used for cooking, but has medicinal value.

Flax is as timid and quiet as clary sage is "loud." Flax's leaves and stems have fibrous tissue that was widely used in colonial days to make cloth. Lately, this plant has been in the news for its cholesterol-lowering seeds and oil. However, I grow it mostly for its soft sky-blue flowers, which add a touch of quiet beauty to the garden.

Hyssop is nice for the border, having evergreen leaves and sturdy, woody stems that send out lots of new growth yearly. Its sprays of bright, bluish-purple flowers complement the glossy green foliage well.

Lavender! Ah, sweet lavender! Few other plants offer so much fragrance. Grow plenty of lavender for use in potpourris, sachets, soaps, and many other fun uses.

Sweet Annie is also an extremely fragrant plant, with a clean, deodorizing scent for sachets and potpourris. Being a tall, almost treelike plant, it's suitable for filling up corners, or along a fence or wall.

Sweet Woodruff, with its glossy, star-design leaves, is a winning ground cover. It's a vibrant, perky plant and readily dresses up bare spots. Starts can easily be transferred to the desired spot.

HERBS FOR ALL USES

Plotting Your Garden

God created herbs for man's pleasure and well-being. Having an herb garden opens up tremendous possibilities of culinary, medicinal, and visual enjoyment. Plus, herb gardening involves low investment, especially if you grow your own plants (or get starts from a friend!). An herb garden concept gives a breath of fresh air to the flower bed tradition, too. Rather than pretty flowers just to look at, you have attractive, useful, edible plants that help you be self-sufficient.

SITE SELECTION

Most herbs love full sun. A rule of thumb is at least six hours of full sun per day. Good drainage is also important. A southern slope is ideal. If poor drainage is an obstacle, you may decide to create a raised bed.

Many herbs will tolerate shade; a few even prefer it. Their foliage might be a bit more sparse than in sunny conditions, and they will need more phosphorus (bonemeal is one source) rather than nitrogen.

The great majority of herbs will thrive in acid to neutral soil (pH 6.0 to 7.0) with the exception of a few: lavender, anise, and fennel, which must have alkaline soil; and sage, basil, and yarrow, which will tolerate quite acidic soil.

It's a good idea to position the herb garden so that it's easily accessible from the kitchen. This gives you the liberty of taking a quick snip even while the soup's on! And also, having the herb garden in a spot where you'll walk past or see it almost every day lets you keep an eye on the growing process, not to mention weed patrol.

If you have limited space, you can plant herbs in containers, placing them on your deck or patio. Another option is a window box.

DECIDING WHAT TO PLANT

The vast smorgasbord of plant choices makes it both delightful and challenging to select. First, decide on the basic purpose of your herb garden. Are you interested mainly in culinary herbs? Medicinal and tea herbs? Herbs that attract bees and butterflies? Specific color groups, such as brilliant reds and oranges or subdued grays? Tough herbs for rock gardens? Most herbs will overlap several categories rather than fit into only one.

Your proposed site will also help you plan. Will you need plants that appreciate full sun? Thrive in shade, or moist corners? Plants for containers?

Start simple and add to your herb garden from year to year. This is important if you are a new herb gardener. Let's say you're planting a new culinary herb garden. Choose several plants you know, like parsley, dill, and mint, and several you don't know as well, perhaps basil, chives, or thyme. This gives you a basis of both familiar flavors and experimental flavors that lead to more discoveries. Next year you can add a few more plants as time and budget allow.

EXPANDING

You can add to your herb garden using the more-plants method or the add-a-section method. With the more-plants method, fill up your new garden's extra space with annuals (nasturtiums, calendula, or basils) and eliminate some of these the next year to make room for permanents. The add-a-section method adds an entirely new section. Using the more-plants method, my herb collection numbers thirty-something after starting with a basic dozen about five years ago.

PLOTTING THE LAYOUT

Considering your chosen site and the plants you expect to plant, the next step is plotting the layout, deciding where each plant will be planted.

Place the tallest plants in the back (in a round bed, put them in the middle) to prevent them from shading the smaller ones. For a most balanced look plant several same plants beside each other rather than scattered throughout the garden. Intersperse different colors, shapes, and textures. For example, broad-leafed sage enhances fernlike dill, and smooth dark opal basil is striking next to woolly white artemisia. You'll want some bright colors throughout the garden, not only on the one end! A unified color theme enhances your layout, with maybe several groups of blue- and yellow-flowering plants in different parts of the garden.

Define the garden's edge with something permanent like rocks or timbers for a finished look. A hedge-type plant like hyssop or thyme planted around the border of the garden is attractive too. Leave some walking space if you cannot reach all the plants from the edge. If you'd like a charming extra touch, a flagstone path, dotted with thyme, is perfect. Even though curves and circles in your layout create visual interest, they cut down on space efficiency.

Gracia's Herbs

KITCHEN GARDEN

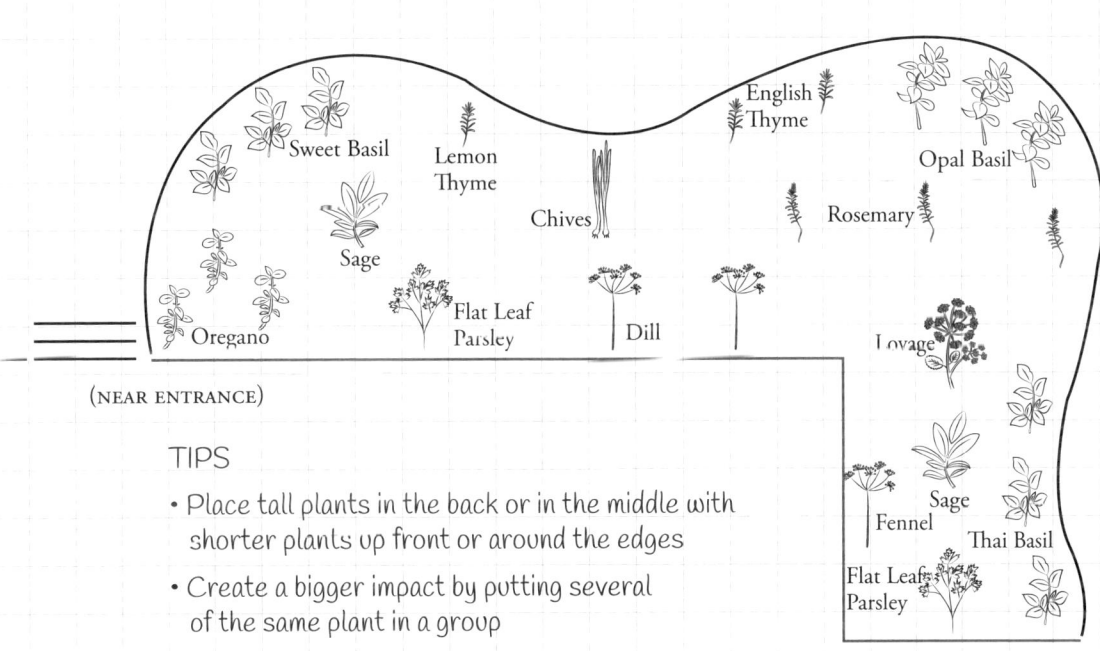

(NEAR ENTRANCE)

TIPS

- Place tall plants in the back or in the middle with shorter plants up front or around the edges
- Create a bigger impact by putting several of the same plant in a group
- Use odd numbers in groups, such as three or five
- Put contrasting colors and leaf shapes beside each other
- Design straight borders for a formal, orderly look
- Choose curved borders for inviting appeal
- Allow some space between plants for an uncluttered feel and easy harvest

PLANTER

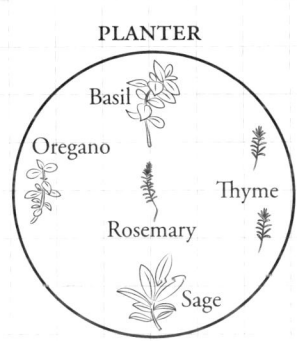

TEA GARDEN

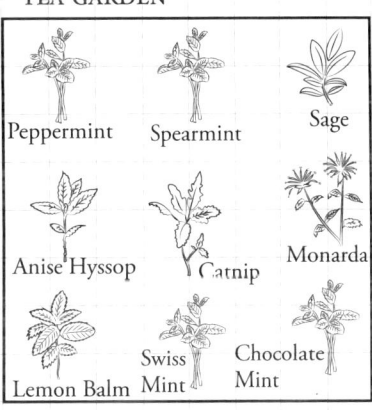

(Plant mints in submerged pots)

PLOTTING YOUR GARDEN |19|

SQUARE GARDEN

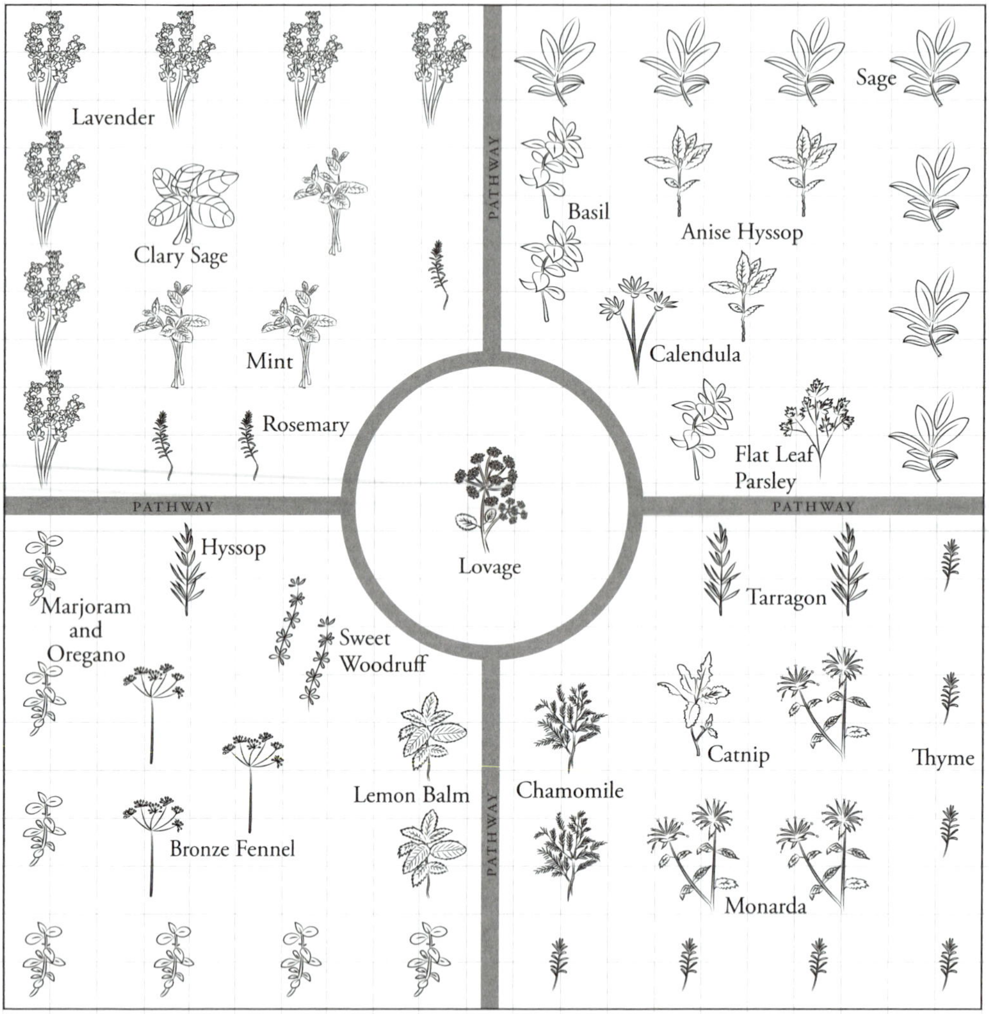

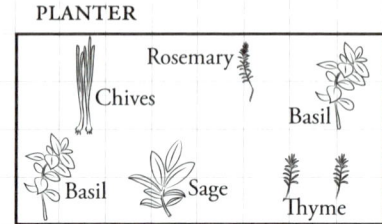

Starting Herbs by Seed

Many herbs can be propagated by cuttings or divisions, but starting from seed has its advantages. It's a very economical option. For the price of a seed packet you can have a number of plants or even a whole row. Seed-grown perennials can be added to your collection with little expense.

DIRECT-SEEDING

Seed starting by direct-sowing in the garden is a low-fuss method, especially for annuals like dill and cilantro. Dill can even be fall seeded by sprinkling seeds in a spot that won't be plowed or tilled in spring. Seedlings will emerge at the first warm spell.

Three factors that must be right for direct-seeding success are soil texture, soil warmth, and consistent moisture. Finely cultivated soil prevents seeds from falling among the clods. Good soil-to-seed contact speeds germination. Most herbs sprout best at 55–60°F. If it's warm enough to go barefooted, it's probably warm enough to plant seeds in the garden. Regular watering should keep the ground well moistened but not flooded. Covering seeds with a light layer of peat moss also helps.

STARTING SEEDS INDOORS

Sowing indoors gives an early start for the growing season. When planting time arrives, plants are ready to set out. Although most annual herbs are easily direct-sowed outdoors, an early start indoors is beneficial if a prolonged cool or rainy spring hampers soil preparation or if you're a resident of a short-season climate. An early start translates to an earlier harvest for annual herbs. Slow-growing perennial seedlings are ready for transplanting at the frost-free date when sown at least six to eight weeks before.

Another benefit of starting seeds indoors is having regulated growing conditions. Tiny seeds and delicate plants do best in a sheltered environment. Overall, though, herb seeds need the very same conditions for growing as do vegetable and flower seeds: consistent light, warmth, and moisture and an appropriate planting medium. Any sterile seed starting mix or fine potting soil works well.

One method that I like for starting herbs indoors is to plant rows of herbs in open flats. Using a piece of cardboard, I make shallow impressions the width of the tray, about two inches apart, then sow the tiny seeds thickly in rows. Thick sowing ensures a good stand, since most herb seeds average 60 percent germination. Planting in rows also allows good air circulation and will simplify transplanting. Larger seeds can be sown singly in pots or cell packs.

If the seed packet doesn't specify a planting depth, cover the seed with soil three times as deep as its diameter. Some herbs germinate better with very little or no cover. Simply tamp firmly into the soil to keep moist.

When true leaves appear (the second set, after the first leaflets), it's time for transplanting. Not only does this give the plant more room to grow, but it helps it become sturdier. Avoid pulling on tender young plants to get them out of the flat. Scoop them out with a spoon, keeping all the soil possible on the roots. I like to plant a small clump per pot, rather than one single plant. Situate them in larger pots or cells and lightly cover the roots with soil, then water down instead of tamping with your hands. Give the newly planted herbs a boost with mild fertilizer or fish emulsion.

Herbs like dill, borage, chervil, and fennel are members of the carrot family and have a taproot. This makes transplanting them a little more tricky. One solution is to direct-seed it outdoors where you intend it to grow. Another option if you want to start it indoors is to plant it in a peat pot or Jiffy pot so the root won't be disturbed when setting it outdoors.

Before planting your herbs in the garden, accustom them to outdoor breezes and temperatures by setting them outside for several hours a day, a process known as hardening off.

HERBS COMMONLY GROWN BY SEEDS

Herb	Days to Germinate at 70°F	Cover/ Uncover	Comments
Anise Hyssop	6	Uncover	
Basil	4	Uncover	Heat loving; keep warm and not too moist to prevent dampening off
Borage	5	Cover	Extremely taprooted
Burnet, Salad	5	Cover	
Calendula	6	Cover	
Caraway	10	Cover	Sow 12 weeks before last frost; needs long growing season
Catnip	5	Uncover	Has low germination; sow thickly
Chamomile, German	4	Uncover	
Chervil	7	Cover	Soak seeds in warm water before planting
Chives	6	Cover	
Cilantro	6	Cover	Needs consistent heat to germinate
Dill	5	Uncover	Needs light to germinate
Fennel	6	Cover	Soak seeds in warm water before planting
Feverfew	5	Uncover	
Lemon Balm	7	Uncover	
Lovage	8	Cover	Somewhat slow to germinate
Marjoram, Sweet	5	Uncover	
Oregano	4	Uncover	
Parsley	8	Cover	Soak seeds in warm water before planting
Sage	8	Cover	Keep well watered
Savory	6	Uncover	
Tansy	5	Cover	
Thyme	4	Uncover	
Wormwood	5	Uncover	

Rosemary

It's Planting Time

It's a warm afternoon in late May, and we head to the garden with a flat or two of plants and a basketful of seed packets. The sun is half-hidden behind filmy clouds—not too bright for these new transplants. Best of all, soon they'll receive a rainwater shower!

I grab a hoe and scrape aside the 2-inch layer of mulch, then plunge my little gardening trowel deep and twist to form a hole. I pause for a moment, while lifting a handful of dark soil to inhale, deeply and slowly, that earthy aroma. Soil—it's much more than just dirt beneath our feet. This complex substance anchors plants and provides the nutrients they need. It even absorbs the old roots, leaves, and stems. What a living, teeming, ever-changing wonder!

Gracia's Herbs

After plopping the scented geraniums and rosemarys and variegated lemon thymes into their holes and giving them a scoop of water right at the roots before covering them up, it's time to prepare spots for seeds. Again, an area of this matted hay mulch is scraped aside and the exposed soil is soon hoed into a fine crumbly texture, ready for tiny, black seeds of basil.

THE BEGINNINGS OF A GARDEN

I reminisce to the start of this garden, twelve springs ago. This farm had been sadly neglected. Trash was strewn everywhere, yet the soil looked promising.

Where would be a good site for a new herb garden? Dad recommended a spot across the lane from the house. It would have full sun all day (ideal for most herbs) and was grassy, mostly free of debris. I liked the old, hand-dug well that would be in the garden's northeast corner, but noted that around it the ground sloped downward. Would that lower area be too waterlogged in spring?

Step one was cutting down the half-grown box elder tree along the garden's south side. Step two was getting rid of the grass. We did this by mowing it very short several weeks in succession, then tilling. The soil was very sandy. What we really needed was mulch from a well-seasoned pile, something that wasn't yet available in our new setting.

Starts of tea plants and perennial herbs had been brought with us and found a place in our vegetable garden. Since the herbs already had a temporary home, we had a year to prepare the new garden. The second year, after the herbs had again been transplanted to the new garden, someone brought us a load of old hay. A thick mat of old hay slabs both suppressed any grass that popped up again and kept the sandy soil from drying out too much.

Twelve years and many layers of mulch later, the soil is rich and dark, loose and crumbly, and teeming with earthworms. There is still a little swale near the well, but nearly the entire garden is four to six inches higher than the lawn around it, which keeps the area high and dry in spring. In summer, the soil stays cool and moist under the mulch, although tiny, new plants get periodic drinks of well water, thanks to a cast-iron hand pump my brothers installed.

The ideal garden? Almost. Part of the box elder stump remains and occasionally my hoe clinks against a rusty tool or piece of glass. The weeds, well, most of the time most of them are controlled with a good layer of mulch. This garden is home to many plants, including an overgrown tansy, a stately lovage, five different sages, lots of lavender, rosemary and tarragon, hyssop, germander, and creeping thyme, and even some Johnny-jump-ups close to the well.

WHAT MAKES GOOD SOIL?

Soil is made out of three basic parts, which vary from place to place. Some is fine and sandy; some is sticky with a high percentage of clay. Some has a blend of sand, clay, and silt. Yet what really makes the soil alive is organic matter. This is any fibrous, porous material that spaces the particles of clay, sand, and silt apart. Organic matter helps water to drain away and creates tiny air pockets that give the soil a light and crumbly texture.

Organic matter is all around us, usually free! Fallen leaves, grass clippings, bark chips, old or rained-on hay (befriend a farmer), straw with horse manure, cardboard pieces, cattails, pulled weeds: all of these are ideal for mulch. A mixture gives the best results. A pile of only grass clippings can become slimy and moldy if not turned properly. Cattails make a super mulch, but they are quite light and it takes a lot of them. Table scraps such as fruit and vegetable peelings need to have drier items like leaves added, or the pile will become too gunky.

The process of heating, decaying, and aeration converts organic matter into a usable form such as compost or mulch. It works well to have the compost pile in a contained area. A deeper pile will break down faster and can be turned easier. We have several 20-bushel apple bins with the bottoms taken

out that hold compost in various stages, but then we also have large piles of old hay, bark chips, and leaves that sit for years. Our local town is only glad for a place to dump their chopped maple leaves.

After it is spread on a garden, mulch eventually becomes humus, the decayed organic matter that is part of the soil, along with clay, silt, and sand. Humus is the life and pulse of the soil. It gives the soil a dark, fertile appearance, and makes a great place for earthworms to live. Do you see lots of earthworm castings in your soil? That's a very good sign.

My favorite mulch in the main herb garden is old hay. Its slabs (or layers, if you have round bales) make it easy to cover a large area quickly. It dries quickly after a rain, and mats down to prevent weeds. In the kitchen garden, which is a stone terrace north and west of the entrance, I like a mixture of well-composted leaves with chicken bedding. It is fine, and very dark brown, nice for the close-up view. For garden paths, bark chips are ideal. They don't break down so quickly.

LOTS OF HUMUS

Having soil with a high content of humus is very important for herb gardens, for several reasons. Good drainage is essential. Many common herbs such as oregano and thyme are native to the Mediterranean area, which has a sunny climate. They thrive when their root zone is dry, not soggy. Raised beds are one option for low-lying areas. Yet it takes only a few seasons to raise and amend a garden by piling on mulch.

Mulch also enriches sandy soil and helps it retain moisture, when otherwise all the water would simply drain away too quickly. For clay soils, mulch will help the soil stay more porous, instead of becoming slick when wet, and hard, sunbaked clods when dry.

An established herb garden falls into the maintenance mode. Weed control and soil health are the main things, because the various perennials don't need a lot of cultivation. I keep spots open for some annuals (and have a separate kitchen garden, too, for annuals), and almost every spring I add or rearrange some plants according to whim. Still, it's not like a vegetable garden that needs large-scale cultivation. A good layer of mulch in spring, after the ground has warmed, usually lasts most of the year. By late summer, a few bare spots may need touching up.

For the past few years, my biggest weed problem has been purple dead-nettle *(Lamium purpurea)*. New seedlings of this overwintering perennial pop up in summer. This year, I diligently uprooted them in late August and spread them on top of the mulch to dry in the sun. After a few days, these plants had dried to a crisp and became part of the mulch.

PLANTS IN POTS

If my garden soil is good, should I use it to fill my pots for container growing, too? The answer is usually no. Even good garden soil will settle too much in a container after watering, leaving a hard chunk of soil. Also, sunlight shines directly onto the root area of window boxes or patio pots, and especially hanging baskets. This dries out the soil even more.

The best soil for growing herbs in containers has a good ratio of peat moss and bark chips. It can be fairly coarse, but fluffy enough for good drainage.

Clockwise from top: Curly parsley, sweet basil, spearmint, thyme

Gracia's Herbs

Herbs Everywhere

When I first started growing lavender, sage, and basil, I thought of herbs as those mysterious plants that belong in a little garden all by themselves. A bit of experience showed that herbs are not that different from all other flower or vegetable plants. Some are annuals; others are perennials. After all, a basil plant behaves much like a pepper plant, or a lavender plant like a daisy.

No, herbs must not be limited to solitary confinement. Where can you grow herbs outside the garden? The possibilities are vast—alongside vegetables, on a windowsill, in a perennial bed, with spring bulbs, or spilling out of a hanging basket.

Of course, a garden devoted to herbs alone provides enjoyment and value. An organized collection of medicinal and culinary is both fascinating and functional. But not everyone who enjoys herbs decides to dedicate a space entirely to these useful plants. Perhaps you prefer to grow herbs on a smaller scale. Maybe a lack of space or time keeps your dream of an herb garden from becoming a reality. This is not a problem, but an opportunity. Herbs can grow anywhere!

ANOTHER ROW IN THE GARDEN

Most vegetable gardens are spaces where annual plants are grown, then cleared out at the end of the growing season. Usually it's not suitable to establish perennial plants in this area. Annual herbs are perfect. Grow them in rows just like other vegetables.

Many annual herbs are easily started from seed. Simply sow seeds in well-cultivated soil and keep moist until germination. If the row of new seedlings is very thick, pluck out the extras and leave 4 to 6 inches between plants.

The all-time favorites—dill, basil, and parsley—are good garden herbs since they pair up so well with tomatoes, cucumbers, and other veggies. Cilantro is another easy-to-grow selection. Other annuals like chamomile, anise, summer savory, and marjoram are also useful, adding variety to your garden. Carefree annual caraway and blue-flowered nigella produce seeds for topping breads.

PERENNIAL BEAUTY AND BLESSING

Herbs often overlap the categories of flowering plants and plants for eating and healing. So when you integrate herbs into perennial beds or borders, you are rewarded with both color and function. With so many different colors to pick from, the many varieties of herbs give immense opportunity. Take advantage of the multicolored hues of variegated herbs like tricolor sage.

Flowering herbs such as lavender clary sage or striking red bee balm brighten the landscape. They also delight nature's nectar lovers—hummingbirds and butterflies. Bees, too, capture the sweetness of flowering herbs in delectable honey.

Early emerging plants like chives are a

Bee balm

good companion for spring bulbs. When the daffodils fade, perky pink chive blossoms hide the spent stalks.

Echinacea, sage, feverfew, and many others have ideal cutting flowers for bouquets. Others like tansy, wormwood, and hyssop retain their color when dried. Lately some new varieties of oregano have been developed. These feature large, decorative clusters of pink and purple blooms for fresh or dried arrangements.

Some perennial herbs will define a border by forming a low, informal hedge. Semi-woody plants like lavender, hyssop, and germander are good choices.

READY FOR ROCK GARDENS

Rock garden plants need to be tough and willing to thrive amid sunbaked rocks and dry soil. Many herbs are right at home amidst the boulders since their native area is the rocky Mediterranean shore or a similar area.

Here's a tip for picking out herbs that tolerate and even prefer dry conditions—check the leaf color. Is it silver, white, or grayish green? Plants of this color, like sage or lavender, require little water. These drought-resistant habits make them good choices to fill up a spot where few other plants can grow. Tough, woody plants like thyme also will grow in the most challenging places between the nooks and crannies of stone walls or outdoor paths.

PRETTY FOR A SEASON

What is the primary attraction in a bed of annual flowers? It's color, isn't it? Here again herbs contribute well. Various annual herbs have showy leaves or blooms, or both.

Basil is one good option. Sweet and lemon basil are just plain green, so choose a Thai or opal variety for some color. 'Siam Queen' and 'Magical Michael' both have dark burgundy flower heads with pinkish blossoms. A dark purple basil, especially a ruffled one, provides beautiful contrast. Imagine what a stunning combination it is with lavender petunias and purple alyssum!

Annual lavenders are too often overlooked (in my opinion). Their fine-cut foliage is a muted silver, but their true elegance is seen in the long stemmed flowers—nearly 18 inches long—with the clearest hues of blue. The scent is faintly camphoraceous rather than floral perfumed like other lavenders, but I grow them for those sapphire-blue wands. How lovely in the garden or in a vase!

CARPET OF GREEN

Grass is the most common ground cover, but not every spot is suited for grass. A steep slope, exposed tree roots, or a dark, shady area can make grass-growing difficult. Creeping herbs come to the rescue.

Creeping thymes spread between stepping stones can withstand a fair amount of traffic. There's a nice variety of creeping thymes, some furry, others more upright. Several also have showy red or pink flowers. Sweet woodruff is a shade-loving plant with lush green leaves. It likes a moist area. Roman chamomile forms a soft, green mat which is mowable. Tread on it for a pine-apple-scented walk!

PERFECT FOR A PATIO

So far, all our herb growing options have been outdoors in the ground. But the possibilities don't stop there. Oh, no! Herbs are excellent plants for containers, indoors and out. If your gardening space is limited, grow herbs in planters, window boxes, hanging baskets—anything that holds a bit of soil! Even though I have plenty of outdoor space, I grow lots of herbs in containers for convenience and decoration.

My favorite containers for herbs are clay pots. They are porous and keep the soil from becoming waterlogged. Besides, herbs blend well with their quaint, earthy appearance. Rustic wooden planters, earthen crocks, and old baskets also make charming containers.

Strawberry pots with side openings are perfect for herbs and allow you to plant a mixture of sizes. For example, a tall plant like chives or rosemary looks good at the top of the pot, while thyme or marjoram can spill out of the sides.

Herbal hanging baskets are another fun project. The wire type with a pressed natural liner is especially pretty.

Proper container size is important. For a single plant, a pot 6 to 10 inches in diameter is probably sufficient. A large semi-permanent plant like lemon verbena which is brought indoors in winter needs a more sizable 12- to 24-inch pot. So does a combination of several plants in a planter.

A combination of herbs brings out the best of container gardening—beauty and usefulness. Herbs can be grouped by use—kitchen herbs, tea plants, medicinal gems—or by color. A handy color tip is to separate plants into the "warm" group or "cool" group. The warm group includes lush greens, goldens, and yellow, orange, and red blossoms. Cool colors are silver, muted green, purples, and blues. The "cool" plants prefer less frequent watering.

Container plantings can be kept from year to year with a bit of maintenance. Lift out the pots and trim and fluff the roots if they have become potbound. Add some new soil. Fertilize occasionally and trim the plants if necessary.

L-R: Thyme, sage, basil

Grow a Crop of Herb Gardeners

ALL GARDENS ARE SCHOOLS

Any garden, whether of vegetables, fruits, flowers, or herbs, holds a wealth of valuable lessons. Many of the lessons are learned by doing. As children dig and scratch and sow, they learn to recognize the essentials of plant life: soil, water, light, warmth, and air. Although we work hard to provide all the right conditions, God alone can awaken a seed or unfurl a flower bud.

In the garden, children learn patience. The seeds are planted, then we wait to see little green sprouts. Fruits and vegetables swell and color, but we wait until they are fully ripe before picking. (Only the first strawberries may be pinkish at the very tip!)

They also learn responsibility. Planning a garden takes foresight. Forgetting to water may cause a tender plant to die. Picking zucchini is a daily job unless giant "baseball bats" are desired.

A garden holds the promise of reward. Youngsters love to lug in the fruits of their labor. Often the output is relative to the input. Can you expect prize-winning pumpkins to emerge from a sea of weeds?

By working side by side with an experienced gardener, children learn common techniques such as planting, watering, thinning, weeding, and mulching. They become familiar with words like germinate, pollinate, and transplant.

HERB GARDENS ARE ADVENTURE GARDENS

Growing herbs opens up a new world beyond the common radish, tomato, and sunflower plot. Children love sensory experiences—things they can see, touch, smell, and taste—and herbs offer all of them. Herbs have somewhat specialized uses which help young gardeners learn to appreciate the finer, more detailed aspects of plants.

In an herb garden, bright colors like the vivid orange calendula and bright blue stars of borage delight the eyes. Pebbly sage, ferny dill, and matted creeping thyme beg to be stroked and touched.

There are plenty of scents to please inquisitive noses. The perfumes of lavender and scented geraniums appeal to the girls. If the boys turn up their noses at such sissy scents, they can sniff rosemary (smells like a piney grove), tansy (no wonder it chases spiders!), or clary sage leaves (someone has been running hard for a long time on a very warm day!).

Tasting is the most exciting sensation, and an herb garden is full of tasty discoveries. Yes, dill pickles are flavored by a plant. Sugar is sweet, and so is stevia. Lovage and salad burnet taste like vegetables we know. Tarragon, when chewed, causes tongues to tingle. Cilantro, epazote, and perilla are familiar flavors to children in faraway lands. And who doesn't think of licorice when nibbling anise hyssop?

As children get to know herbs, their plant vocabulary enlarges. Even the little ones love to roll around the funny names. If Mary knows which is oregano, you can assign her to fetch a handful for the pizza you're making.

Throughout history herbs have been an important resource for seasonings, remedies, and even the coloring of fabric. In our modern age of store-bought spices and easily obtained medicines, many of these skills are no longer passed down to the younger generations. Perhaps if herbal basics are taught to children, they'll be inspired to recapture some of these arts once they're older.

HANDS ON HERBS

Keep it informal, and don't expect a grand-scale garden. A preschooler might be delighted with one plant to call her very own, complete with a tag. School-age children can plan their own little row or a larger plot. Depending on your location, plants in pots may be the best choice. Children love tools that are their size—small scratchers, trowels, and downsized rakes, shovels, and watering cans.

Quick-growing annuals are ideal for a child's garden. Since they last only one year, you can try something different in the same spot next year. Annuals generally have larger seeds, which are easier sowing for small hands, and can be sown directly into the garden. Dill doesn't even need to be covered. Simply tamp the seeds firmly into moistened soil. Basil needs warmth to germinate. Sow when the soil is warm enough for planting corn and beans. Cilantro, chervil, and anise are additional easy-to-sow annuals.

In an undisturbed plot of their own, self-sowing annuals like nigella and chamomile return yearly. Calendula will do the same when seeds are allowed to mature and drop.

You may also decide to start out with potted plants, which have an "instant garden" advantage. With guidance, little helpers can dig holes, water, and pat the soil in place.

Chances are, that as a mom of little ones, your gardening time is limited to the basics. You might choose to have a collection of versatile perennial plants that need minimal care. This could include chives, mint, oregano, thyme, feverfew, bee balm, or lemon balm.

Children love to be included in the action. They can soon catch on which plants are good and which are weeds. Little ones can hold the basket as you snip herbs for drying, an excellent time for a plant identity quiz.

Gracia's Herbs

CHILDREN—DO YOU LIKE FUN PROJECTS?

Germination is one of nature's miracles. For a close-up look at the process, lay cilantro seeds onto a saturated sponge. Keep warm and moist by regular spritzing. You'll see the tiny balls cracking, then sending out green sprouts.

Rosemary can be trained into a little tree. Select a healthy, vigorous plant 12 inches tall with a straight stem and plant it in a pot. Trim off all the leaves and branches along the bottom two-thirds of the stem. Place a stake alongside the stem and fasten with twist ties to keep it nice and upright. As the plant grows, pinch the growing tips to make a bushy lollipop shape. When kept indoors in winter, a rosemary tree can grow for years.

For an informative stroll, have the plants in your garden labeled. Smooth wooden slats with permanent marker writing make inexpensive signs.

Keep a gardening journal to increase your observation skills. A notebook is all it takes to get started. List sources and sketch garden plans on the first pages. Staple empty seed packets to keep track of varieties. Record date of planting, bloom time, and other facts throughout the summer.

Herb gardens are havens for insects and other critters, so keep a magnifying glass handy. Watch for the good bugs like ladybugs and praying mantises. Can you spy butterflies or even a hummingbird? They love the abundant nectar of blooming plants. Peel back the mulch, and you might discover a host of pill bugs and earthworms in their cool earthy home. In my herb garden, a giant toad has its home in a thick clump of lovage!

Herbal vinegars are an easy project. Place mashed herbs (basil, dill, thyme, or tarragon are good) into a glass jar and cover with mild vinegar such as apple cider, or rice, or wine vinegar. Let set for two to three weeks, then strain and bottle. Now you have a uniquely flavored vinegar for salad dressings.

Do you like to press leaves and flowers for cards, bookmarks, and mottoes? You'll find plenty of variety in a plot of herbs. Fabric sachets are another nice item, filled with lavender and other pleasantly scented herbs. All you need is a square of cotton cloth and a handful of dried flowers and leaves. Place in the middle of the square, gather up the corners, and tie with a piece of ribbon.

Herb gardening is rewarding for the young (and not so young), but one of my favorite sayings comes to mind, "The highest reward for a person's toil is not what they get for it, but what they become by it."

Spikenard and saffron; calamus and cinnamon, with all trees of frankincense; myrrh and aloes, with all the chief spices.

SONG OF SOLOMON 4:14

SECTION II

GETTING TO
Know Herbs

Rosemary

"This section walks you through my garden to acquaint you with the most common (and a few not-so-common) herbs for culinary and medicinal use. You'll see the plant and its growing habits. You'll experience its distinctive flavor. And finally, you'll see how it's put to use. Come and discover!"

—*Gracia*

Anise Hyssop

In the tea section of my herb garden a clump of anise hyssop stands tall. A second one occupies a spot in the kitchen garden just outside the north entrance door. These plants have certainly gotten their share of admiring (and inquiring) comments like, "What is that plant with pretty purple spikes?" or "Amazing, this tastes like licorice!" Even those who know anise hyssop well can hardly resist snatching a leaf or two to nibble when passing by.

Exactly what is anise hyssop? It's not related to anise, although both plants share a sweet, licorice taste. Neither is it related to the medicinal herb hyssop, a woody perennial which also has showy flower spikes. A host of nicknames like licorice mint, root beer plant, and giant blue hyssop surround this unique plant, but many catalogs and handbooks use its botanical name *(Agastache foeniculum)*, or simply agastache (pronounced ag-uh-STACK-ee).

Can its square stems and paired leaves give a clue to which plant family anise hyssop belongs? Sure. Anise hyssop is a member of the same family as are other tasty tea plants like mint, catnip, and bee balm. I love its stately yard-high stalks, with plenty of dark green, heart-shaped leaves—slightly toothed—to form a well-balanced clump. In full sun, the stalks are sturdy and don't need staking. They may be a little wobbly in partial shade. As a tall herb, anise hyssop is best situated as a center focal point in the garden or the back row of a border. In my kitchen garden it neatly hides the corner of our house. In the main herb garden it contrasts nicely with woolly gray horehound and cheery white and yellow German chamomile.

Anise hyssop attains its prime in midsummer as flower spikes burst forth at the end of every branch, first lavender, then maturing to a deep purple. Looking closely, you will see that each 4-inch spike is densely packed with tiny, two-lipped flowers—perfect nectar-sipping stations for bees, butterflies, and hummingbirds. This purple profusion provides a dramatic herb garden focal point, and it lasts from late June to nearly frost. You can capture the beauty by adding anise hyssop to fresh bouquets or preserving it for use in dried bouquets. To dry, simply hang bunches to air dry in a breezy spot, out of direct light.

A NATIVE PLANT

Many of our favorite herbs such as sage and oregano claim a Mediterranean heritage, but anise hyssop is a Native American plant. During the 1830s botanist Thomas Nuttall encountered it as he crossed the Midwest. He was so fascinated with these sweet, nectar-filled flowers that he introduced it to beekeepers in his native Europe. It remains a favorite among beekeepers today. Its use among gardeners has been somewhat limited. Recent new varieties, especially 'Golden Jubilee', have increased its familiarity.

'Blue Fortune', a widely available variety, is a cross between *Agastache foeniculum* and *Agastache rugosa*, a closely related plant known as Korean mint. It has the aroma and taste of *A. foeniculum* with periwinkle-blue flowers and sharply pointed leaves. It reaches the height of 4 feet when in full bloom.

'Golden Jubilee' is a compact 20-inch plant. This true anise hyssop offers a unique color variation of chartreuse-yellow leaves and purple flowers. The name refers to the celebration of Queen Elizabeth's fiftieth year of reign.

I've never grown any of the white varieties such as 'Snowspike' or 'Alabaster'. Some wide-range perennial and herb catalogs list even more kinds, including additional agastaches with red or orange flowers.

FROM GARDEN TO KITCHEN

Most of the references I checked indicate that anise hyssop is a perennial that grows in Zones 4 to 9. In my garden it seems to be a short-lived perennial. Younger plants may overwinter well, but I allow at least a stalk or two to reseed, just to be safe. In spring you can quickly scuffle the unwanted sprouts with a hoe or scoop out a section to transplant (or share with a friend!). About reseeding, here's a suggestion: Goldfinches and other winter birds love the tiny black seeds. You may see them perched on the stalks in late fall, extracting seeds from the now-brown flower heads.

Anise hyssop seeds germinate easily. Sowing can be done outdoors after danger of frost. This herb tolerates a variety of soils and is usually a carefree plant with little disease or pest problems. Full sun is best. It does not have underground root runners like mint, but may form a clump several feet in diameter if well established.

With its delightfully sweet anise flavor, anise hyssop is a favorite tea plant. Its flavor has been compared to fennel or tarragon, but it possesses a special sweetness of its own. Leaves can be used for tea, fresh or dried. Anise hyssop is a good choice for creating homemade tea blends, so I like to have a good winter's supply of dried leaves. Try adding it to spearmint for special effects.

All aerial parts of anise hyssop are edible. In early spring, gather tender new leaves for a savory salad green. Use flowers to add a sweet anise touch to fruits and desserts. Pluck tiny individual flowers from the spikes and drop into mixed fruit or sliced peaches. Sprinkle onto cake instead of frosting, or use as a garnish with frosting. The purple blossoms look pretty with white frosting in cupcakes.

Another delicious item made with anise hyssop is a syrup. Heat 1 cup water and 1 cup sugar until boiling, then toss in a handful of anise hyssop flowers and leaves. Simmer over medium heat for 2 to 3 minutes, then strain. Drizzle over fruit or pastries or use to sweeten tea.

Sweet basil

Basil: Lots of Variety

Sweet or spicy, green or purple, ruffled or smooth, bushy or tall: all these describe different kinds of basils. With such variety, it's no wonder that basil is among the most popular herbs. In fact, if I were asked to name my favorite herb (what a hard decision—to pick just one!) I just might settle for basil. Basil is an annual, and that's another thing I like about it. Every year you can try new kinds or plant them in a different spot.

SWEET BASILS

Sweet basil includes the common green basil and Italian types. These sweet-scented types have plenty of smooth, bright green leaves that soak up

BASIL |43|

the sun like chlorophyll factories and convert it to a spicy sweetness. These fast-growing plants benefit from rigorous trimming to keep them leafy and productive.

'Genovese', an Italian favorite, is extra sweet and flavorful. Lettuce leaf has extra large leaves. Its mild sweetness is well suited for salads and sandwiches. 'Nufar', a newer strain of sweet basil, is resistant to Fusarium wilt.

PURPLE BASILS

Purple basils taste a lot like green sweet basil, but offer a unique color variation. These reddish-purple plants have lavender or pink flowers and add a bright splash of color to salads, vinegars, or jellies. Older varieties like 'Opal' may have some mottled plants or even some with partly green leaves. 'Red Rubin' is a newer, nearly all-dark basil. The highly ruffled leaves of 'Purple Ruffles' glow with a very deep purple hue.

'Opal' basil

BUSH BASILS

The saying, "Good things come in small packages," holds true for bush basils. These plants with compact, globe-like shapes are useful for several reasons. For one, they fit perfectly into containers and small spaces. Second, the tiny leaves are packed with big flavor. They carry a strong, sweet flavor with undertones of spice.

Bush basils are sometimes labeled compact, dwarf, or miniature basil. Depending on the kind, they range from 6 to 12 inches tall with tiny leaves. When growing bush basil from seed, expect some variation in leaf size and growth habit between plants.

'Spicy Globe' is one of my favorites. Its sturdy, uniform plant, about a foot tall, is loaded with scent. Compact basil forms a cute green pom-pom. Regular pinching helps keep the rounded form.

Fine leaf basil

SPICY BASILS

Two characteristics of basils in this group are a spicy flavor and attractive foliage. You can use them for vinegars, jellies, and desserts, and they make attractive selections for planters and flower beds, too. Thai basil has smooth, pointed green leaves with purple stems. Its striking symmetrical form grows at least 2 feet high. 'Siam Queen', an All American award winning Thai basil, is slightly more compact. Cinnamon basil is lovely for bouquets, and repels insects at the same time.

Thai basil

LEMON BASILS

Need a burst of lemon flavor for teas and desserts? Try lemon basil, fresh or dried. Compared to other basils, lemon basil can be more slow growing, sometimes with a leggy appearance. 'Sweet Dani', an All American award winner, grows in a robust, bushy form, with good lemon flavor. 'Blue Spice' is the result of crossing lemon and sweet basil. Its leaves are tinged with purple and contain hints of vanilla. Once, when making potpourri, I threw together 'Blue Spice' basil flowers, lavender blossoms, and blue salvia flowers. It was a lovely combination.

Although these brief descriptions cover the basics of basil, many other basils are available for the adventuresome gardener. Check seed catalogs for a wide variety of basils for both culinary and ornamental use.

GROWING BASIL

Like other annuals, basil grows from seed. Warmth and adequate moisture speed the sprouting process. At 90°F, basil germinates in three days. When sown outdoors, wait until the soil is warm.

For a head start, the plants can be started indoors four to six weeks before the last frost date. A basil seedling's worst enemy is damp coolness. By keeping the temperature warm and the soil a little on the dry side, diseases like mildew and botrytis are avoided. Outdoors basil thrives in full sun, with well-drained soil.

Throughout the summer, pinching back the growing tips when flower buds appear will keep the plants bushy. I like to trim back sweet basil down to the inner framework of the plant. The new flush of leaves that follows is extra sweet.

Leaves are ready for picking at any stage. To dry, strip from the stems and lay flat (screens work well) in an area out of direct sunlight. The leaves may darken as they dry, but this does not affect the flavor.

Don't overlook basil's edible flowers, valuable for salads and more. I allow some plants to mature into the flowering stage. When the seed heads are brown and fully developed, they are ready for saving.

IN THE KITCHEN

Basil enhances many foods, but most of all anything with tomatoes, from salsa to pizza sauce. It blends well with vinegar, garlic, and other herbs like oregano, thyme, and rosemary. Use them fresh, dried, or even frozen, chopped with a bit of water to make cubes. The frozen form is good for soups.

When a recipe calls for dried basil and you want to use fresh leaves, double or triple the amount it asks for, according to your taste. Fresh leaves can be minced with a kitchen shears or, if you are using a lot for a canning project or pesto, chop in a bowl or blender.

I find it convenient to have basil flakes in a shaker with large holes, ready for frequent use. I add liberal amounts when mixing bread sticks or cooking a pot of spaghetti. I also reach for the shaker when making pizza to add a good sprinkle of basil flakes before topping with cheese.

Basil is essential for herbal vinegars, marinades, herb butters, jellies, and more. It flavors meats from roasted chicken to grilled salmon. Just like the many forms of basil, there are many, many ways in which you can taste the sweet, spicy, or lemony flavors.

Sweet basil

Borage

Compared to some annual herbs like dill and basil, borage doesn't share such widespread popularity. Yet I consider it a fascinating plant for two reasons. First, its bright blue flowers add a burst of brightness to any garden, like bits of the clear blue sky brought down to a gardener's level.

Second, borage *(Borago officinalis)* has an uncommon flavor. Most references describe it as cucumber-like. It does have a cool, neutral flavor like that of cucumbers, but I detect a delicate sweetness, too, edged with salt. Try it. You might have yet another interpretation of the taste!

Borage is native to Europe and northern Africa, but is now widely grown around the world. It was among the first plants brought to America by the early colonists. Since the days of ancient Rome, people held borage as a symbol of courage and happiness. Its blue flowers were said to banish sadness and dispel sorrow, to impart gladness and lighten the spirits. It's no wonder. The sky-blue stars bring irresistible cheer. Now, recent research has shown that the plant does indeed have mild antidepressant qualities.

TROUBLE-FREE ANNUAL

Borage is very easy to grow—great for children's gardens. You can get started simply by scattering its triangular seeds into good garden soil after danger of frost is past. An earlier start is possible by planting indoors, but use a method such as sowing into peat pots that won't disturb the taproot when transplanting. Space plants at least 15 inches apart.

Borage freely self-sows, and it seems that once you have it, you'll always have it. Since the seeds are viable for eight years, seedlings sometimes pop up in unexpected places.

The borage plant stands tall at 2½ to 3 feet, with a majestic, rounded form. The slightly fleshy leaves are oval and have a silvery green cast. Both leaves and stems are lined with clear hairs, fuzzy on young growth, becoming more prickly as they mature. In late summer its hollow stems are often prone to collapse. To prevent flopping you can either provide support or plant it alongside a sturdy plant, such as a rosebush.

STARS OF BLUE

Despite the plant's gangly appearance, the flowers are always pretty. The nodding clusters at the tips of the branches don't have long stems, nor are they long lasting, so their use as a cut flower is limited. But the blossoms are fully edible and lots of fun. Their flavor is neutral, so you can use them in many different ways.

Borage flowers have two parts. The five blue petals and five slender green sepals fit onto each other like hands on a clock. You can use the entire flower. Or, if you wish, snip off the pointed black anthers and lift the blue petals free, now with a perfect circular hole in the middle.

These blossoms can be frozen into ice cubes or floated on drinks just before serving. Tossed into a salad, they add a splash of unexpected color. These blue stars can be pressed into herb butter or fruit dip, or used atop a cake as an alternative to frosting. If you wish to admire the blossoms, but prefer not to eat them, they can be strewn amid place settings as a garnishing accent.

If you wish to crystallize them, dip flowers into beaten egg white then into extra fine granulated sugar. Repeat several times, allowing to dry between coats. They keep for a long time stored in a glass jar.

Borage flower

Borage flowers and leaves can be used as salt substitutes. They contain lots of potassium and calcium as well. See what happens when flower clusters are placed onto glowing embers. Unlike most plants that simply turn black, borage stems sparkle and shimmer as the natural salts meet the heat.

Borage leaves add a refreshing cucumber taste to salads and sandwiches. The tender young leaves are best, but well-rinsed older leaves are good, too. Most sources do not recommend frequently eating large amounts of borage due to the possibility of elevated alkaloid levels building up in the liver, but sensible occasional use will be okay.

COMPANION PLANTING

Beekeepers and orchardists sometimes plant patches of borage, knowing that bees are fond of the nectar-laden blue flowers. In fact, a nickname for borage is bee bread. If you wish to enhance pollination for your fruit trees or strawberry patch, consider planting borage nearby.

Other insects like borage as well. Borage acts as an attractant to grasshoppers and tomato worms. Since it tolerates having holes chewed into its leaves, plant some near tomatoes or mints to reduce insect problems.

MEDICINAL

Borage is mainly used as a culinary herb, but it also has some medicinal use. Borage tea is soothing and has diuretic properties. When mashed, the leaves are mucilaginous and make a cooling poultice. Most borage that is commercially grown is used for seed production. Borage seed oil has a high omega-3 content and is a useful ingredient for both food and cosmetics.

Calendula

A FLOWER WITH FLAVOR

Sometimes the line between herbs and flowers becomes a bit obscure. Calendula (pronounced kuh-LEND-yoo-luh) is a prime example. Its bright petals provide spice and color for food, and soothing, healing merits for the skin and stomach. It does all of this and adorns the garden. Its colorful blossoms appear continually from early summer until frost. Did you know that calendula's name indicates this long blooming habit? It comes from *calend*, a Latin word meaning "first of the month." Our word *calendar* derives from the same root.

Calendula's favorable reputation began long ago according to its host of nicknames, including Marybud, summer's bride, and holygold. The most common nickname, pot marigold, is used today, referring to a spice thrown into the cooking pot. During the Middle Ages petals appeared in European spice markets by the barrel. Calendula was vaguely similar to expensive saffron and much more affordable. The colorful petals also provided medicine and fabric dye. Apparently calendula seeds were tucked in some trunk on the Mayflower voyage, for it was a valued plant in the Pilgrims' gardens.

Dried calendula

Calendula plants of long ago produced pale green leaves and single yellow flowers. After many years the leaves haven't changed much, but the flowers have developed some variations. Brighter, more vibrant shades such as orange, apricot, and lemon yellow appear. Numerous named varieties offer single and double blossoms ranging from 1 to 3 inches across. Depending on the space you want to fill, you could choose from a compact 10-inch plant or taller ones that reach from 18 to 24 inches.

NOT JUST ANY MARIGOLD

Calendula or pot marigold should not be confused with our common garden marigold, a totally unrelated family known as Tagetes. Calendula is native to Mediterranean regions while garden marigolds come from Central America. The flowers have similar colors and shapes, but only calendula is suitable for culinary use. (A few Tagetes such as 'Tangerine Gem' are exceptions.) Calendula blossoms have a mild but tangy taste while garden marigolds emit a bitter odor. Most garden marigolds are toxic—although not highly poisonous—and their unappetizing smell is a built-in warning.

A GARDENER'S DELIGHT

Calendula does best in full sun, in nearly any soil except very rich, moist soil. Sandy or meager soil is rarely a hindrance. It also tolerates both cold

CALENDULA

and heat, growing in Zones 3 to 10. In Zones 8 to 10 treat it as a cool-weather annual. I've noticed that calendula in my garden blooms prolifically as cooler fall weather approaches. Its sunny yellow contrasts nicely with other cool-weather flowers, especially purple pansies.

Calendula blossom

Knobby, curled calendula seeds germinate readily, perfect for young gardeners. Seeds are most often direct-sowed outdoors, sprouting within a week. Thin to 10 to 12 inches apart. For an earlier start, seeds can also be started indoors four to six weeks before frost-free date.

Flowers are prime for picking just as fully opened. Even if you're not harvesting flowers for use, remove the faded ones to encourage new buds. A plant whose flowers all mature to seed will wither and die. Although calendula reseeds easily, it's not invasive. In spring you can thin and resituate seedlings with a garden trowel.

After picking, flowers can be used fresh or dried. Drying is simple. Just place the flowers on a screen. I prefer drying the whole flowers, and if a recipe calls for petals only, pluck them from the bitter center disk, but you could do this step while the flowers are fresh and scatter only petals on the screen. Even when dried, petals will have a chewy texture rather than crispy. To prevent mold, make sure they're fully dried before putting in a jar. Store out of direct light to preserve color.

GOLDEN OPPORTUNITIES

Although calendula's primary use is medicinal, the bright yellow and orange petals provide some interesting options in the kitchen, both for flavor and color. They impart a unique taste—like honey with a touch of vegetable oil and hints of squash—while adding a golden color. Use calendula in dishes in which the combination of earthy flavor and sunny color are compatible, for example, broth-based soups, gravy, rice, and noodles. Add to the liquid at the beginning.

With a neutral yet sweetly resinous taste, calendula will enhance baked goods and desserts, such as pumpkin bread or cookies, cornmeal muffins, or carrot cake. Use your favorite recipe and add 2 to 3 tablespoons dried petals (a bit more if fresh) for an interesting color and texture. Fresh calendula petals dress up salads, especially egg salad or one with dark greens like spinach or kale. These appealing petals also color herb butters and omelets a sunny yellow.

SKIN CARE AND STOMACH CURE

Soothing skin is calendula's best-known virtue. Many natural skin care products—lotions, salves, creams, tinctures, or ointments—contain calendula. Researchers are not certain exactly what makes calendula effective, but it seems to have anti-inflammatory compounds. Products with calendula relieve irritated, chapped, or sunburned skin and heal wounds, scrapes, and scratches. Its astringent action will tone facial skin with large pores or acne, yet is gentle and safe for babies' diaper rash.

Calendula blossom

Another use involves gastrointestinal health. The same astringent action settles the stomach, easing ulcers and intestinal cramps when taken as a tea. Deep golden calendula tea is rich in vitamin C and phosphorus. Steep 1 teaspoon petals in a cup of water for 5 minutes.

Catnip and Its Cousins

Have you met the Nepeta (pronounced NEP-uh-tuh) family? The most familiar member, catnip, is a well-known tea plant. After centuries of use, this soothing herb still occupies an important spot in herb gardens. Besides catnip, the Nepeta family includes a group of decorative perennials called catmint. These don't contain the medicinal power their cousin catnip does, but they give carefree, aromatic beauty to herb gardens and flower beds.

Catswort, catsmint, nip, nep: catnip's nicknames are many. To add to the confusion, the names "catmint" and "catnip" are sometimes interchanged! They are closely related, but they are not one and the same. Identification is simple by using the botanical name, Nepeta, followed by the specific name.

CATNIP

Five hundred years ago, not a single catnip *(Nepeta cataria)* grew in North America. Instead, the plant inhabited only the gardens and fields of its native Europe. Historical lore says catnip flourished near a certain Roman town named Nepeti, and received its name there.

Multipurpose catnip was one of the main medicinal herbs grown in monastery gardens, for both internal and external uses. In Europe, catnip tea was a favorite beverage before tea was imported from the Far East. It was often given to children (sweetened with honey) to ease stomach disorders like colic and diarrhea. A preparation of the leaves treated skin sores, scalp irritations, and bruises.

After early settlers brought catnip to America, it rapidly naturalized, so even the native Americans discovered its usefulness. The Cherokees treated colds and coughs and made a parasite-killing potion. The Iroquois gave it to infants and children to ease stomach complaints and sore throat and to promote sound sleep. The Chippewas found it useful to reduce fevers.

Modern herbalists still recommend catnip tea for a relaxing drink to take before bedtime or anytime a calming tonic is needed. Catnip is also a fine remedy for upset stomach, cold, and flu. It controls diarrhea and relieves headaches. Because it stimulates sweating, catnip helps break a fever. It has also shown usefulness for relieving allergies, hemorrhoids, arthritis, and rheumatism.

Catnip contains compounds that repel mosquitoes and other insects. Research shows these compounds to be just as effective as DEET. Rub bruised catnip leaves on arms and face for a quick, natural, and safe mosquito deterrent.

Today catnip grows nearly everywhere, thanks to its self-sowing abilities. Because of its adaptable growing habits, you may see it flourish at creek's edge or in high, dry meadows. Another sure catnip habitat is any abandoned farmstead. The buildings may be sagging in disrepair, but in the old, neglected garden, catnip thrives!

Catnip from the wild is fine for harvesting. Yet for convenience and quality, I grow it in my garden. Cultivated plants do have larger, more abundant leaves. I also snip off the flowers soon after bloom, which prevents self-sowing.

You can dig a clump from the wild for your garden or grow it from seed.

Germination may be 50 percent or less, so sow thickly, indoors in early spring or outdoors after danger of frost.

Catnip's square stems and paired leaves show its relation to mints, but it doesn't have runaway roots like mints. It has a clump that enlarges yearly. Occasionally it might be good to lift out the old, woody clumps and keep only a newer section.

Catnip is no dazzling herb, but I like its downy heart-shaped leaves, grayish green on top and silvery white beneath. In midsummer, tiny lavender flower clusters appear on the stem tips. The flavor of catnip is hard to describe. It's somewhat minty, yet not sweet, with hints of thyme and camphor.

The plant is tall, up to 36 inches when flowering. In early spring, its lush, well-balanced look is striking in the garden. After bloom, it tends to become a bit shaggy. A good trimming that reduces the height to half or one-third will stimulate a flush of new growth.

Lemon catnip *(N. cataria citriodora)* looks and grows much like other catnip, but has a mild citrus flavor which makes a pleasant tea. The intensity of lemon flavor may vary from plant to plant.

Do cats actually like catnip? Yes, the same plant that calms people will excite cats. Given a chance, many cats respond to the plant with sniffing and licking, paw-swatting, or even a frenzied rolling among the stems. Catnip-filled cloth toys for kitties can be bought in pet shops. Catnip response seems to be an inherited trait. About a third of cats ignore it.

CATMINT

After taking a look at the medicinal Nepeta, catnip, let's acquaint ourselves with the beautiful Nepeta, catmint, which is one of the most gardener-friendly plants around. It's vigorous and hardy but seldom needs division. The flowers in shades of soft lavender or vivid blue are long-lasting. Sounds like the ideal plant, doesn't it?

Catmint is a sort of broad title for the various decorative Nepetas. All have mildly aromatic leaves and lots of flowers. Full sun and dry soil is best for all except *Nepeta*

Catnip

siberica. Because they have different heights and colors, we'll focus on each one separately.

Nepeta faassenii (also known as Faassen's catnip) is a showy catmint, growing to 18 inches. It thrives best in sandy or well-drained soil. This low, bushy plant has tiny, silvery foliage and a profusion of lavender blue flowers. It's perfect for rock gardens or underplanting among roses and irises. Butterflies and bees love its abundant blooms.

Catmint

Bloom time is through June. When old flowers are clipped, it will bloom again in late summer. The flowers are sterile, so don't worry about self-sowing! Two hybrid cultivars, 'Blue Wonder' and 'Walker's Low', make spectacular silver-leaved, blue-flowering ground covers in sunny areas.

Nepeta siberica is the biggest, boldest catmint. It stands 36 inches tall, with upright branches in a shapely form. This catmint actually prefers somewhat moister soil and will tolerate partial shade. *N. siberica's* vivid blue flowers resemble veronica. It benefits from a bit of shearing after the flowers are spent to promote another round of flowering and to control the plant's shape. Several outstanding cultivars of *Nepeta siberica* include 'Six Hills Giant', a tall extremely cold-hardy cultivar, and 'Souvenir d'Andre Chaudron', also known as 'Blue Beauty', which has long-lasting flowers and grows vigorously.

SLEEP PILLOW

Sew an 8x8-inch bag using prewashed muslin fabric, leaving one side open. Blend ¼ cup each dried catnip leaves and lavender blossoms. Pick out any sharp stems. Place dried mixture into the bag and sew shut. Slip this scented bag between your pillow and pillowcase. Enjoy the soothing sweet fragrance. It will help you relax! Zzz…

CATNIP TEA

Pour 1 cup boiling water over 1 tablespoon fresh or ½ tablespoon dried catnip leaves. Let set 5 minutes. Strain and sweeten with honey or stevia if desired. Adults can drink 2 to 3 cups daily. This tea is also safe for children in smaller doses. To improve flavor, add peppermint or chamomile to catnip.

Chamomile

Chamomile (pronounced KAM-uh-mile) holds the honor of being among the oldest herbs in continuous use. Some old herbal guides give almost no description of chamomile. Why? None was necessary because it was so well-known and widely used.

ONE, TWO FOR TEA

The name chamomile refers to two totally unrelated plants, although both have a mild, sweet apple-pineapple flavor that's valued for tea. Both have fine, light green leaves and daisy-like flowers. Both are very easy to grow. But there the similarities end. German chamomile is an annual that grows tall, up to 18 inches, while Roman chamomile is a ground-hugging perennial.

In midsummer, German chamomile *(Matricaria reciutita)* has cheery white flowers with a yellow button center, almost an inch in diameter. They dot the plant abundantly and beg to be used for a flavorful tea. Any chamomile tea you buy is German chamomile, which has far more medicinal value than Roman chamomile. Depending where you live you may be able to find German chamomile growing in vacant areas or along a roadway. Some guidebooks even call it wild chamomile, although that is still another plant.

ONE FOR THE LAWN

Another name for Roman chamomile *(Anthemis nobilis)* is lawn chamomile and with good reason. It's a sturdy ground cover that releases a pleasant pineapple scent when crushed. Before modern lawn-trimming equipment was available, wild chamomile often covered hard-to-mow corners, around the barnyard, for example. True Roman chamomile, though, forms a soft, creeping mat which is very pleasant for bare feet. English herb gardens often have a quaint feature: a chamomile bench. This is basically a raised bed of bricks or stones laid to comfortable sitting height with Roman chamomile for the "cushion"! Roman chamomile can be started from seed, but a started plant is easier. Quick-growing and water-loving, Roman chamomile puts out eager shoots that soon root to the ground. Still, it's not invasive.

GROWING AND HARVESTING

Now we're back to discussing German chamomile. Growing it is extremely easy and as simple as scattering seeds! Choose a spot with full sun and well-prepared soil. In early spring, sow the tiny seeds. Keep evenly moist and weed-free. Within several weeks you should be rewarded with tiny chamomile plants.

Given a sunny place to grow, chamomile takes care of itself. Flowering time, in June, is delightful, with bees and insects buzzing by to enjoy the wealth of blossoms. After you've harvested blossoms and the remaining ones have gone to seed, the plant tops can be trimmed off. Sprinkle some seeds onto the ground for next year's crop. Remember, German chamomile is an annual.

Dried chamomile blossoms

HARVESTING

Chamomile's most active ingredients are found in the flower heads, so that's the part to harvest. When the flowers are in full bloom, in mid-June, snip or pull them off, and place on screens to dry. Store the dried flowers in glass jars.

IN THE KITCHEN

Chamomile takes second place to other herbs when it comes to flavoring food. Its primary culinary use is making tea. Chamomile jelly, made with tea, has a honey-like flavor. Here's a little hint about tea: brewing chamomile tea for too long can make the tea bitter. Prepare the tea and serve soon.

MEDICINAL USES

Chamomile's beneficial properties are so many and varied, it's hard to keep count! It is proven to be one of the safest herbs, suitable even for children.

However, beware if you have hay fever; experts say those who react to ragweed might also react to its relative, chamomile. Use cautiously at first, if there's a possibility of allergies. If you notice no ill effects, go ahead and use it.

Chamomile tea is mild and soothing, and is the traditional first choice herb for aiding digestion. It makes sense to drink chamomile tea after a meal. I've heard that even the most distinguished restaurants offer chamomile tea as an after-meal beverage. Both hot and iced tea are effective.

Another use for chamomile when taken as tea or tincture is to help calm upset stomach and other digestive ailments such as heartburn or ulcers. It also counteracts insomnia and eases stress. That's why so many teas with names such as "Good Night" and "Sleep Tight" have chamomile as their main ingredient. In Beatrix Potter's famous story, Mrs. Rabbit gives little Peter Cottontail chamomile tea at bedtime. Chamomile essential oil effectively relieves muscular aches and pains when applied externally.

Gingivitis, inner ear infection, cough, and other respiratory concerns—with regular use, chamomile helps conquer and prevent these conditions. To relieve a stuffy nose, prepare chamomile infusion in a bowl and inhale the steam deeply. The stronger the infusion, the more results.

NIGHTTIME TEA

Ingredients Needed:

1 part mint   1 part catnip
1 part chamomile

Directions:

Variations for chamomile tea: Sweeten with honey and serve with a slice of lemon. Add a pinch of grated ginger before serving.

CHAMOMILE FACIAL SCRUB

Ingredients Needed:

3 bars Dove® soap, grated   ½ c. dried sage leaves, crushed
1½ c. dried chamomile flowers 1 c. oatmeal flakes (optional)

Directions:

Blend all ingredients. To use, enclose a tablespoon of mixture in a muslin bag or doubled cheesecloth and tie with string. Wet both the bag and your face. Rub with circular motion to stimulate circulation and remove dead skin cells.

Chamomile blossoms

Chives

Cheerful and charming, it's easy to have chives for a favorite herb! In early spring, chives is often the first in the herb garden to bravely peek its head through the soil and proclaim, "Spring is here; it's time to start growing." Few other herbs are as gardener friendly, as fuss-free, and as useful in the kitchen.

COMMON CHIVES

A clump of chives *(Allium schoenprasum)* might look like a mere bunch of grass, but it's much more! Chives has long slender leaves that are hollow (like thin straws) and taper to a point. In spring, the plant blooms, with globelike lavender-pink flowers. Chives, an onion family member, has tiny onion-like bulbs that grow closely together to form clumps.

Mostly, chives is known only by its common name, yet there are some named varieties: Profusion produces leaves and flowers prolifically, but the flowers do not develop seeds. 'Grolau' is a good choice for indoor windowsill gardening, being developed for greenhouse forcing. A newer variety, 'Grande', has exceptionally large leaves and flowers. 'Forescate' has flowers that are more pink.

GARLIC CHIVES

As its name suggests, this kind of chives has a garlic flavor. The leaves are flat and ribbonlike rather than hollow, and its flowers are white and larger than the pink of the common chives. It reaches a height of about 10 to 12 inches. Garlic chives are very easy to grow, tolerating both sun and shade. Interestingly, there is a form of garlic chives, mauve garlic chives, that does have pink flowers. Garlic chives *(Allium tuberosum)* is sometimes called Chinese chives, due to its wide usage in Asian cooking.

GETTING STARTED

The quickest way to establish chives is by obtaining potted plants; or if your neighbor or friend has chives, you may divide an existing clump. Whether you wish to add to your existing amount or begin a new stand, it's as easy as grabbing a shovel! Lift out a clump after loosening all around, then divide it by pulling apart sections of ten or more bulblets. The sections can be planted from 8 to 12 inches apart. After replanting, I often trim off the green leaves about 2 or 3 inches above the ground to minimize transplant shock. Water regularly and you'll see your new chive plants thrive!

Garlic chives

Starting chives by seed is another way to begin, with both indoor or outdoor sowing. Using fresh seed is important for best germination. Sowing indoors, at least four to six weeks before your area's last frost-free date, gives a head start on the season. Sow the seeds thickly in packs or trays and keep evenly moist, at around 65–70°F. Even with the best of conditions, chive germination can be a bit slow, up to fourteen days. Generally, garlic chives sprout sooner and easier than the common chives. After sprouting, however, chives grow rapidly, and can soon be transplanted outdoors in small sections, with several plants per section.

When sowing outdoors, sow about one-half inch deep in finely cultivated soil. Covering with peat moss helps keep the area moist and prevents weed competition with the tiny, new plants as well. It could take several years to have a sizable clump of chives started by seed. Regular trimming helps develop a thicker stand.

GROWING

When I was a beginning herb gardener, I was unaware of the secrets of growing lush, vibrant chives. By the second year, none of the beautiful clumps that I had envisioned along the south edge of the herb garden existed. Instead, there were rather limp, scraggly-looking heaps of dull green leaves, with barely enough flowers to prove that they were chives. How disappointing! What was wrong?

Then a fellow gardener shared some valuable tips: Clip regularly and give it the sunniest spot in your herb garden for perky growth. Keeping the plant well-manicured spurs it to grow.

In early spring, as chives bravely emerges, little maintenance is needed. Simply watch it grow—the true signal of spring's arrival! Even the very first tender stalks can be snipped with moderation, to enjoy that distinctive taste.

Soon after, flower buds form and mature. Now's the chance to dry a bunch of those. Delightful as these flowers are, I am careful not to let them go to seed. Chives gone to seed can be a real problem, spreading especially to grassy areas like yards and pastures.

After flowering time, clip off your clumps of chives and water well for a new flush of growth. I clip off just above the ground. Whenever you harvest, the leaves should be clipped off just above ground level. Only tipping the leaves slows growth, and causes the leaves to brown, making an unsightly harvest later on. Perhaps clipping off the whole clump seems a bit drastic and you want to keep the looks of the clump rather than topping it. Clip only about half of the plant, with a random thinning effect and then later, once new growth has sprung, you can thin the other half.

Regular harvest throughout the summer usually provides all the clipping your chives need. With all the possible uses for chives, regular harvest shouldn't be a problem! Sometimes, though, with a lot of chives, a clump or two may have escaped the shears and could benefit from a good trimming. Then, with one eye on the approaching rain clouds that will soon drench the ever-thirsty chives, I dash out with the kitchen shears and clip, clip.

Chives are also useful as container plants, indoors or out. As patio plants in pots or boxes, chives' spiky leaves provide a touch of contrast, plus the pink or white flowers are an added delight. Potted chives require little particular care besides regular watering and occasional trimming to keep the plants looking their best.

During winter, chives brought indoors provide a handy harvest of the flavorful leaves. A clump can be lifted out and potted for windowsill growing. Keep in mind that chives might have a period of dormancy before regrowth; therefore, keep it cool, dark, and a bit dry for several weeks, then water and promote growth.

EDIBLE "FROM HEAD TO TOE"

With their delicate onion flavor, chives are a charm in the kitchen! Best of all, not one part of the plant need be overlooked, for every part of the entire plant is edible, from the bulblike roots to the showy pink flowers, as well as the green leaves between them. Chives also have the side benefits of being rich in calcium and vitamins A and C. Chive blossoms, pink for common, white for garlic, also have the same mild onion flavor. Added to a salad, they provide an unusual burst of color. Fully opened flowers can be separated into tiny individual florets for smaller pieces. Partly opened buds with just a bit of color showing are also nice for tossing with a salad. Fresh chive blossoms are also useful as a garnish.

Chive blossom vinegar is both pretty and easy to make. Place two or more blossoms (several leaves also, if you wish) in a glass jar and cover with apple cider vinegar. The vinegar becomes a lovely light pink. I let the flowers remain in the jar as long as there's sufficient vinegar to cover. This vinegar is useful in salad dressings, bean salad, and marinade.

Another fun thing to do with chive blossoms is drying them in a bunch. Simply select a good-sized bouquet of flowers that have just fully opened. Hang upside down to dry, out of direct light. The stems tend to fade a bit, but the flowers keep their

Chive blossoms

cheery pink hue quite well. Tie with a coordinating bow and hang in your kitchen.

Of course, the most widely used part of chives is the leaves, both fresh and dried. Because chives has a long growing season—the first plant up in the spring, last plant to settle for winter—using fresh chives is possible for most of the year. This is a real plus since chives in their fresh form are far more flavorful than dried chives.

Using fresh chives is quick and easy. A kitchen shears works well for cutting a bunch of leaves, then mincing them finely. Rinsing the leaves before mincing or chopping them is usually not required. Sometimes a few yellowed leaves or other plant debris need to be picked out, but proper plant trimming prevents a lot of unusable leaves.

Chopped fresh chives can be substituted for onions in many dishes for a different twist; for example, haystacks, pizza, or meat loaf. Chives are also an excellent nutritious condiment, served with coneys or other sandwiches.

Chives' bright green leaves do wonders in dressing up light-colored foods such as creamy soups or stuffed eggs. Just a few sprinkles add a touch of attractive green, plus that delicate onion flavor.

Yet chives seem to rise to their best when served with potatoes. Chives, sour cream, and butter seem to be the perfect trio with potatoes in various forms—baked, or simply cooked and drained.

Let's not forget the roots! Remember, they're like tiny, tiny onions. After trimming off the hairlike fibers and rinsing, chive roots can be minced and used as you would onions.

Chives are easily dried, though some flavor and color is sacrificed. Often, dried chives are used in recipes that require baking, such as breads. To dry your own chives, cut fresh leaves into tiny bits and place in your oven (not turned on) or other slightly warmer spot for quick drying.

Another method of preserving chives is freeze drying. Spread chopped leaves onto a cookie sheet, single layer, and pop into the freezer for several minutes, or until the pieces are frozen. Keep frozen in a freezer container or bag.

Minced chives

Is Comfrey
IN YOUR GARDEN?

I've never heard anyone oohing or aahing over a comfrey plant. Yet it's one of the most useful plants in an herb garden. Who would guess that this tall, slightly unkempt mass of broad, prickly leaves has so much potential?

Few plants are as green—simply chlorophyll-laden green—as comfrey. It emerges from the soil in early spring and simply grows and grows all summer. The leaves are fleshy and slightly prickly, like those of its relative, borage, although much bigger, up to 2 feet long and as wide as my hand. Eventually the plant puts up some taller stalks (3 to 4 feet), topped with tiny, nodding white

Comfrey blossom

to pinkish flowers.

Both common comfrey *(Symphytum officinale)* and Russian comfrey *(Symphytum uplandicum)* will tolerate full sun, but they really prefer patchy or partial shade. Comfrey loves moisture too. It takes a lot of water to support the high moisture content in its roots and leaves. Yet it is also quite tough and will survive even when the temperature dips to 40°F below zero.

I rarely bother with winter protection. In late fall, the mass of leaves mats down to form its own mulch. In spring, these should be cleared away to make way for the new sprouts.

New plants should be spaced at least 2 feet apart; farther if you want easy digging for the roots. Leaves can be harvested as soon as possible from young plants. It takes at least one growing season to have sizable roots.

COMFREY, CONTROLLED

Comfrey has a reputation for being an aggressive grower. Yes, when left alone, the roots (actually rhizomes) will spread relentlessly. My comfrey grows in our north garden, alongside the rhubarb in a well mulched area. I like it there because the roots are easy to dig in good garden soil, compared to hard, packed ground in some grassy area. In loose, cultivated soil, the roots are reasonably straight and have good size.

Because I dig lots of roots every year for salve making, there isn't a big risk of it spreading out of control even though it has the best of growing conditions. Left unchecked it might take over the entire garden in two or three years! Once comfrey has spread out of control, it's hard to eradicate. A physical barrier such as landscape timbers or an upright piece of roofing will help contain it, or, better yet, plant it alongside a slab of concrete.

By midsummer when I need roots, the plants are top-heavy and the flower stalks sprawl over to the side. It doesn't hurt to be ruthless with comfrey, so with several mighty chops of the shovel, I quickly deal with any stems that interfere with my digging plans. Discarded parts go into the compost bin. The high nitrogen levels in comfrey leaves make them an excellent mulch and help other things break down faster as well.

For ease of preparation, I like to go for the biggest roots, which are about an inch thick. By carefully tugging at an exposed end rather than chopping off anything visible with the shovel, it's possible to extract pieces up to 12 inches long. A thin, nearly black, skin-like layer covers the root. The German name for comfrey is, indeed, *Schwarzwurz*, that is, black root.

Although roots can be peeled or scrubbed with a stiff brush, I prefer dry-cleaning with a cloth to keep the black layer intact. Pieces of old denim or knit fabric are ideal. Twisting and rubbing with both hands will soon remove all traces of soil. The black layer is smooth and almost shiny. Keeping this layer makes the roots less messy to handle up to the point when you will peel, chop, or mince them. The interior is white and mucilaginous (slightly sticky and slimy). Peeling the roots will make a lighter-colored salve or tincture. I've used unpeeled roots, too, to save time.

Most times I use comfrey roots immediately after digging, but they can also be dried by slicing thinly and letting them dry on screens in a warm area or in the sun. Dried roots can later be powdered.

HARVESTING LEAVES

Comfrey leaves are best used fresh, but they can also be dried by cutting before the flowers appear. Place leaves in a single layer out of direct sunlight. Leaves are dried when they have changed color, but are still a bit pliable. They can be stored in jars, crumbled, if you wish to save space, or packed in layers in boxes, just like burdock leaves.

SHARE IT

Your clump of comfrey can be seen as an opportunity to share this useful plant with others. Almost any piece of comfrey root, large or small, will grow if it is placed in good soil and kept watered. I've had good success with early spring propagation by selecting root pieces about as thick and as long as my little finger that have a green growing tip attached. Place them in a container with potting soil. The young green leaves may wilt; keep them out of direct sunlight and give lots of water. They're sure to perk up soon! In fact, within a week you can have an assortment of vigorous little plants!

A FODDER CROP

Since it grows fast and yields a mass of nutrient-rich leaves, comfrey is also a useful forage plant for animals. Its thick green leaves are excellent fodder for goats, rabbits, and other nibblers. When I was a little girl, I would join my cousins to cut comfrey leaves for their hogs. They loaded leaves onto a two-wheeled wooden garden cart known as the "comfrey cart," then wheeled it to the hog pens. How we liked to watch those greedy eaters! After being cut, comfrey rebounds and may produce up to three or four cuttings in a season.

There is even a southern Minnesota town named Comfrey. The story goes that, in 1878, the new postmaster of that area had just read a U.S. government publication on growing comfrey as animal fodder, when the need to name the new town arose. In 1998, Comfrey was hit by a severe tornado and nearly wiped off the map. Living up to the healing reputation of its namesake, the town rallied together and was rebuilt.

A GREAT MENDER

Comfrey popularity as a healing plant is evident in its name, derived from Latin and meaning "to grow together." In fact, its nicknames include knitbone, boneset (not to be confused with another plant by that name), and bruisewort. These bring out the plant's ability to heal broken bones and damaged muscles. It can also give soothing, cooling relief to soft tissue injury. But most of all, comfrey salve and tincture are indispensable for the many scrapes and wounds, even burns, that inevitably occur. Yes, make sure your herbal first aid kit includes comfrey!

While comfrey is also rich in calcium, potassium, and vitamins A and C, plus other trace minerals, two separate compounds are responsible for its healing action. Rosmarinic acid deals with inflammation, and allantoin works to repair cells and promote their growth. Both leaves and roots have these properties. The roots have more, but the leaves taste better, so take your pick!

IS COMFREY SAFE?

Nearly any herbal health reference will mention the controversy of internalizing comfrey; that is, using it for tea, drink, or food. These precautions are based on fairly recent studies despite comfrey's widespead use for hundreds of years. Supposedly, the plant's roots and tender, young leaves have higher levels of a substance that could cause liver damage. It doesn't hurt to be cautious, so you might decide to use only full-sized, mature leaves for making tea. For myself, I don't have qualms making a decocted tea from the roots, either.

Comfrey is often mixed with other tea herbs for respiratory cleansing, and for taking care of inflammation. If I were laid up with a sprain or broken bone, I would also drink comfrey smoothies—blended fresh leaves with anise hyssop or mint to improve the flavor, along with pineapple juice.

Thankfully, there have never been any warnings surrounding external comfrey use. Comfrey leaf may freely be applied as a poultice on soft tissue injuries such as sprains. My brother has had frequent bouts with bursitis in his knee. A thick poultice of comfrey leaves, scalded until limp, then placed between two layers of gauze and wrapped around the knee brought relief. Another option is to peel and mash fresh roots and apply topically. Be careful with comfrey on deep, open wounds, especially puncture wounds, if there is risk of infection. You don't want the surface of the wound to close up before the inside heals.

Comfrey salve is probably the most convenient way to use it for small scrapes and burns. Infused oils and tinctures are still other ways to use it externally.

Comfrey leaves

Coriander or Cilantro

Two names for one plant? "Hmmm," you may ask, "may I just use the name I like best?" Well, it depends on which part of the plant you're describing. Say "cilantro" and you're talking about the green, leafy part of the plant; say "coriander" and you're naming the dried seeds. For the plant as a whole, use the word coriander.

Cilantro (a Spanish word pronounced see-LON-tro) is also sometimes called Chinese parsley. Cilantro and parsley, especially flat leaf, do have a lot in common. Both have a chlorophyll-rich green color, and grow in similar size and shape. Even the seed heads in later summer are similar. But one major difference is their taste. Cilantro's flavor outdoes parsley, with a rich, musky flavor hinting of celery and onion. The dried seeds offer yet a slightly different flavor, a blend of spice and citrus, with a somewhat sweet aftertaste.

People all over the world use cilantro, especially in Asia and Latin America, and it has long been associated with Southwestern cooking. In North America, cilantro has rapidly gained popularity in recent years. Its increased demand has partly been created by many immigrants who wish to continue cooking with this favorite herb. Even the Spanish word *cilantro*, which has become the name for the fresh leaves, reflects Latin American influence.

My past experience with coriander *(Coriandrum sativum)* was humdrum. I sowed it, watered it, observed it, nibbled it (a little), and in the fall pulled out the brown stalks. After a visit to Central America, where cilantro appeared time and again to give a delicious touch to tacos, rice, beans, sauces, and salads, my appreciation for the plant was truly rekindled! Now I sow lots of it, anticipating an abundance for cooking. I'm also fascinated how manna was "like unto coriander seed" (Numbers 11:7). What a miracle it must have been to gather these tiny balls.

SELECTING CORIANDER

Depending whether you wish to grow lots of cilantro or gather many seeds, there is a coriander suited for it. Corianders are annuals, and grown from seed. Seed coriander, or just plain coriander, has feathery leaves like Queen Anne's lace. It will set seeds readily in midsummer, sending up a taller stalk of nearly 30 inches, and blooming white blossom heads, which mature to seeds. The immature seeds actually smell unpleasant; don't worry, the delightful scent is gained at ripening. Leaves of seed coriander can be used like cilantro, but since they are fine and delicate, they're much more difficult to gather.

For a leafy cilantro plant that is slow to bolt, choose one of the named corianders: 'Longstanding' or 'Santo'. Pot cilantro is a generic term. These have broad leaves, similar to flat parsley, with slightly notched edges. They remain a bushy, compact dark green plant, unlike seed coriander, and allow repeated leaf pickings. Eventually they will produce seed heads, but successive planting helps keep a plentiful supply of tender young plants. Pot cilantro is good for potted plants and windowsill gardening.

Mexican coriander *(Eryngium foetidum)* is a tender perennial, not related although they taste very similar. It has thicker, almost fleshy leaves, which some prefer.

GROWING IT

Coriander is an annual with several growing habits to consider. First, it dislikes being transplanted, so sow outdoors where you intend it to grow. It should be sown in prepared soil at a depth of about ¼ inch, and kept evenly moist to soften the outer seed coat. I like to sow mine in little rows, with the seeds about an inch apart, and 12 inches between the rows. About ⅓ or ½ packet is ample for a single sowing.

After the seedlings emerge, thin them to about 6 inches apart. The thinned-out plantlets are ideal to add to salads. You could begin to harvest leaves when the plants are 6 inches or taller.

Coriander is a cool-weather plant. It can be sown early, even a week or two before your frost-free date since it thrives in the cool temperatures of spring. Successive plantings about three weeks apart help keep a good supply of fresh cilantro. In summer, it may help to plant it in a partially shaded area. Sowing again in July ensures an ample supply for canning salsa and other tomato-based foods. In warmer areas, a late summer or fall sowing might overwinter successfully.

Cilantro

Like lettuce, coriander has a tendency to bolt when it is stressed by poor soil or overcrowding and summer's heat and drought. It shoots up a tall stem and produces a batch of seeds. No more leaves, no more cilantro, only coriander! Weed it diligently, keep it thinned, and water if necessary. A bit of mulch or natural fertilizer such as liquid kelp mixed in with the water helps the plant to stay in the leaf-producing mode.

But coriander varies a lot from plant to plant. Sometimes there's a nice row of leafy plants, except for one, reaching skyward and adorned with a crown of seeds. Some plants may have finely toothed leaves; others have leaves with few or no toothed edges. It's interesting to watch it grow.

PUTTING IT TO USE

To harvest cilantro, pick the outer, mature leaves at the base of the plant. New leaves emerge out of the center of the plant, so leave that part undisturbed.

Unfortunately, cilantro does not dry well and must be used fresh. Its storage life can be prolonged, though, by refrigerating it. Place either an entire plant or just leaves in a plastic bag and moisten it a little. Too wet is not good. Even when a bit wilted, it is still okay.

When using cilantro in cooking, snip it finely with a knife or kitchen shears. It has a dominant flavor, and mincing it well helps to blend the flavor throughout the food.

If cilantro is a new herb for you, become acquainted with it by adding small amounts to foods you already know, such as chili, or rice with vegetables. Cilantro really enhances tomato-based dishes like salsa. Garlic, paprika, and chili pepper are good seasonings to blend with cilantro.

For a simple but tasty salsa, combine tomato chunks with chopped onion and minced cilantro and enough vinegar to cover. If you prefer some heat, use diced habanero peppers instead of tomato. Serve this condiment with chicken, rice, beans, tortillas, or other main dishes. Use a fork to serve, draining off the vinegar. Replenish vinegar as needed with fresh chopped vegetables.

To collect coriander seed, watch the seed heads in late summer to observe the ripeness. When the seeds turn brown, they are ready. The seed heads should be clipped off before the seeds are ripened to the point of loosening and falling. Hang them in an airy place to dry fully, then store in a glass jar. The seed heads can also be used in dried arrangements for a touch of interest and varied texture. Their spicy scent also lends a delightful flair to sachets and potpourris.

When a recipe asks for coriander seed, it usually refers to ground seed. Seeds can be ground by crushing them with a mortar and pestle, or other heavy object. The round seed is actually the seed coat, encasing two or more little moon-shaped seeds. The seeds have a citrus-like flavor, and add a nice zest to cookies, rolls, or other baked goods.

Coriander seed

Cilantro is a good source of chlorophyll and helps maintain joint health. It can help stimulate an appetite when brewed as a tea, about one teaspoon chopped fresh leaves per cup of water.

CORIANDER OR CILANTRO |75|

Dill Delights

Thanks to the popularity of dill pickles, dill is a familiar flavor for most people. Since ancient times, dill *(Anethum graveolens)* has been an important cooking herb, but it also had other roles. For example, traces of dill weed have been found in Egyptian tombs. The Greeks nibbled dill seed to cure hiccups. In pioneer days, dill was called "Meetin' Seed" because the settlers' children chewed dill seed during lengthy sermons!

Dill is also among the tithing plants mentioned in the Gospels. Jesus rebuked the self-righteous crowd: "Woe unto you, scribes and Pharisees, hypocrites! for ye pay tithe of mint and anise (dill) and cumin, and have omitted the weightier matters of the law, judgment, mercy, and faith: these ought ye to have done, and not to leave the other undone."

Dill's native area extends beyond the Mediterranean region, from southern Russia to western Africa. In Spain, dill grows as a weed in cornfields.

I love the elegance of a tall dill plant, a smooth, shiny stalk that branches out with graceful, fernlike leaves and a symmetrical flower head. Dill with its upright growing habit makes an ideal background plant in flower beds and gardens, especially when the plants are spaced far enough apart that each one grows into a full-branched form.

Dill and other related plants like carrot, celery, fennel, and parsley all have umbrella-like flower clusters that mature into seed heads. Dill's airy yellow flower heads add texture and interest to bouquets. It's best to cut the flowers when the umbels are about two-thirds open. At this stage the flowers may still shed a bit of pollen, but if you cut them earlier, they are almost too delicate and tend to wilt soon after cutting. You can also cut the semi-mature seed heads when they are still bright green for an edible or strictly decorative portion of a bouquet.

Dill head

'Long Island Mammoth' or 'Common' is the most widely planted variety and found in many seed packets simply labeled "Dill." It matures quickly and produces lots of seed heads, which makes it a good choice for dill pickle lovers. It reaches a height of 3 to 4 feet. But not all dill is created equal. Compared to the generic dill often found in seed packets, named varieties produce more consistent plants. 'Bouquet' is slightly more compact, while 'Dukat' has a high flavor content and more uniform growth. 'Fernleaf' and other dwarf dill plants are slow to go to seed and are desirable for dill weed production or container growing.

SOW AND SOW AGAIN

Sometimes it seems like a challenge to synchronize the dill crop with the pickle crop, and here's why. As a cool-weather plant, dill is sensitive to increasing day length, which speeds its growth rate. Early-sown or self-sown plants from the previous year are very prone to premature bolting, going from seed to bloom in six weeks. After the summer solstice in late June, dill grows more slowly. During August or September it may take eight to twelve weeks to grow from seed to bloom and the plant is a picture of perfection.

Successive sowing ensures a steady supply of dill for all uses. Sow the next set of seeds four weeks after the first, followed by a third sowing in midsummer.

Plant your first row of dill early: at least four to six weeks before the last frost date. The young seedlings can withstand cool temperatures, and you get a head start on growing.

The ideal site for dill is sunny, with well-drained, fertile soil. Dill will tolerate poor or compact soil to some degree, but with slower growth. Dill is best started by seed outdoors, due to the fragile taproots that resent being transplanted. Cultivate the soil well before sowing. Dill can be sown in rows or blocks. Sow seeds thickly (and plan to thin later on), or space at least 6 inches apart. Water the area, then tamp seed gently into the moist soil. There is no need to cover dill seed because light speeds its germination! A thin sprinkling of peat moss helps retain moisture. Keep well watered. Germination time is approximately 21 days.

When seedlings emerge, thin to 10 inches apart and keep the area weed free. Weeds can easily overtake those tender young seedlings until the plants are big enough to shade the soil.

For those who use companion planting methods, dill is an excellent partner for cabbage, broccoli, and other cole crops, but carrots have a distinct dislike for it. Interplanting dill and tomatoes reportedly deters tomato hornworms. Keep dill and fennel at a distance to avoid cross-pollination.

Dill is usually free of diseases. Aphids, however, can be a severe problem. The best control for aphids is to remove infested plants and sow a new crop.

Fresh dill weed, as the leaves are known, can be snipped from the plant at any stage. Dill weed can be harvested as soon as the plants reach 6 inches or so. 'Fernleaf' can be harvested earlier. Pick the outer leaves, not disturbing the inner growing point. Dill weed can be refrigerated for several days. It also dries well. Place on racks in a warm spot or hang to dry in small bunches. When dry, crumble and store in an airtight container.

To collect seeds, clip the seed heads at maturity. The seeds should be brown and should loosen readily. Place the seed heads in a paper bag, allowing several days to dry, then shake to loosen seeds. Save the seeds for culinary use, or to sow next year's crop. Immature (green) seed heads can be used for pickling and in other recipes, including dill vinegar. To collect ripe seeds, wait until brown then snip into a paper bag. When still green, dill seed heads can be refrigerated for several days or even frozen.

Gracia's Herbs

Yes, dill does self-seed! One advantage to this is that self-seeded plants are hardier and mature earlier than others. Simply allow the seeds to mature and drop at liberty. Avoid cultivating this seeded area in the following spring. One disadvantage of self-seeding dill is the possibility of having dill plants everywhere! Harvest seeds regularly during the summer to prevent this, or allow only designated plants to self-seed.

After heavy frost, your dill will be "done." Tug out the plants and transport them carefully to your compost area to keep seeds from spreading. You can extend the dill season by growing a plant indoors during cold months. 'Fernleaf' is well-suited for indoor growing.

DILLY DELICIOUS

Did you know recipe books never call for dill *leaves*? Instead, the proper term is dill weed. This is the leafy part of the plant, whether fresh or dried. Dill seed is the dried mature seed. Green immature seeds often used for pickles are called dill heads.

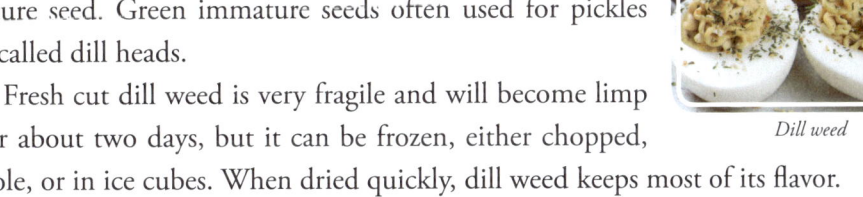

Fresh cut dill weed is very fragile and will become limp after about two days, but it can be frozen, either chopped, whole, or in ice cubes. When dried quickly, dill weed keeps most of its flavor. A teaspoon of dried dill weed equals a tablespoon of fresh.

Dill combines very well with a number of foods. Of course, we all know about pickles, but dill and eggs is also a winning combination. When making stuffed eggs, liven up your favorite recipe by adding chopped dill weed or a bit of dill vinegar or pickle juice to the filling. Garnish with a sprinkle of paprika and a sprig of dill. Egg salad, egg sandwiches—add a bit of dill for something different.

When adding dill as a variation, use about 1½ teaspoon fresh dill, or ½ teaspoon dried, for every four servings. Add fresh chopped dill weed or seed heads to any oil/vinegar dressing for a quick vegetable marinade.

Dill also makes a beautiful garnish. Its fine, dark green fronds add an attractive touch to light, creamy soups or dips.

Dill also is a good salad herb, whether for leafy green salads,

Dill weed

Dill weed

pasta, potato, chicken, or tuna salad, or coleslaw. And don't forget to add a dash of dill vinegar to the salad dressing.

When paired with milk products such as sour cream, cottage cheese, or yogurt, dill is a key ingredient for dips, spreads, and herbal butters. Its flavor is almost too delicate for most meats, although dill and fish are compatible, especially baked salmon with a drizzle of melted butter and dill weed. Dill seed is valuable for breads, salad dressings, and various pickling recipes.

Dill is not usually thought of as a medicinal herb. Yet its name, taken from the old Norse *dilla*, means to lull gently. Dill is a carminative herb, beneficial to the stomach and aiding digestion.

Some say using dill weed instead of dill seed gives a more uniform flavor when baking or for soups and salads.

YOGURT DILL DIP
Ingredients Needed:
1 c. plain yogurt
1½ tsp. fresh or ½ tsp. dried dill weed
chopped onion to taste
dash of vinegar

PICKLED EGG VARIATION
Add to your favorite pickled egg recipe: chopped fresh dill weed and/or dill vinegar
chopped onion

Garnish eggs with dill.

SWEET DILL PICKLES
Place in bottom of jar:
1 head dill and 1 garlic bud (I use 2 to 3 heads of dill)
Fill jar with sliced cucumbers (not too thin) and place 1 head dill and 1 garlic bud on top.

Mix together and heat:
2 c. water   3 c. sugar
2 c. vinegar   2 Tbsp. salt

Pour over cucumbers and seal. Cold pack until water boils, then remove immediately.

Echinacea for Health

Echinacea, also known as purple coneflower, is a beautiful perennial flower which crosses over to the herb category because of its tremendous usefulness in medicine.

Echinacea's healing power is not a new discovery. Native Americans on the Great Plains used this native prairie wildflower to treat all kinds of ailments—even snake bites. Before antibiotics began to replace it in the early 1900s, it was the best-selling herb in the United States. In recent years, echinacea (pronounced eck-i-NAY-see-uh) regained popularity in medicinal use as people again began to appreciate natural remedies.

ABOUT THE PLANT

Echinacea reaches high, with a height of 3 to 4 feet. The flower's center is a pointed, bristly cone, earning the name coneflower and the nickname hedgehog plant. When the flowers are in bloom, the cone is orange; once the seeds mature, it's brown. The surrounding petals have the unique tendency to slant away from the cone, giving the flower a somewhat triangular shape. Most echinaceas are colored with a strikingly rich blend of pinkish lavender and purple.

Being tall, echinaceas are well suited as background plants in the perennial border or along fences and stone walls. Dwarf varieties could be planted in the foreground.

MEET THE CONEFLOWERS

The coneflower family includes nine species. Here are the four most common: purple coneflower *(E. purpurea)*; narrow-leaved coneflower *(E. augustifolia)*; yellow coneflower *(E. paradoxa)*; and pale purple coneflower *(E. pallida)*.

Purple coneflower is the easiest to grow and most widely grown as a perennial. Narrow-leaved coneflower is the top medicinal choice, although all species are effective medicinally.

Several named strains include 'Bright Star', lavender-pink in color, and 'Bravado', which has huge, 4-inch flowers. 'Magnus', 1998 Perennial of the Year, has more horizontal petals in a deep rose shade. 'Kim's Knee High' is a delightful dwarf plant, 12 to 18 inches tall. There are even some white varieties—'White Swan' is one—which provide great color contrast in the perennial garden. 'White Swan' has the added benefit of a honey-like fragrance. And believe it or not, *E. paradoxa* is a cheery yellow!

"Cone" of echinacea flower

A TOUGH PLANT

Echinacea is a tough plant, appearing regularly on easy-to-grow and top-ten lists. It doesn't know what fussy means. Cold hardy to Zone 3, and extremely drought tolerant, it's hard to go wrong when growing echinacea. Echinacea is comfortable both in full sun and part shade. Average, well-drained soil is okay, but the plants do produce more roots in rich soil.

The echinacea in my garden has proved tough already. One spring I happened to slice off all the tender, new sprouts of one plant hiding under some mulch. This rough treatment evidently didn't harm the plant. By midsummer it couldn't be picked out from the rest. One summer some tiny echinacea seedlings, only a few inches tall, traveled along when we moved from Holmes County, Ohio, to Lyndonville, New York. By the time they were planted—and in newly broken sod!—the plants looked rather raggedy and I questioned if they would thrive. They responded by growing vigorously and even produced a crop of flowers!

CHILL BEFORE PLANTING

Echinacea can be started from seed or by root division. When starting from seed, germination is best when seeds are stratified (kept moist and refrigerated) first. Stratify for 21 to 30 days before planting into regular potting mix…or let nature do the stratifying by planting outdoors or in a cold frame in the fall. Purple coneflower is the least ticklish to start. It doesn't hurt to stratify its seed for a week, but it's not as necessary. I have used nonstratified seeds with decent results. Germination takes up to three weeks. After danger of frost is past, transplant outdoors. When sown indoors in February or March, echinacea often blooms the same year.

BEAUTIFUL BLOOMS . . . BUTTERFLIES

In midsummer, echinacea's glory unfolds as the flowers appear. People aren't the only ones who enjoy the blooms. Butterflies love the nectar stored in the cones. When planting flowers to attract butterflies, definitely include echinacea. Echinacea's strong, stiff stems make it a good cutting flower. On or off the plant, the blooms are very long-lasting. New flowers appear all summer long, often until frost. As the flowers grow older, their color fades to a light lavender. After the blossoms are spent, the dry cones can be used in dried arrangements for visual interest.

Echinacea flower

HARVEST

The effective medicinal parts of the plant include the leaves and roots, especially the spreading, horizontal roots (rhizomes). After drying the leaves, they can be ground and put into capsules, or stored whole in glass jars until ready for use. To dry roots, dig, shake off soil well, and rub clean with a dry cloth. Keep in a warm, dry spot until dried. Store whole in glass jar, or grind and put into capsules.

When getting your plants ready for winter, trim down the stems neatly to several inches above the ground. Protect with mulch. Scatter some seeds on the surrounding area to be stratified during winter. In spring you'll be rewarded with many new volunteer plants!

NATURE'S IMMUNE SYSTEM BOOSTER

Echinacea seems to be the natural cold and flu fighter, boosting the body's own disease-fighting white blood cells. Extensive research has shown that echinacea has the ability to help halt infection by strengthening the immune system. It may even have anti-tumor properties. When taken after cold and flu have started, it can help to ease symptoms and speed recovery.

Medical experts agree that echinacea should not be taken on a regular basis, only at the first sign of symptoms or when you have increased risk of becoming sick after exposure to germs.

The most common way to use echinacea is as a tea, which can be prepared by steeping 2 or 3 tablespoons of dried leaves or grated roots in a cup of boiling water for five minutes. Six to eight hours later, take another cupful. Tincture is also an effective way of taking the herb.

When applied externally to wounds to prevent infection, echinacea is a very gentle antiseptic. Using tea or tincture might be just as effective.

Taking echinacea may give your tongue a tingling sensation. This is normal and harmless. In fact, some people take the tingling as a sign that they're taking the real thing. Sometimes echinacea products are mixed with other herbs as fillers. Look for standardized capsules or extracts at your health food store to avoid this. Or better yet, grow your own!

Gracia's Herbs

Fennel

"Do you like licorice?" It's hard to find someone with a neutral answer to this question. Most people either love it or loathe it. Those who love it will also love fennel, one of the several herbs that have this flavor.

A TRIO OF FENNELS

The term fennel can indicate three different plants. Common fennel *(Feoniculum vulgare)* is sometimes called wild fennel. This is the fennel grown for its leaves and seeds, for cooking, and medicine. Common fennel resembles dill in color and shape. These two plants are so

Sweet fennel

FENNEL |85|

similar that it's hard to tell them apart from a distance. Fennel, though, grows taller, up to 5 feet. The stems widen at the base, branching out in a fascinating herringbone pattern.

The leaf base of Florence fennel *(F. vulgare var. dulce)* forms a pronounced bulb, crisp, succulent, and sweet. It's also called sweet fennel or raddiccio. Florence fennel could almost be classed as a vegetable rather than an herb, since it grows to only 18 inches and rarely gives seeds. Its bulb can be sliced and eaten raw in salads. Some other serving options are adding it to stir-fry or steaming it along with other vegetables.

Bulb of Florence fennel

Florence fennel is a cool-season crop that thrives in spring or fall gardens. To make the bulb even more mild and crisp, cover it up with a hill of surrounding soil as it grows and water it often.

I've observed that many seed racks, in garden centers and Walmart, for example, frequently offer only Florence fennel. Check the botanical name to make sure you're getting what you want.

Bronze fennel *(F. vulgare 'purpureum')*, a showier version of common fennel, has dark burgundy leaves. It's pretty enough for a border or butterfly garden, one of my favorite tall plants. Imagine the contrast when a swallowtail butterfly lands in its dark ferny fronds! Many kinds of butterflies are attracted to fennel, but black swallowtails especially like its flat flower clusters.

SOW AND WATCH IT GROW

Some books list fennel as a perennial hardy to Zone 6. I've found that fennel does sometimes overwinter, but I treat it as an annual. Once a bronze fennel, probably self-sown, came up alongside the concrete slab that edges my herb garden, and persistently returned several years even after I tried to chop out the roots. Maybe bronze fennel is somewhat hardier.

Bronze fennel

To start fennel, sow seeds in spring outdoors where you intend it to grow, ideally in full sun. Like dill, it also has a taproot and doesn't transplant well. Beware that fennel and dill can cross-pollinate if planted too closely. Keep the two plants separated unless you don't mind seeds that have a funny licorice/pickle flavor.

AN HERB FOR THE FRUGAL HERB GARDENER

Every part of fennel is edible, from the bulby base to the celery-like stalks, the fine leaves and spreading flower heads, and finally, ribbed green seeds. Fennel leaves can be snipped even when the plant is still young. That's when they're most sweet and tender. They should be used fresh or frozen, since it loses flavor when dried. Fennel is good paired with fish, eggs, and other mildly flavored main dishes that don't swallow up its delicate flavor. Try adding finely snipped fennel leaves to lettuce, cucumber, or fruit salad.

Seed heads should be dried, but still green in color when they're harvested. The brighter green, the higher the quality. Hang them out of direct light to retain the nice green color.

Fennel seeds, either whole, cracked, or ground, are used to flavor breads, muffins, and cakes. Some meat recipes (like sausage) also call for fennel.

Not only are fennel seeds packed with licorice flavor, but also with helpful medicinal compounds. Brew fennel seed tea, a teaspoon of seeds in one cup of hot water, for a variety of uses. Fennel is best known as an anti-colic, anti-bloating herb, safe even for babies. Taken as a hot, soothing tea, it will help settle the stomach. An old herbal remedy guide, Pastor J. Glaesser's *Kräuterbuch* says (translated from German): "Take fennel tea readily, for its effects are rapid and sure. Colic may strike quickly, followed by cramps. Do not hesitate. Prepare a tea by steeping a teaspoon of fennel in a cup of milk for 5 to 10 minutes. Drink as warm as possible. Meanwhile, apply this same tea externally to the abdomen." Another bit of old lore recommends chewing fennel seeds Sunday morning to prevent embarrassing stomach noises during church.

Fennel tea is also good for nursing moms since it promotes milk flow, but avoid it when pregnant. When cooled, fennel tea is also an effective rinse for conjunctivitis, applied three times daily.

Fennel can also improve the taste of other herbal tea. One herbal mixture I like for cough and sore throat is mainly marshmallow and echinacea root. But because it also has fennel seed, some whole cloves, and a bit of dried orange peel, the earthy root flavor is pleasantly masked.

Garlic

Garlic is the wonder bulb that defies being categorized. Is it an herb, vegetable, or medicine? Why is it loved by some and scorned by others? My opinion is that garlic *(Allium sativum)* is one of the greatest wonders in the plant world. This mere bulb contains unsurpassed safe and natural healing, a must when dealing with wintertime coughs and sniffles, or worse.

Throughout history garlic was thought a strength-giving food. During the pyramid-building era, the Egyptians fed their slaves large amounts of garlic. The Israelites even wished for garlic and other foods of Egypt as they traveled through the barren wilderness (Numbers 11:5). The athletic Greeks and Romans consumed much garlic before their games, and garlic was a major part of the Roman soldiers' rations. Even today, garlic in the diet is highly recommended!

More than 500 million pounds of garlic are grown annually in the United States. Four-fifths of this crop is used for dehydrated garlic products, including flavorings and food supplements. Gilroy, California, home of the famous annual Gilroy Garlic Festival, is the "garlic capital of the world."

Easy to grow with little effort, garlic is a rewarding crop for beginning gardeners or children who love to plant their own crops. Do you love to cook? Discover the pleasure of using fresh, homegrown garlic. Are you attracted to garlic because of its many health benefits? You will find homegrown garlic fresher and more appealing than capsules out of a can.

GARLIC GROUPS

Peeled garlic bulb

Before I grew my own garlic, I thought all garlic was alike. But there are many, many garlics! They're distinguished by color, size, and shape, along with flavor, how well they store, and what climate they need. Nearly all garlics belong to one of two groups, softneck and hardneck, according to the main stem. Hardneck types bolt and send up a flower stalk which eventually becomes hard and woody. The non-bolting types are softnecks.

Both hardnecks and softnecks can be broken down into a number of subgroups that include hundreds of true varieties and many passed-down kinds with informal names. Even garlic experts sometimes disagree on how a certain kind should be classified. To complicate matters, factors like climate, soil, and growing methods can make a particular variety do something unexpected. For example, a southern softneck may grow a flower stalk at first when planted up North, or hot garlic may be milder at a different altitude.

Chances are, you could plop nearly any old clove into the ground, even China-grown stuff from a supermarket, and get some sort of harvest. But you'll have more predictable success by starting with locally grown stock, from a neighbor or a nearby farmers' market. Sometimes gardeners have no choice but ordering from a distant mail-order source. Not a problem. Most garlics adapt to the local climate within a few years simply by planting and replanting.

I tend to stick with a handful of favorites that fit our family's needs. A hardneck or two for canning and cooking. One softneck for winter-long eating and another for decorative braids. I plant these kinds year after year by saving my own seed garlic. I'll admit, I'm intrigued by detailed garlic descriptions in catalogs. Rare garlics from Europe and Asia. Others, famously hot and aggressive on the tongue. Clove colors ranging from deep burgundy to the lightest of lavenders. My dream garlic collection…

SOFTNECK GARLICS

Since softneck garlic bulbs consist of tightly packed cloves layered inside a tight wrapper, they have a long storage life. Their pliable, leafy stems are suitable for braiding. Most garlic found in stores is softneck because of better shelf life, and because it's less labor intensive to grow.

Softneck subgroups include artichoke types which are by far the most popular for both home gardeners and commercial growers. Artichokes are very productive and adapt well to various climates, even mild winters in the South. Creole types also tolerate mild winters, but tend to have smaller bulbs. Silverskin types have exceptional storage ability with an intense hot flavor. Turban types are quick growing and early maturing.

Suggested varieties: **'Italian White'** (Artichoke)—snowy white bulbs; **'Okrent'** (Artichoke)—easy to grow; **'Mild French'** (Silverskin)—ideal for South.

HARDNECK GARLICS

If allowed to mature, hardneck flower stalks will produce little bulbils that can be planted. Most growers, however, snap off the stalk soon after it starts to grow to keep the plant's energy going into the bulb. Hardneck bulbs have a circle of large, easy-to-peel cloves surrounding the woody flower stalk. As a rule, hardnecks have richer, more robust flavors than softnecks, but don't store quite as long.

Rocambole and porcelain types both require a long growing season (plant early!) and thrive nearly anywhere but in the Deep South. They do especially well in northern areas, despite harsh winters. Many cooks consider rocamboles the best tasting of all garlics while porcelain types have bigger cloves.

Suggested varieties: **'Music'** (Porcelain)—consistently large bulbs; **'Georgian Crystal'** (Porcelain)—huge cloves; German varieties like **'Northern German'** and **'German Red'** (Rocambole)—dependable and tasty; **'Spanish Rojo'** (Rocambole)—an excellent flavor.

ELEPHANT GARLIC

Despite its name, elephant garlic *(Allium ampeloprasm)* is not a true garlic. Instead, it's closely related to the leek. Its size and taste are distinctly different from regular garlic. Judging from its name alone, you can guess that it's big! Under good growing conditions, the bulbs can weigh as much as half a pound. One elephant garlic clove equals about ten regular garlic cloves.

Elephant garlic with its garlicky, yet very mild, flavor can be used raw, in large amounts. Growing requirements are similar to softneck garlic, except plant it 6 inches deep. One curious trait of elephant garlic is the tiny yellow bulbils that grow attached to the main bulb. When planted in fall, these often produce a round, or one-piece, bulb, which in turn will grow into a full-size bulb.

GROWING GARLIC

If you have yet to grow a bulb of garlic, here's a brief summary of garlic growing habits. Like tulips, garlic is planted in fall and emerges in early spring. It grows to maturity by midsummer. A garlic bulb, or head, can be separated into sections, called cloves.

Our family received our first garlic growing lesson from John Watt, a customer at our fruit tree nursery. An avid gardener and an Italian cook, John informed us, "Garlic is a six-month crop. Get it into the ground early, so it's ready to grow at the first touch of spring."

Folklore maintains that mid-October (if you wish for a trick to remember, think Columbus Day) is a good time to plant. This gives the bulbs enough time to establish their roots before the ground freezes. In Zones 5 and colder, or other areas with short growing seasons, fall planting is a must.

In warmer zones, spring-planted garlic, particularly softnecks, will grow with fairly good success. According to our friend John, even late winter is a suitable time to plant garlic. "If you can get into the ground in January, get the cloves into the ground and cover them up with mulch. They'll grow."

Loose, fertile, and well-drained soil in full sun—these are essential for the best garlic production. We reserve the best spots in our garden for garlic, usually following a rotation of cover crops. It's also a good idea to avoid a spot previously occupied by onions or leeks, just to minimize any possibility of disease.

In preparation for planting, choose the biggest bulbs, break them apart, and select only the plumpest cloves. The cloves used for planting are sometimes called *seed* at this point. Place them root end down, 6 to 8 inches apart, 3 inches deep. Save the smaller sliver cloves for eating or for growing garlic greens.

I usually make furrows for planting, but I've seen dibbles that poke individual holes for the cloves. After planting the cloves, I use a hoe or rake to cover up the furrows again. Last, I put in wooden markers at the end of the rows. If you're planting lots of different kinds, you might also want to draw a map of the row layout.

Some growers mulch their garlic plot in the fall and others don't. Mulch will prevent weeds, but in the spring, it will also prevent the sun from warming up the soil early.

Depending on the weather, little green sprouts are soon visible, and may even poke up through a light snow cover. In early spring, as plants actively begin to grow, fertilize with organic matter or foliar feeding to encourage growth.

Once the bulb begins to form, fertilizers no longer benefit. Bulb size is directly affected by available moisture, so keep garlic well watered, especially in dry weather.

Garlic's greatest enemy is weeds. A weed-free patch and good bulb size go together. Cultivate the soil around the bulbs regularly, just like any other garden plant. I like to use a narrow onion hoe. Be careful not to nick the bulbs.

Garlic is rarely bothered by insect pests. In fact, it can be used as a companion plant with roses, tomatoes, and other plants to deter plant pests. Remove and discard any plants that show signs of stunting or disease.

If you're growing hardneck garlic, watch for flower stalks in early summer. These stalks, also known as scapes, grow from the center of the plant. I love to watch them form fascinating graceful coils. If left long enough, they straighten upward and flower at the very tip to produce little bulbils. But they should be snapped off soon after they appear to help all the plant's energy go into the bulb. These scapes are delicious for eating in salads, stir-fries, soups, and more—anywhere you want a mild, gourmet garlic taste. They keep for a long time when refrigerated.

Hardneck garlic scapes

HARVESTING

Most varieties mature in mid to late summer. For signs of maturity, read the plants—they have their own ways of letting you know when they're ready. Wilted or yellowing leaves near the soil level signal that the plant is no longer actively growing, but is ready for harvest. Once nearly half the leaves appear spent, dig up a bulb or two and check the size and the skin. The bulb should be plump and the wrapper fully intact.

Just harvested hardneck garlic

Determining when to harvest is very crucial. Harvest too soon, and you will sacrifice bulb size. Harvest too late, and the protective papery skin will loosen and expose the cloves inside. When fall arrives, and the cloves still remain in the soil, they will spread apart and prepare to grow for next year. Remember, garlic is actually a perennial crop.

It's easy to pull the stalk off the head, so for best results, first loosen the soil with a shovel or spade. Gently lift the bulbs out of the loosened soil and shake to remove any soil clinging to the roots. Resist the urge to wash the bulbs, even if they appear dirty.

CURING AND STORAGE

After garlic is harvested in midsummer, it needs to be cured by air drying for at least two weeks. The stalks and roots should remain attached. Hang the garlic in loose bunches, or spread out single layer on racks or screens in a well-ventilated place under cover. Once it's cured, most garlic will keep until early spring if stored properly.

When curing is complete (two to six weeks), trim the roots and stalk close to the bulb. Place the bulbs into baskets or mesh bags and store in a cool, dry, airy place. For long-term storage, garlic needs temperatures as close to freezing as possible, without actually freezing. Cold air keeps garlic bulbs crisp. It also slows down the natural sprouting process so the bulb stays intact longer.

Don't refrigerate garlic, though, because the moisture in the refrigerator is detrimental. One of the best ways to store garlic is to hang bunches or braids in a cool, well-ventilated area. For garlic not hanging or braided, use wooden crates or mesh bags instead of cardboard boxes, which tend to absorb moisture. Cold and dry—that's what garlic needs for storage. Ideal storage temperature is 45–55°F. Most garlics have a storage life of at least six to eight months. Partially sprouted bulbs are still okay to eat.

Garlic

GARLIC | 93 |

BRAIDING

Braiding is an attractive and easy way to preserve garlic. Use softneck garlic varieties, freshly dug so the leaves are still pliable. Start with three bulbs, braiding together and adding other bulbs (like French braiding) as needed to continue. The bulbs can be tightly woven, with little or no leaves visible, for a more showy braid, or loosely woven for best air circulation and ease in cutting a bulb loose. Once your braid reaches the desired size, braid the last leaves into a loop, which can be reinforced with twine or wire, and hang to cure.

THE GREEN SIDE OF GARLIC

Every part of garlic—from the flowers to the root—is edible! Garlic leaves, often called garlic greens, can be snipped off and used like chives or green onions.

To grow garlic greens, plant cloves closely together in spring or fall. You can use any odds and ends—cloves that were sorted out at planting time, or beginning to sprout in storage, and even hardneck bulbils if you have some. The greens can be harvested several times in early spring and again in late summer. Allow a little break during midsummer for the bulbs to recover. A patch of garlic greens can continue to produce for at least three years. For an extra twist try blanching garlic greens by covering the plants with a clay pot. The blanched leaves are a light green and have a pleasing snap.

Garlic greens can be grown indoors, too, especially in winter. Simply place cloves into a pot with potting soil, about an inch underground, and water well. A small pot is perfect for a windowsill, while a larger pot has more capacity. Soon there'll be tender sprouts that can be clipped again and again. They contain large amounts of vitamin A and C. Add them liberally to salads and soups, or use to top baked potatoes. They can also be substituted in any recipe that calls for chives.

GARLIC IN THE KITCHEN

No matter where you go all over the world, garlic, basil, and olive oil team up with tomatoes. Spaghetti, salsa, chili, pizza sauce, tomato-based soups, ketchup, tomato juice—all these are enhanced by adding garlic. Garlic and

Braided garlic

Garlic bulb beginning to sprout

dill are perfect partners for making pickles and relishes. Many pickle recipes call for one garlic clove per jar.

Garlic bulbs can be kept close by, ready for use, hanging in a braid or setting in a basket or crock. The cloves come in handy, premeasured form inside their own package. Garlic's scent is enclosed inside its cloves unless they are crushed or sliced.

PREPARATION

Each garlic clove has a thin paper skin. Peeling can be time consuming if you're preparing a lot of garlic for a recipe. One helpful tip is to lay a clove on a cutting board, then press hard with the flat side of a broad knife. The gentle pressure will crack open the skin, ready for removal by hand. An even quicker way to peel garlic is to put cloves in a stainless steel bowl with a lip. Place an identical bowl on top, clamp the two together with your hands and shake hard! *Thump, thump, thump, thump,* then rinse. This works well with garlic that will be minced, because tumbling about in the bowls can bruise it a little.

Garlic can be minced or chopped with a sharp knife, but my favorite tool is a garlic press. With a single pressing action, the clove is peeled and minced. Once, at a yard sale, I found a Tupperware® garlic press and by now it's one of our indispensable kitchen tools.

ONE BULB, DIFFERENT FLAVORS

Hardneck garlic and garlic press

Garlic's flavor is formed by a complex combination of natural chemicals. Each variety of garlic has a unique flavor. (Check catalogs for descriptions, such as "has lots of heat.") Depending how garlic is used, the same bulb will present different flavors. Of course, raw garlic has the strongest flavor, especially when pressed and allowed to stand for a bit. Cooking garlic will remove a lot of the heat, especially when the cloves are whole or sliced.

Roasting will bring out the mild side of garlic, almost nutty and sweet. In wintertime, when our cookstove supplies steady heat, I like to roast garlic. Take a head of garlic and slice off the top quarter, place it into a square of tinfoil, then drizzle with olive oil. Wrap the heads and place onto a cookie sheet. Bake at 325°F for 45 minutes, or until the pulp is soft enough to squeeze out of the clove. Try roasted pulp on crackers or whole wheat bread, or as a side dish with meat or vegetables, like cooked carrots. It can also be mashed with potatoes. Mix with sour cream for dip, or add to beef gravy. Mmm.

When cooked too long, garlic flavor practically disappears. Therefore, when cooking most dishes, put garlic in late, minutes before serving.

GARLIC BREAD

Ingredients Needed:

½ c. butter
¼ c. cream cheese
2 Tbsp. garlic powder
sour cream & onion powder, optional
1 loaf of bread (we like to use homemade bread braids, which have smaller slices, similar to French bread)

Directions:

Let butter and cream cheese stand until soft. Add powder and mix well. Spread onto bread slices, both sides. Put loaf back together again, wrap in foil, and warm slowly in oven. Serve warm. Delicious with spaghetti or soups!

GARLIC BUTTER

Ingredients Needed:

1 c. softened butter
4 small garlic cloves, finely chopped
minced chives

Directions:

Mix together and refrigerate in a tightly covered container. Use with warm bread, soft pretzels, rice, or hot vegetables.

GARLIC VINEGAR

Ingredients Needed:
½ c. chopped garlic
2 c. apple cider vinegar

Directions:

Let stand for 2 to 3 weeks. Strain (chopped garlic can be used in cooking). Place into bottles, inserting a clove for appeal. This vinegar offers a handy liquid garlic flavor. Add a dash to marinades, salad dressings, and dips.

INSECT REPELLENT

Ingredients Needed:
10 to 15 finely chopped garlic cloves
1 pint mineral oil

Soak 24 hours. Strain and dilute with water before spraying. Test on a few plants before applying to a large area.

STAY HEALTHY WITH GARLIC

Recent medical research has created newfound respect for garlic. But, unfortunately, many still share the same sentiments as an 1870 medical journal which classed garlic as "a quaint and absurd medicant, now obsolete among physicians." Don't let embarrassment prevent you from using nature's most powerful antibiotic. There's nothing as effective as garlic to clear up a cough, bronchitis, ear infection, and more cold weather complaints. Garlic also lowers blood pressure, reduces fatty buildup in arteries, and fights cancer cells.

One important feature of garlic is its self-storage capabilities. The medicinal chemicals in garlic become active only when exposed to air. In fact, they are at their best when garlic is minced or chopped and allowed to set for about ten minutes.

For medicinal purposes, you can choose from all kinds of capsules, oils, and mixtures. But the simplest—and probably most effective—method is to eat raw garlic in small quantities, but consistently. Nibbling a clove three times a day will almost instantly cure a cold or cough. After indulging in garlic, eat a juicy apple, fresh parsley, or leafy green vegetables to neutralize the strong taste.

Since raw garlic is strong, it's a good idea to eat it with other food. Pressed garlic can be hidden in applesauce. For the most sensitive stomach, dip cloves in boiling water before mincing. Or make garlic chips by slicing cloves ⅛ inch thick, spreading them single layer, and dehydrating at low heat until dry. Store in a tight container. Chew on a chip whenever you feel a cold coming. After eating garlic, crisp, juicy apples are refreshing.

A daring garlic fan I know shares this secret for sinusitis, and I'd recommend it only for adults: Select thin sliver-shaped cloves of garlic that will stay when inserted in your nostril. With a sharp paring knife, trim off the very point of the clove, just enough to expose a tip of raw surface, but not so large that it will irritate the sensitive nasal lining. Plug into one nostril and breathe deeply. The garlic fumes will take care of infection.

An alternative to eating raw garlic is to add lots of minced garlic to soup, just before serving. The simmering steam is also effective.

PROVEN MEDICINAL POWER

Garlic is nature's number one antifungal, rivaling tea tree oil. In many cases, garlic is just as effective, if not even more so, than commercial creams. Apply garlic oil (crushed cloves steeped in olive oil for several days, then strained) to infected areas once or twice a day. Athlete's foot may be relieved with a foot bath of several crushed cloves and a bit of rubbing alcohol in water.

Softneck garlic

Researchers have confirmed that garlic consumption of a clove a day boosts heart health. Garlic helps lower artery-clogging cholesterol while increasing levels of the good cholesterol.

Garlic's anti-clotting properties are most potent of all natural substances, even more potent than aspirin. They reduce the risk of heart attack by making the blood less likely to clot and block the arteries. They also help to control high blood pressure, improve circulation, and counter altitude sickness.

For most people, these anti-clotting properties are good news. However, for people with bleeding disorders or blood pressure issues, they can be dangerous. Seek professional medical advice before consuming heavy doses of garlic.

Horseradish

KNOWN FOR ITS BITE

Horseradish is a plant which I consider a sort of extra, something to grow that adds an additional zest to your eating, and experience to your green thumb. It doesn't have a wide range of uses nor grand medicinal value, but can give you the satisfaction of growing and processing your own food.

According to folklore, horseradish *(Armoracia rusticana)* received its English name through mistranslation. Early German and Dutch colonists who brought the plant from its native Europe called it *Meer* (sea) radish. English colonists, using the same sound, changed it to Mare radish and eventually to horseradish.

SPRING

A sure sign of spring is horseradish plants pushing up their tiny new leaves! Try nibbling several or adding to salad for some early spring greens. In springtime there is still time to harvest roots, if you've not done so already.

If you don't have horseradish plants, spring is a good time to plant some. Choose a spot where it can grow year after year, with plenty of space, since it will spread unless regularly harvested. Horseradish is not a particularly striking plant, with large, rough leaves on upright stalks. The stalks tend to droop in late summer, giving the plant a spreading, floppy look.

SUMMER

At this time of the year, the plant is growing actively; not only are the rough, dark green leaves in full size, but underground, the roots are increasing in diameter. Mulching to keep the soil moist and weed-free is beneficial. Very few pests, if any, ever bother the plant. The main thing you will need to do in the summertime is keep an eye on the plant. Is it spreading anywhere you don't want it? Make a mental note to harvest accordingly to prevent overcrowding.

In mid or late summer, flower stalks appear, with white flowers similar in form to its relative, mustard. After flowering, these stalks produce seedpods. These seeds are rarely good for planting. Instead, root cuttings are used.

If you would travel through southern Illinois in late summer, you could see the majority of U.S. commercial horseradish fields. Here, horseradish thrives in the fertile Mississippi River floodplains. These fields have up to 40 feet of topsoil in some places. Can you imagine what huge roots this produces?

FALL AND WINTER

During September and all other months with an *r* in their name, it is time to dig horseradish roots for grinding. Horseradish can spread invasively, but proper harvest manages it quite easily.

Any root part left in the ground will grow again, so dig up the entire plant. Set aside several crowns (roots with leaf stubs left on) for replanting. Whatever you do not wish to grind, discard. Replant the crowns in desired area. When given a place with loose, deeply cultivated soil, horseradish responds by producing large, straight roots. It will tolerate nearly any soil, though, except very wet areas.

It's hard to believe, but slashing roots actually encourages growth. Even a small piece of root will form a new plant. Generally, roots older than two years are too woody for best grinding. Well-managed plants have crisp, young roots.

Tough plant that it is, horseradish needs little or no winter protection.

Horseradish root

HARVEST & PREPARATION

Time for tears!! Use a spade or fork to dig the branched roots, which resemble parsnips. Roots of any diameter can be ground, but large roots are easiest.

After digging, prepare the roots for grinding. First scrub and rinse the roots to remove soil, then peel with a sharp paring knife, gouging out any dark parts. Cut large roots into chunks. Thin, pencil-like roots should be cut into small sections for easier grinding.

Now for the sad part! We like to do our grinding outside, for plenty of fresh air to dilute the pungent fumes. After the roots are peeled and chunked, it's fairly important to grind soon, or the chunks will begin to turn grayish from air exposure.

Grinding horseradish is truly a test for having brave eyes. Compared to onions, it's quite a bit more pungent. It's not too bad when working as a pair and you can trade off at the grinder. We grind ours with a small manual meat grinder with good results. Other options include grating or using a blender.

After grinding, add enough vinegar to give it an easy-to-spread consistency, yet not too watery. You can always add more vinegar later if needed. Also add some salt. Spoon the finished horseradish into glass jars. We've found that using small jars (half-pints are a good size) helps preserve the strength. Otherwise, when stored in large jars, it's exposed to air too much. Screw on caps tightly and refrigerate. One store-bought brand has a catchy tip: "Keep cold to keep hot." It's true; room temperatures and open-air containers are bad for preserving the bite of horseradish. The zip becomes less and less, until nearly bland.

When stored properly, horseradish keeps for several months.

ON THE TABLE

Horseradish is most popular as a partner with meats and sandwiches. It deserves a place with all-time favorite condiments, ketchup and mustard.

Nearly all meats—hamburgers, meat loaf, hot dogs, ham, sausage, fish, and shrimp are enhanced with zesty horseradish. Also try horseradish with cheese slices or with eggs, especially hard-boiled. Serving horseradish is quite easy. Simply open a jar and spread with a spoon.

Horseradish is mainly a condiment to enjoy, yet it does have some medicinal value. For one, it's a great reliever for a stuffy nose or clogged sinus passages. Simply eat straight by the spoonfuls, if brave, or in liberal amounts mixed with other foods. When eaten regularly, horseradish can also help your body be less sensitive to allergies.

ZINGY HORSERADISH DIP

Directions:

Mix equal parts of ketchup and prepared horseradish. Delicious with burgers or seafood.

CREAMY HORSERADISH DRESSING

Ingredients Needed:

¾ c. sour cream or yogurt
4 Tbsp. prepared horseradish
4 Tbsp. cream

Directions:

Serve with greens or vegetables.

SWEDISH HORSERADISH SAUCE

Ingredients Needed:

2 Tbsp. freshly ground horseradish
¼ c. lemon juice
2 Tbsp. butter
2 Tbsp. flour
1 chicken bouillon cube
1 c. hot water
½ c. heavy cream

Directions:

Mix horseradish and lemon juice; set aside. Melt butter and stir in flour until well blended. Dissolve bouillon cube in hot water and gradually add to flour mixture, stirring constantly until thickened. Remove from heat and stir in cream and horseradish mixture. Serve warm with fish fillets or chilled with sandwiches.

Lavender to Love

Lavender is an herb to be enjoyed by the senses. As you stroll through your herb garden, rustle the lavender leaves to release some of the pleasing scent they possess. Bury your nose deep in the woolly spikes and inhale deeply. Ah! Wonderful! Bees adore it, too. They probe into the tiny blue flowers in search of sweet nectar. Once you have started growing lavender, it seems you can never get enough of the charming, fragrant herb. It truly is one of the most fragrant plants in the garden.

An aromatic perennial, lavender *(Lavendula sp.)* has upright stems, 2 to 3 feet tall, that are covered with narrow gray-green leaves. Spiky flower stalks sprout from the main plant in midsummer to fall. The color lavender is named after the purplish-blue flower. It is grown commercially for its oil, which is used in perfumes and other cosmetics.

Most lavenders are native to the Mediterranean region, but are grown all over the world. Lavenders are grouped into two main types, hardy (English) and tender (French). There are over dozens and dozens of lavender varieties. Some popular hardy cultivars include 'Lady', which flowers the first year after starting from seed, and 'Munstead', a dwarf lavender suitable for colder climates and container gardening. 'Hidcote' is also a well-known English variety, with large, dark purple blossoms. French lavenders have larger, showier flowers and bigger, fuzzier leaves. They tend to have a more spicy, camphoraceous scent.

STARTING LAVENDER

Lavender's tiny dark seeds have a hard outer covering that needs coaxing to germinate. The first important step is to chill those seeds before planting. Pop the seed packet into a storage bag and into the freezer. Let the seeds chill for two or three days, then remove them from the freezer and plant them. There is seemingly no significant difference in germination either way. Start your plants early, eight to ten weeks before the frost-free date.

Another secret in getting lavender to germinate is using peat moss or vermiculite as the growing media. If you do use potting soil or a seed starter mix, cover the seed with peat moss or vermiculite. The seedlings emerge slowly; it could take up to three weeks for the first one to peek through.

Keep the soil moist but not wet. If the soil is overly moist, the plant is more liable to rots like "dampening off," which are a great threat to the fragile new plant. Transplanting to a larger container is necessary. Transplant outdoors only after the plant is reasonably large and weather conditions are moderate. Harden off the plants prior to outdoor planting.

Lavender blossom

MORE METHODS OF PROPAGATION

Lavender can be propagated from established plants by stem cuttings or layering. These methods are perhaps more reliable than starting from seed because the new plant will not vary from the parent. Seedlings are more variable. Layering is so very simple. Choose a healthy-looking branch and strip off most of the leaves, leaving the tip. Bend it downward and bury the stripped part in loose soil. Weight the branch with a stone. After a few weeks, roots will begin to form. The following year, you can clip the branch from the main plant and transplant the new one. Or just clip it and leave it in place for an extended lavender bed.

IN THE GARDEN

Lavender thrives in full sun with well-drained sandy soil. Even hardy lavenders require winter protection for survival. (In climate Zone 4 and colder, the normally perennial lavender may have to be treated as an annual.) Keep this in mind as you consider a site. For example, situate your plant along a stone wall or a southern slope where winter winds will not hit directly. Lavender lends itself well in a rock garden.

Lavender will not grow in compact clay soils or soils that are too acidic. A pH of about 7.0 is preferred. The plant will tolerate drought. In fact, a hot, dry climate produces the best lavender plants for oil production. So you can more or less ignore the watering of your lavender plant and it will still be happy!

Space the plants approximately one foot apart. Work sand or pea gravel into the planting hole along with a few tablespoons of lime if your soil is heavy. Water the plant to get it established, but don't overwater.

Harvest the flower stalks when the tiny flowerets nearly all have opened, but none are faded. Clip the stem where it joins the main plant. The flowers can be used in fresh-cut arrangements (and later dried), or hung in bunches to dry. The dried flowers have a lovely dark blue color.

Depending on variety and climate, your plant will flower most of the summer, perhaps going through intense flowering spurts with a few stragglers in between. If you do not harvest the blooms as they form (I do! Each single flower is precious!), trim off the spent blooms to keep the plant looking attractive.

Let your lavender experience some frosts unprotected to toughen it up! Once the weather threatens to

'Lady' lavender

turn wintry, cover your lavender plants with slabs of semi-composted hay or straw to protect them from cold winter blasts. Situate the slabs as uprightly as possible so they don't crush the plant. In spring, remove the slabs after danger of frost is past.

PRUNING FOR GROWTH

Lavender also benefits from pruning in early spring. Trim the plant way back to the woody portions. Don't be afraid to trim hard, because this encourages fresh new growth and more flowers.

This spring all my lavender plants got a good trimming. Last year I didn't trim the lavender, and it had a slightly unkempt look all summer, instead of being completely covered with a new flush of growth.

For awhile, I was afraid I trimmed the 'Lady' lavender too hard. I made a round with the pruning shears on a mild March day, then cool, wet weather set in for longer than I ever remember. Even by the first of May, all twenty-some plants just sat there, waiting for the warmth of summer. Little sprouts of green assured me that it was still alive, though. But would it grow?

I needn't have worried. The row is now just one swath of purple, with bees humming all around it. It looks so pretty near the 'Mr. Lincoln' and 'Gold Nugget' roses along the stone wall on the southeast corner of the house. Whenever one walks past, those lavender wands just beg for a rustling touch to release the perfume. Since 'Lady' had rather short stems, I let it bloom freely and pick flowers from other kinds for drying.

The largest, oldest 'Munstead' lavender—the trusty plant that usually gives bunches and bunches of long-stemmed flowers to dry—is another story. This summer, only ten, maybe twelve, spindly little flower stems developed. Maybe it was the hard trimming or the cool weather. Or maybe it's simply time to replace that plant.

THE SCENT OF CLEANLINESS

By now you can tell that lavender is one of my favorite plants, can't you? Its scent is so sun-kissed clean, so sweet and soothing, and yet invigorating. Of all herbal scents, lavender remains the most popular for soaps, shampoos, and lotions.

Lavender's powerful, clean fragrance makes it a great natural air freshener, whether placed in a basket or tucked in a fabric sachet for lending its sweetness to linens or clothing. A slight crush is all it takes to renew the scent. For the best fragrance, I replace all the dried lavender each season with the new crop.

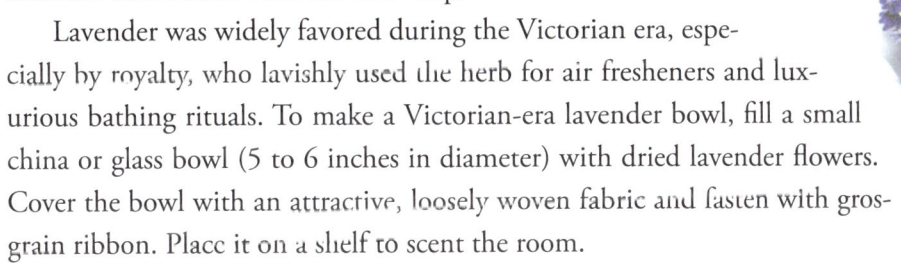

Lavender blossoms

Lavender was widely favored during the Victorian era, especially by royalty, who lavishly used the herb for air fresheners and luxurious bathing rituals. To make a Victorian-era lavender bowl, fill a small china or glass bowl (5 to 6 inches in diameter) with dried lavender flowers. Cover the bowl with an attractive, loosely woven fabric and fasten with grosgrain ribbon. Place it on a shelf to scent the room.

THE SCENT OF SOOTHING

I love lavender as a flower, but recently rediscovered its efficacy as a medicinal plant. After reading the chapter, "An 'Essential' Oil," in *Be Your Own Doctor* by Rachel Weaver, I was motivated to find out more about lavender's best usable form—essential oil. This light-colored oil can be obtained from any herbal care product source. Look for a clear, light-colored, high-quality oil, not necessarily the cheapest.

An essential oil is made by distilling the oils from a plant's flowers and leaves into an extremely concentrated form. Essential oils are strictly for external use, and most how-to resources recommend diluting them with water (as in a bath) or mixed with another neutral oil such as high-grade olive oil before applying to the skin.

Lavender essential oil is an exception, though. It is usually safe to use undiluted. So, why should your medicine cabinet or herbal first aid kit have a bottle of lavender essential oil? Its compounds are quickly and easily absorbed for pain relief and muscle relaxation in a variety of situations. Lavender also has some antibiotic properties and it even discourages lice infestation.

A combination of apple cider vinegar and lavender essential oil can be used in the final rinse water when doing laundry.

Lavender oil does wonders for the skin. Its cooling, soothing feel will remedy a bad sunburn, blister, or even a deeper burn once it has been properly

LAVENDER

cooled. The area should dry between applications. In other words, don't keep a bandage saturated with lavender. Apply the oil, let it dry, and later, reapply. A quick salve can also be made with lavender oil and honey. Some may find lavender oil helpful for skin conditions such as acne, dermatitis, or eczema.

Use lavender as a first aid for bee stings, immediately after removing the stinger. It also helps lessen the itch of mosquito and other insect bites.

Lavender has mild sedative action for calming nerves and loosening muscle tightness. Try a few drops of oil in warm water for a foot soak or up to ten drops to a bath to relieve stress and aid sleep. When dabbed into the temple and nape area, then massaged into the skin, lavender oil relieves tension headaches. The scent of lavender has also been proved to help concentration. And it works! I'm writing this with a drop or two on each wrist.

Dried lavender

LAVENDER WATER

Ingredients Needed:

1 qt. cold water with lavender flowers   1 Tbsp. lemon juice

Directions:

Let stand 10 days. Strain. The lemon juice acts as a preservative.

Lavender blossoms

ROSY LAVENDER POTPOURRI

Ingredients Needed:

2 c. dried lavender blossoms and leaves
1½ c. dried rose petals
3 to 5 drops of lavender essential oil
1½ c. fixative (dried calamus root or corncob chunks)

Directions:

Drop the essential oil onto the fixative and mix well. Add the flowers; mix and put into a glass jar with lid. Keep the jar covered for a week so the scents can blend. After a few months the scent may begin to fade. You can give the fragrance a boost by adding several drops of essential oil.

LEMON LAVENDER REFRESHER

Ingredients Needed:

½ c. dried lemon peel, crushed into quarter-sized bits
½ c. lavender blossoms

Directions:

Mix and display in a glass jar or use as a drawer scenter. Crush the lemon peel occasionally to release more scent as necessary.

LAVENDER COOKIES

Ingredients Needed:

½ c. margarine
1 c. sugar
2 eggs
1 tsp. dried crushed lavender leaves
1½ c. flour
2 tsp. baking powder
pinch of salt

Directions:

Cream margarine and sugar. Add eggs and lavender. Sift flour, baking powder, and salt and blend into other ingredients. Mix well. Drop a teaspoonful at a time onto an ungreased cookie sheet. Bake at 375°F for 10 minutes. Yields: 2 dozen. These cookies are delicious, with a delightfully sweet taste of lavender!

Lemon balm

Lemony Herbs

The flavor of lemon is unique—refreshingly tart, yet with an appealing tanginess. Our taste buds enjoy this tantalizing zip of citrus in drinks—from cold lemonade to soothing honey lemon tea—and in desserts like lemon meringue or lemon cakes and cookies. Even certain main dishes of meats and vegetables benefit when a dash of spicy lemon is added.

    Lemon aroma also has its special traits. Doesn't it give us a refreshed, invigorated feeling when inhaled? That is why many household cleaners and polishes are lemon scented, imparting a crisp, spick-and-span cleanliness.

    Where does lemon come from? Of course, the main source is the bright yellow fruit of the lemon tree. If you reside in a warm climate, perhaps you

Gracia's Herbs

have an abundance of lemons within easy access. Those who don't live in the tropics can still enjoy the taste of lemon from their own garden by growing lemon-flavored herbs that taste very close to the real thing.

The five lemony herbs featured here are not related. Even though they share a similar flavor, they have quite a variety of shapes, sizes, and growing habits. They also have different degrees of lemon-ness, which are suited for various uses. But whether you grow one or all of them, you are sure to be delighted by the taste of lemon!

Here's a brief description of each plant's lemon flavor, found in the leaves.

Lemon Balm—mild but tasty, with a hint of mint.
Lemon Basil—spicy lemon peel flavor; strongly citrus.
Lemon Geranium—tongue-tingling! Bursting with tartness!
Lemon Thyme—intense lemon with an undertone of thyme.
Lemon Verbena—warm, robust true lemon, but not overwhelming.

LEMON BALM—A DEPENDABLE FAVORITE

This lemony plant has truly earned its place as a dependable perennial, and for several reasons. First of all, its reliable year-after-year presence, despite cold winters or poor soils, is remarkable. Lemon balm grows in Zones 3 to 10.

Another likable habit of lemon balm is its beautiful growing form. It grows to a lush green bush, well rounded and balanced, about 2 feet high and also that wide. Even each individual leaf has a pretty, symmetrical shape, somewhat like a heart and full of a minty lemon aroma.

Besides the standard green lemon balm, there's 'Aurea', a variegated cultivar with gold-splashed leaves. 'All Gold' is a bright, golden-hued green. These add color to shady corners and variety to herb gardens.

Nearly any well-drained soil is a good home for the plant. Full sun, part sun, or shade—all will do. Shade is advisable in southern states, especially for the golden or variegated forms.

Planting seeds or dividing existing plants are easy propagation methods. Seeds can be planted outdoors after danger of frost in well-prepared soil, kept evenly moist until germination. Division can take place in early spring, as soon as new growth appears, or in late fall, when the growing season is done. To divide plants, dig

Lemon balm

out a chunk of the outer part of a clump, and move to a new location. Mulch both the old and new patch.

Throughout the summer growing season, lemon balm is a carefree, self-sufficient plant requiring little special attention. Pinching the growing tips occasionally helps keep the plant compact. The plant has few plant pests; its citrus scent repels them.

Lemon balm is susceptible to powdery mildew, a fairly mild fungal disease. Simply remove the diseased parts, and new, healthy growth should follow. To help prevent mildew, allow sufficient space between plants for air circulation.

In late summer, tiny white flowers appear along the stem, and then you may notice that this plant is not only a favorite for gardeners but bees as well. A member of the mint family, lemon balm is a virtual magnet for honeybees and other insects. In fact, its botanical name *(Melissa officinalis)* is Greek for bee.

Lemon balm

Flowering time continues to late summer. To direct the plant's energy back to new growth, trim back the entire plant to a height of 6 to 10 inches. (Allow some flowering time for the bees to enjoy, though!) This second growth is ideal to harvest for drying.

To harvest leaves for drying, pick fresh new growth, either prior to flowering or second growth in late summer. The lowest leaves on the plant have the richest concentration of lemon oils. Snip the leaves off the stems and dry on nonmetallic screen. Some references say the leaves darken when dried, but I've found that drying the leaves quickly (in an oven warmed by the pilot) helps prevent darkening.

If you do not wish to have an invasion of lemon balm plants (which can happen if allowed to freely self-sow), simply clip off all blossoms. The plant can spread rambunctiously by self-seeding and ever-enlarging root clumps. It does not, however, have spreading underground runners as do mints.

When preparing lemon balm for its winter nap, trim the plant to about 6 to 8 inches and cover with mulch. Though the clump may appear lifeless, come early spring, it will reliably come back!

Lemon balm, with its rich, lemony flavor, offers special culinary opportunities. Its striking green leaves are a beautiful and edible garnish for drinks, desserts, and salads. Chopped fresh leaves can be substituted for lemon zest (grated rind). A combination of tarragon and lemon balm makes a tantalizing vinegar. Or try lemon balm jelly, substituting lemon balm for mint in the recipe.

Despite all other exciting uses, lemon balm as a tea is the ultimate favorite. Served hot or iced, lemon balm tea's light, pleasant lemon flavor hits the spot. Using fresh leaves is best—drying causes some flavor loss. Dried leaves can be used, though. Simply steep longer, up to 10 minutes, to draw out the fullest flavor. Try using lemon balm tea as part of the liquid in gelatin salad, or using frozen tea cubes in drinks.

For a basic lemon balm tea, use 1 to 2 teaspoons dried or 2 tablespoons fresh lemon balm leaves per cup of water. Steep up to 10 minutes and sweeten with honey. Optional: Combine one part lemon balm and one part spearmint for lemony mint tea.

Lemon balm

LEMON BASIL—EASY ANNUAL

Lemon basil is a quick and easy annual that can be sowed directly in the garden. Simply sprinkle seeds into finely tilled soil. Once the soil is warmed (corn and bean planting time), cover with a thin layer of soil and keep evenly moist for seven to ten days. Thin out the seedlings, keeping only the sturdiest plants.

Compared to sweet basil, lemon basil plants are a bit smaller and more sparse, with leaves of a yellow-green hue. Pinching back the tips with your fingers every few weeks or when you see a flower head forming will help the plant become more bushy. Several newer hybrids, 'Mrs. Burns' and 'Sweet Dani', are sturdier with more leaves. They also supposedly have a greater concentration of citrus oils, but I never did notice a substantial difference.

Lemon basil leaves have a tangy, lemon peel flavor, somewhat spicy yet enjoyable. They can be used for tea or substituted whenever a recipe calls for lemon peel.

In late summer, seed heads form, first with tiny inconspicuous flowers, then forming seeds, and finally browning to maturity if left that long. I like to clip these bristly stems 6 to 8 inches long and hang them to dry in a bunch. Tie with a ribbon or place in a sachet for a closet and drawer scenter. Unlike leaves, these stalks do not crumble when squeezed to release the fragrance.

LEMON GERANIUM—FASCINATING PERFUME

For a profound lemony experience, grow a lemon-scented geranium. Just the slightest touch to its crinkly leaves will release a burst of intense aroma, lively and vibrant. Nibble a leaf, and you will discover a tart, crisp profusion of lemon that leaves your taste buds amazed.

Lemon geranium

There are a number of lemon-scented geraniums, including the named varieties, 'Frensham Lemon', 'Prince Rupert', 'Mabel Grey', and 'Fingerbowl'. Most have a compact growing habit with curly, crinkly leaves like curled parsley, but more fleshy. These plants are good windowsill pots in the winter and can be set outdoors in the summer.

One of the best uses for these citrus-scented gems is for potpourri, since the leaves do not crumble as easily when dried because of their slight thickness. Even though lemon geraniums are fully edible, they are almost too pungent for best flavor in foods unless used sparingly.

In olden times lemon geraniums were used as a sanitizer by floating sprigs in a shallow bowl of water. This bowl often stood in the center of the table to provide a refreshing cleanse, done by a quick dip of the hand, hence the "fingerbowl."

LEMON THYME—CHARMING CREEPER

Now we'll take thyme (pronounced TIME) to explore a few more lemony plants. Among the creeping, ground-hugging family of many thymes are several citrus-scented varieties in a medley of colors.

Lemon thyme *(Thymus x citriodorus)* appears nearly identical to regular culinary thyme—same dark green color, same low-growing, spreading habit. But after rubbing a sprig between your fingers, you will immediately sense that it is no ordinary thyme, but a delightfully scented one with the taste of lemon.

Golden lemon thyme

Gracia's Herbs

My favorite of this group, golden lemon thyme (*T. x citriodorus* 'Aureus'), is undeniably beautiful, with creamy white edges marbled onto tiny green leaves. This showy variegation is so pretty in mixed planters or among other plants in the garden. During June and July, it has the added accent of lavender flowers. Golden lemon thyme is somewhat sensitive to winter's cold, so I always make sure to protect it well with a thick layer of mulch.

I added another lemon thyme to my collection called 'Doone Valley'. It makes the perfect contrast for the variegated one, having very dark green leaves randomly flecked with yellow as if a dripping paintbrush had been held above the plant.

Lemon thymes are showy and tasty! The sprigs are at their peak flavor when used fresh. What a striking, edible garnish they make!

For showy lemon ice cubes, place a sprig of golden lemon thyme into each compartment of an ice cube tray. Freeze. Serve with a fruit drink or iced lemon tea.

LEMON VERBENA—ULTIMATE IN TASTE

Sweet, authentic lemon; robust, but not overpowering; prized in the kitchen—this is lemon verbena. Because of its balanced, warm citrus flavor, it is one of the most favored lemony plants.

Just by looking at the plant you may not guess that it holds such flavorful potential. It is apt to have a leggy appearance, like a gangly forsythia, slightly woody with tender green tips. Lemon verbena *(Aloysia triphylla)* is a warm climate native, so it must overwinter indoors in the North (Zone 7 and colder). If you prefer, grow it as an annual. The plant will be smaller than if kept from year to year.

Lemon verbena

Having the plant in a big pot makes it easiest to overwinter. Clip the long stems and place the pot in a protected area like a basement or garage. Don't overwater, just enough to keep the soil from completely drying. In spring, water, fertilize, and set outdoors. The extra effort is worth it!

Lemon verbena leaves are excellent both fresh or dried. To dry, simply strip the leaves from the stems and spread on a screen. Store the dried leaves whole in glass jars and crumble only as you need. The flavor will keep very well this way for several years.

To make a single serving lemon tea, place three to five leaves of lemon verbena (dried) into a teacup. Don't crumble. Pour in boiling water and allow leaves to soften, then bruise with a spoon to release the lemony oils. Sweeten to taste with honey, stevia, or sugar. If you wish, you can lift out the leaves with a fork before drinking the tea.

LEMON BALM FOR COLD SORES

Lemon balm has been known for centuries to have soothing, sedative effects, and gained popularity as a safe, caffeine-free tea for regular consumption. In recent years, renewed attention toward the plant focuses on its powerful antiviral and antioxidant properties.

Lemon balm's antiviral action on outbreaks caused by the herpes simplex virus (cold sores, fever blisters, etc.) proves effective. At the first symptoms, drink lemon balm tea. Repeat at least twice daily. Prepare a strong infusion of 3 to 4 teaspoons dried or 3 to 4 tablespoons fresh lemon balm leaves per cup of water. Once it's cooled to a comfortable temperature, apply directly to the cold sore with a cotton ball or sterile gauze. Apply several times hourly. Discard unused infusion after one day and prepare a fresh batch. My younger brother seems to be prone to recurrent cold sores and this lemon balm treatment relieves the symptoms greatly and shortens the healing period.

Lemon balm

There are a few standardized lemon balm creams available for cold sore treatments. Check at your local drugstore or natural food market.

Lemon balm oil, made by diluting 2 to 5 drops of 100 percent lemon balm essential oil to 1½ ounces of almond or wheat germ oil, can also be applied. Apply to cold sores, shingles, or insect bites. Use as a massage oil to soothe aching muscles or rub onto temples to help relieve migraine headaches. Lemon balm oil can also be used to make ointment.

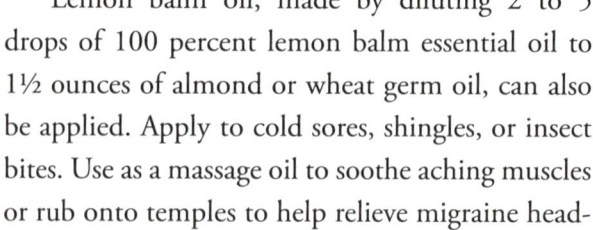

Several drops of lemon balm essential oil in a simmering pot disperses the fresh scent of lemon throughout a room. Dried lemon balm is also a great addition to any citrus-based potpourri or sachet.

Lovage

In an herb garden, picking out the lovage plant is usually quite easy. You see, as one of the biggest and boldest of herbs, it thrusts its glossy green leaves up to 6 feet high! Because its taste so closely resembles that of celery, lovage (*Levisticum officinale*) is definitely a useful plant for any cook. You can think of it as a perennial celery substitute.

IT'S HUGE AND HANDSOME

Envision a bunch of giant celery stalks grouped together and you get a picture of what lovage looks like. Well-established plants in good soil can reach a height of 5 or 6 feet, and form a clump 4 or 5 feet in diameter. It is not a spreading plant, like mint; it simply grows tall, strong, and sizable over the years.

Though it tastes and looks much like celery, one difference is found in the stems. Celery has fleshy stalks; lovage is hollow. The slender outer stems where the leaves are attached are not hollow, though, and can be chopped to form tiny "celery" bits.

In my herb garden, lovage occupies a prominent spot right in the middle, like a stately centerpiece. And a good centerpiece it is! Its towering but well-balanced shape and lush, shiny leaves are truly beautiful. The foliage is suitable for bouquets, or for dressing up meat platters before serving.

In late summer, the plant sends up flower stalks (pale green heads that reach even higher!) which mature to seeds by fall.

It's Easy to Grow

Lovage can be started by sowing seed outdoors in early spring at the intended site. It can also be sown in summer to have a plant for transplanting the next spring. Another method of starting is division of the root clump.

Rich soil with lots of humus is best for growing lovage. Very hard, dry soil, or sites with poor drainage, should be avoided, or amended before planting. Both sunny areas or partial shade are okay. Lovage is quite hardy, growing in Zones 3 to 8. Actually, it needs some winter cold for a period of dormancy, but can be grown as an annual in warmer areas.

Lovage is ideal for companion planting near tomatoes because it helps to lure away tomato hornworms. It also tends to attract aphids to its seed heads. Keep them trimmed off or apply insecticidal soap to deter them. Another insect that loves to burrow into the hollow stalks is called the brown leaf miner. Affected stalks have yellow leaves and should be pruned out.

A lovage plant is usually at its tallest, greenest, best in early summer. After that, its vibrant look declines somewhat, but a bit of manicuring, such as keeping the flower stalks clipped off, does wonders, although if you're wanting to get seeds from it, you should leave a few flower stalks. I like to clip the stalks off down far enough so that the stubs are hidden among the bushy leaves.

Any other yellowing or brown leaves should be trimmed out. It is not unusual for the plant to appear considerably shorter by late summer, with all the

Lovage seed head

Lovage leaf

trimming and not much new growth after the flower stalks appear. In fall, a cover of mulch, such as straw, hay, or leaves, is beneficial for winter protection.

Another secret for lush lovage is keeping the roots young by dividing the clump every four years or so. This can be done in early spring or fall, taking out any old or tightly massed roots, and replanting younger, vigorous ones. With a bit of maintenance, lovage is a very long-lived herb.

If space is limited and you are unsure whether such a large plant will fit, keep the clump small by removing a large portion of the roots each fall.

IT'S A PLEASURE TO USE

Lovage proves to be very useful in the kitchen, mainly because it is a perfect celery substitute. Since it is a perennial that appears in very early spring, you can harvest lovage a good part of the year. It can be used fresh or dried, and all parts are edible, from roots to seeds.

The very first shoots of spring are tender, mild, and crisp, and can be eaten as greens in salads or with sandwiches. Once the plants are a little larger, the stems close to the leaves are suitable for dicing like celery, for potato salad, dressing, or soups.

The leaves, finely chopped or minced with a kitchen shears, also lend a rich celery flavor to soups, meats, and other main dishes. The leaves have a fairly strong, well-bodied taste, so use them accordingly, especially with light dishes such as chicken noodle soup, pasta, or rice.

Lovage seeds taste much like celery seed, but are much larger. For the best even flavor, crush the seeds before using in salad dressings or when pickling.

Supposedly the large taproots can be dug and cooked as a vegetable; I have not tried that yet. I imagine it would be similar to parsnips.

When drying lovage, flavor and color are best preserved by drying quickly. My favorite quick-drying method is clipping the leaves from the stems and placing them

Dried lovage

LOVAGE |119|

single layer on a screen. Next, put them into the oven (not turned on), where there is just enough warmth for rapid drying. Once the leaves are crispy, store in glass jars.

Dried lovage flakes, when mixed with other dried herbs such as basil and parsley, make an excellent soup flavoring mix. Keep it readily handy for adding to stews and soups or tomato sauces.

IT'S GOOD FOR YOU

Lovage tea is a helpful digestive aid and soothes the stomach. Use about 2 tablespoons fresh or 1 tablespoon dried per cup. Cover with boiling water and steep. James A. Duke also mentions its potency as a diuretic in his book, *The Green Pharmacy*, and recommends using it to relieve bladder infections. Persons with kidney problems and who are pregnant should avoid excessive use.

The plant is also rich in minerals and vitamin C. Keep this in mind as you cook!

Fresh lovage leaves make a healing nonstick wound dressing for cuts and burns. Place several layers directly on the area and wrap with gauze or tape. Also, lovage tea is an antiseptic soak for puncture wounds.

ZIPPY TOMATO JUICE

Ingredients Needed:

8 qt. tomato juice	¼ tsp. garlic salt
1 c. sugar	1 c. ReaLemon
3 tsp. salt	2 tsp. dried lovage flakes
2 tsp. onion salt	

Directions:

Serve with a section of hollow lovage stem for a straw.

Mint

When you hear the word mint, what comes to your mind? Quite likely, you think of tea! That's because the mints are popular tea plants all over the world. Mint flavor is also used in toothpaste, chewing gum, and medicines, plus candy and other food products. In floral language, mints speak of wisdom and virtue.

ABOUT THE MINT FAMILY

Mints come in a rainbow of greens: light, dark, and variegated; and in a range of textures: smooth, woolly, and crinkly. There are many fascinating scents and tastes, too! But all mints have square stems and leaves growing in pairs, one on each side of the stem. They grow up to 30 inches tall. Mint roots, called runners, spread underground and send up new plants every few inches.

MANY TO CHOOSE FROM…

There are many, many different kinds of mints. Mints readily cross-pollinate to form many, many variations! Here are several of the most common mints.

Spearmint *(M. spicata)* — A lighter, more yellowish-green with a slightly jagged edge and milder taste. Pointed flower tips. Leaves and stems are the same color. Some varieties are woolly. This is the most used mint. When a recipe calls for "mint," it means this one.

Peppermint *(M. piperita)* — Darker green leaves, reddish stems, rounded or oblong leaves. Rounded flower clusters. Intense flavor. Peppermint flowers are sterile and can't produce seeds. Start with cuttings or plant division.

Field Mint *(M. arvensis)* — North America's only native mint. Easily recognized by its flower clusters, which are tucked along the stem above each pair of leaves.

Additional mints include apple (fruity flavor), pineapple (variegated, very fragrant), chocolate (peppermint patty flavor), ginger (spicy taste), lime, orange, and grapefruit (citrus flavors).

For true-to-variety plants, start them by division or cuttings. Because mints cross-pollinate, seed-grown plants are often not reliable. Mint division couldn't be easier—grab a shovel and dig a clump!

NO GREEN THUMB NEEDED!

Mint seems to grow at a gallop; in fact, it almost seems too easy to grow! When growing mint, keep two things in mind: it can spread and it loves moisture.

Plant mint along a building or stone wall to control its spread. Some gardeners confine their mint in a sunken watering trough. Chimney flues or ceramic tile will work if smaller space is needed. Yet another idea is to sink strips of tin between the plants. Mint roots can grow to a depth of 10 inches, so make sure your barrier is deep enough.

Wild mints ramble along creeksides and roadside ditches to satisfy their thirsty habit. So give your mint a moist home. Plant some close to an outdoor faucet—it will love the drips and splashes. A partly shady place is ideal. Mulch the area with composted matter, but avoid manure, which can cause rusty-looking spots on the leaves.

Every few years breathe new life into your mint patch, by lifting out old, woody growth and replanting new, tender shoots.

TIME TO HARVEST

It's late summer, the mint is lush and green, and little flower buds can be seen on the young tips. It's tea harvesting time! Mint can be harvested at most any time throughout the growing season. However, late summer growth has much more flavor than the very first leaves peeping through the March mud.

Clip the tea stalks about 6 inches above the ground. For the best tea flavor, strip the leaves from the stems before drying! Place the leaves on screens and dry till crispy, then store in glass jars.

THE IMPORTANT MENTHOL

The active ingredient of mint is menthol, a natural substance in the plant's oils. It provides the flavor and medicinal effects. Minus menthol, a mint would hardly be a mint!

Menthol gives a tingly, candy cane flavor, warming and cooling at the same time. Many brands of toothpaste, mouthwash, and chewing gum contain this refreshing taste. Through tea or cough drops, menthol's penetrating effects help clear stuffy noses and soothe itchy throats. Some analgesic creams have menthol, for reaching deep into aching muscles, easing the soreness.

Menthol occurs naturally in all mints, but some have more menthol than others. Peppermint ranks most powerful and is the preferred mint for medicinal use. Other red-stemmed, dark-leaved kinds like chocolate and candy mint are also good, followed by spearmints. Mild, fruity mints like apple and pear contain a minimal amount of menthol. (Your nose and taste buds are the best menthol detectors. The more minty, the more menthol.)

MEDICINE AS YOU SIP

Mint tea is a healthful alternative to coffee, and even children can drink tea safely. Did you know that coffee disrupts proper insulin function? Or that caffeine, a harmful drug found in coffee and soft drinks, disturbs cell growth?

Drink tea instead of coffee and your body will thank you for it!

The best-known medicinal use for mint tea is as a digestive aid. Mint, especially peppermint, contains carminative properties which relax the stomach muscles and intestinal tract. So a cup of tea is a simple but effective tonic for a queasy stomach. Even those who suffer from chronic digestive disorders like irritable bowel syndrome find relief in peppermint.

Spearmint tea

By relaxing the stomach, mint also curbs nausea, so it's worth a try for morning sickness. Most resources recommend staying away from peppermint oils and supplements during pregnancy, but a cup of mild tea on occasion should be fine.

Mint also has analgesic or pain-relieving effects, especially for headaches. Try a cup of peppermint tea to help break up that migraine. For a more intense treatment, dab a bit of peppermint oil diluted in vegetable oil directly on your temple. (Do not take by mouth.)

Nine different expectorant compounds are found in peppermint, so reach for a cup of tea to clear up a stuffy nose or congested airways. Even the warm steam alone helps penetrate the clogged areas.

To make a natural mouthwash, make tea with your favorite mint and let it cool to a comfortable temperature, then rinse. The menthol in mint is a natural bacteria fighter.

Two other important compounds in mint are rosmarinic acid and perillyl alcohol. Research shows perillyl alcohol to slow the formation and growth of cancerous cells, while rosmarinic acid relieves the runny nose symptoms of allergies and hay fever.

The next time you have a cupful of mint tea, whether for its flavor, its fellowship value, or its tonic virtues, take a moment to appreciate this valuable brew.

Gracia's Herbs

ICED TEA TIPS

Mint is perfect as a base for your own homemade tea blends. Use cotton cloth to make custom tea bags.

For fuss-free tea brewing, I like to use loose-leaf teas and a mesh ball. A large 3-inch ball easily holds enough tea to make a pot of tea. Smaller single-size tea balls or stainless steel perforated infusers are just right for your own mug.

For nice, light-colored iced tea, strain out tea leaves as soon as possible and chill the tea immediately.

Iced tea can be frozen in ice cube trays or pint-size freezer boxes. When added to drinks, this "ice" doesn't water down the flavor like plain ice would.

Use mint tea as part of the cold liquid when making gelatin desserts or fruit punch.

One quick method for iced tea is to puree tea leaves in water in the blender and strain the juice. Add sweetener and water. This results in a strong green flavor. A friend of mine puts a bunch of bruised leaves in a pitcher of water and lets it set in the refrigerator for a week or so.

CANDIED MINT LEAVES

Pick large, pretty leaves of spearmint or peppermint. Wash and dry them, then dip in a mixture of 1 egg white, beaten and ½ teaspoon water. Immediately dip into granulated sugar and place on waxed paper to dry.

MINT JELLY

Ingredients Needed:

3 c. water

1½ c. fresh spearmint or peppermint leaves

2 Tbsp. vinegar

⅓ c. powdered pectin

4 c. sugar

½ tsp. butter

food coloring, optional

mint sprigs, for garnish

Directions:

Mix the prepared tea with the vinegar, pectin, butter, and food coloring. Mix well. Put over the highest heat, stirring constantly until mixture comes to a full boil that cannot be stirred down. Mix in sugar. Continue stirring, return to full rolling boil, and boil hard for exactly one minute. Remove from heat. Stir and skim off foam with a metal spoon. Immediately pour into hot, sterilized jars with mint sprig in the bottom of each. Seal. Yield: approx. 40 oz.

Note: With no food coloring added, this jelly is an attractive light yellow-green.

MINT NUT BREAD

Ingredients Needed:

2½ c. flour

1 c. firmly packed brown sugar

3½ tsp. baking powder

3 Tbsp. oil

1½ c. milk or ¾ c. milk and ¾ c. apple juice

1 egg

1 c. chopped walnuts

1 c. chopped fresh mint (⅓ c. dried)

Directions:

Preheat oven to 350°F. Mix the flour, sugar, and baking powder in a large mixing bowl. Whisk together the oil, milk, and egg. Blend the mixtures together. Add the walnuts and mint. Bake in greased bread pans for 50 to 60 minutes. Cool and slice. Ages and freezes well.

Woolly spearmint

Oh, Oregano!

Oregano is among my favorite herbs, and here's why: it's easy to grow and it's pretty too! Culinary oreganos are packed with flavor and capture the essence of herbs. Decorative oreganos are versatile for ground covers or dried flowers.

Most culinary oreganos are perennial herbs, which reach a height of approximately 12 inches. They bear oval-shaped leaves on semi-erect stems. In late summer, tiny tubular flowers appear in shades of pink, lavender, or white, depending on variety.

There are several species of oregano, including common *(O. vulgare)* and Greek *(O. prismaticum* or *heracleoticum)*. If you want to use oregano in the kitchen, go for Greek strains, which far surpass the other strains in flavor! The dried oregano available in your local bulk food store or supermarket is liable to be disappointingly bland compared to homegrown Greek oregano. Even common oregano is more tasty than most store-bought oregano flakes! Before buying oregano plants in a garden center, be brave enough to pluck and taste a leaf so you know what you're getting.

'Golden' oregano is a prolific ground cover, showy in chartreuse green with light pink flowers. It grows rapidly across areas you want to cover and can spread to areas you don't want covered. So keep it managed by defining the edge with a shovel.

'Herrenhausen' oregano is an attractive plant. It's suitable for a perennial bed or a hummingbird garden with its tall flower stalks that bloom in a rich raspberry purple. I like to dry these for arrangements and swags.

'Herrenhausen' oregano

PROPAGATION

When starting oregano from seed, use a finely textured seed starting mix. Oregano can also be sown outside after danger of frost is past; prepare the seedbed well with fine soil or peat moss to accommodate the tiny seeds. Seed-grown oregano plants may vary in quality of flavor. Root division and layering guarantee true-to-variety plants.

Dividing an oregano clump is easy. In spring or fall, use a shovel or garden knife to cut the root mass in two. Water well after dividing.

GROWING

Oregano thrives in common garden soil. Loose, sandy, or gravelly soil with good drainage is best. In clay soil the roots are prone to disease. The plant is a sun lover; in shady areas it survives, but grows more slowly.

Oregano's root clump will grow larger from year to year and will spread somewhat. However, as it grows older it tends to die out in one spot and sprout fresh new growth in another direction. Reposition younger clumps or layer stems as needed to keep your oregano bed looking full.

Throughout the summer, harvest liberally as needed for cooking and drying. Just before flowering time, trim back the long stalks to encourage continued leaf growth. In Zones 5 and colder, prepare the plants for winter by mulching.

COOKING USE

Oregano is versatile both fresh and dried. Use it fresh to make herbal vinegar, or to garnish main dishes, or as a refreshing touch of greenery in mini bouquets. Fresh oregano can be stored in your refrigerator for up to a week by placing unwashed leaves in an airtight plastic bag.

To dry oregano, tie into bunches and hang. After about two weeks, once the leaves are crispy, the drying is completed. Strip the leaves from the stems, crush or grind them, and store.

Oregano is the perfect seasoner for tomato-based dishes, soups, and pastas. Sprinkle oregano flakes onto pizza before putting on the toppings.

Oregano is best known for its crucial part in Italian cooking. But don't limit its uses to pizza and pastas! Use oregano to enhance breads, meat dishes (especially beef), and cheese spreads. Add oregano vinegar to salsa and barbecue sauces.

ITALIAN MIX

A blend of dried herbs for use in cooking.

Ingredients Needed:

1 Tbsp. Greek oregano	2 tsp. each of thyme, marjoram, and sage
1 Tbsp. basil	1 tsp. each of summer savory and rosemary

HERB BREAD

Make your regular bread recipe. When ready to form the loaves, add 1 tablespoon dry oregano flakes and ½ teaspoon garlic powder per loaf. Knead into dough. If desired, 1 teaspoon each of parsley and basil may be added.

Parsley

Parsley, the familiar green herb, is seen everywhere! Perhaps it is tucked beside juicy meat loaf, or dotting buttery red potatoes. Maybe you savor its flavor with spaghetti or herb bread. Browsing through a store's produce section, chances are you'll see parsley garnishing displays of vegetables. Keep a lookout, though, for fake plastic "parsley" sometimes used. Don't admire that stuff!

ANNUAL OR PERENNIAL?

Actually, the answer is neither. Parsley *(Petroselinum crispum)* is a biennial; it grows for one year, overwinters in most climates, and goes to seed in the summer of the second year. After it goes to seed, the plant never resumes its young, new growth. For this reason, parsley is often grown as an annual. Parsley varieties divide into three groups: curly leaf, plain leaf, and rooted. All are biennials which grow from 12 to 18 inches tall, preferring full sun, but tolerating part shade also.

Curly parsley

CURLY PARSLEY FOR LOOKS

Curly parsley has tightly crimped leaves, giving it a frilly look. The newest leaves are the most curly. As the leaves become older, they droop outward and are replaced by new growth in the plant's center. Curly parsley is among the most widely grown herbs in the country, with tons being used yearly for garnish in stores and restaurants. Commercial growers know that "the curlier, the better" for discerning chefs. Growers also prefer long stems for harvesting and bunching ease.

'Banquet' is attractive with extremely curly leaves. A good choice for any gardener, it is winter hardy and fast growing. 'Forest Green' is ideal for repeated harvests and holds its color well. Gardeners in the South might try 'Green River', which is heat tolerant. 'Moss Curled' is a very popular cultivar for gardeners and bedding plant growers. Dwarf curly parsley varieties, such as 'Curlina', are excellent potted plants for windowsill gardening.

PLAIN LEAF PARSLEY FOR FLAVOR

Plain leaf, single leaf, celery leaf, Italian: they are all one and the same! Plain leaf parsley is often an overlooked plant, which is unfortunate because it has some definite benefits. For one, you can harvest more, due to its prolific, fast-growing habit, plus being slow to go to seed. The plant also has better winter hardiness than curly types. Yet the most significant benefit is more flavor—rich, sweet, and intense. True, plain leaf parsley doesn't have the fancy curl most people picture when they think of parsley. Yet its smooth, dark emerald leaves are beautiful in the garden and kitchen and their flavor is appreciated by many.

Plain leaf parsley has few named varieties. One recommended strain is 'Italian Dark Green'.

Rooted parsley *(P. crispum tuberosum)* is grown mainly for the white, carrot-like roots, yet its leaves, similar to plain leaf, can also be used. The roots grow up to 7 or 8 inches, and can be harvested in fall, winter, or spring. It stores easily in the ground over winter (just like carrots or parsnips) when mulched. 'Bartowich Long' is available from Johnny's Selected Seeds and is recommended for its surprising flavor. It can be eaten raw or cooked. 'Hamburg' is a well-proven variety.

SOWING PARSLEY

The best way to propagate parsley is growing from seed. Since parsley does not like root disturbance, plant in trays or small pots filled with a good potting medium for best success. When transplanting time comes, simply tap out the plant and surrounding soil, and situate with little shock to the thin, spindle-like taproots.

Parsley germinates and grows rather slowly. Plan ahead; it takes approximately 12 to 15 weeks after planting for a sizable plant to develop. Seeds sown in January or February will be maturing plants in late spring. March or April sowings produce large plants by late summer. By April or May, parsley can be directly sown outdoors. However, I've always preferred to sow indoors, getting a head start and regulated growing. A midsummer sowing will give you well-established plants by fall. Keep well protected from winter cold and come spring you'll have nicely growing parsley.

There are several methods to speed germination time. One is to soak the seeds in water for 12 to 24 hours prior to sowing. Remove from water and plant immediately. A quick trick is to sow dry seeds in potting mix, as usual, then pour hot water over the soil until saturated. (I pour it right out of the teakettle.) Water frequently to keep soil evenly moist.

Once danger of frost is past, the parsley plants should be showing some true leaves, and be ready to plant outdoors. Give the plants plenty of room, spacing them 8 to 10 inches apart. Keep well watered and mulch to retain moisture and cut down on weeds. Mulching also helps provide additional soil nutrients, which parsley readily responds to. An added fertilizer can also be used.

Parsley can be harvested at any stage of the plant's growth. Of course, don't overharvest young plants to the point of stress. One idea is to plant some extras and pick some entire plants when they are quite tiny yet.

It's best to take off the leaves and the entire stem down to the main stalk when selecting parsley for picking. Who likes to see the stubs left by only pinching off the leaf tops? Besides, taking off the whole stem promotes faster regrowth.

Flat leaf parsley

If the parsley plant is in its second year, you should be able to get several pickings in early summer before it goes to seed. By this time, the new plants are green and growing, and replace the old for a nonstop parsley source.

Curly parsley is one of the few herbs that must have artificial heat to dry. After spreading small sprigs single layer on screens or trays, place them in a slightly warm oven (100°F). Too much heat will darken the parsley and give it a burned taste. The leaves should retain their bright green color when dried carefully. It is fully dried when the leaves readily crumble to flakes.

Store in glass jars, preferably without crumbling. What a pretty sight to have a jar filled with dried, early parsley sprigs!

Plain leaf parsley dries faster and usually needs little additional heat. Spread out on screens in a dry, airy place. Store in jars when drying is done. More flavor is preserved if the leaves are still whole. It takes only a few seconds to reduce them to flakes by rubbing as you are cooking. Or prepare a small amount ahead of time and keep in a handy shaker.

Fresh parsley can be stored in the refrigerator, or in water as a bouquet. Mince with a sharp knife or kitchen shears.

PARSLEY—COOK'S DELIGHT

The mild flavor of parsley makes it a good addition to vegetables and main dishes. A melted butter/parsley blend is a favorite with young red potatoes, as well as cooked carrot slices. Chopped parsley also adds delicious flavor to dressing and baked potatoes. Meat loaf, meatballs, and hamburgers are enhanced by parsley's subtle, yet rich taste. Don't forget to use fresh parsley as a garnish when the main dish is ready to serve!

Any form of tomatoes, whether sauces, salsa, or soups, accommodates parsley well. Spice up tomato juice with parsley flakes, seasoned salt, and a dash of lemon juice. When adding parsley to soup, put it in only a short time before serving so that the flavor is not simmered out.

Parsley is also a good addition to golden noodles and creamy, light-colored soups, both for taste and color. For something different, try parsley with scrambled eggs or breakfast casserole.

Many uses for parsley are mentioned here, but perhaps your favorite use hasn't been touched! The possibilities with parsley are vast, so use parsley often. After all, it's such a healthful plant! Read on.

SUPER HEALTHFUL HERB

By far the greatest amount (in fact, 90 percent) of parsley used as garnish in restaurants is only looked at, then thrown away. How unfortunate! An excellent source of vitamins and minerals is being discarded. In parsley, vitamin A, vitamin C, and calcium abound. In fact, compared to oranges, there is more vitamin C per volume in parsley. Plain parsley surpasses curly parsley in vitamin content.

Besides containing calcium, parsley also helps your body utilize the calcium absorbed from other sources. It also is a source of naturally occurring fluorine, a bone-building substance. For these reasons, parsley is recognized as an osteoporosis-fighting herb, whether an individual has it or is at risk.

The dark green leaves of parsley are rich in chlorophyll, a natural breath freshener. Nibble a small portion to leave your mouth feeling clean and refreshed.

To receive the health benefits of parsley, use liberally in cooking, adding to hot foods shortly before serving. Make a habit to nibble some fresh parsley occasionally, or take a capsulated form for concentrated strength. Last of all, don't ignore that sprig of parsley garnish!

HABITAT FOR CATERPILLAR GREEN

Have you ever studied the cover of the children's book, *Caterpillar Green?* You'll see a picture of parsley, the favorite host plant for the black swallowtail caterpillar. In the story, a caterpillar is found on a green parsley plant and taken to school, where Miss Rose and her students observe his keen appetite for the "little green plant," before becoming a chrysalis and finally a beautiful black swallowtail butterfly. Parsley definitely deserves a place in a butterfly garden.

Rosemary

For centuries, rosemary with its aromatic leaves and tiny, pale blue flowers has symbolized friendship and loyalty. In fact, it is often known as the "herb of remembrance."

Rosemary's botanical name *(Rosmarinus officinalis)* literally means "dew of the sea." Along the Mediterranean coast, rosemary plants flourish in the moist ocean air. Their roots tolerate—even prefer—the dry, rocky soil. Knowing rosemary's native habitat helps gardeners in other areas grow the plant successfully.

PICKING A PLANT

Rosemary has narrow, dark green leaves, an inch or two long, on upright stems. As the plant ages, its stems harden to form woody trunks and branch-

Rosemary in bloom

es, almost like a little shrub. When grown as an annual, it may reach a height of 2 feet or more. Older plants may grow from 3 to 5 feet with a sizable spread. A mature rosemary specimen can be impressive!

Rosemary seeds can be very slow to germinate, and seedlings may not all be true. Stem cuttings are a much more reliable way of propagating rosemary. If you buy a healthy potted plant, it probably began as a stem cutting.

There isn't a huge difference between rosemary cultivars—they all taste fresh and spicy, almost piney, with rather insignificant little flowers in later summer. Still, I have some favorites such as 'Gorizia'. This cultivars was discovered in Italy and grows beautifully full and stately with an abundance of broad, flavorful leaves. In comparison, 'Arp' is more spindly, but it has better winter hardiness. Well-protected and well-mulched, it survives our western New York winters more often than not. It also tolerates summer heat better in the South. 'Barbecue' has extra sturdy stems. Use a branch for kabobs or for a disposable barbecue brush!

Compared to upright types, prostrate rosemary has more needle-like leaves and an interesting, somewhat cascading habit. I love to grow it at the top of a retaining wall, where it trails down in front of the rocks.

GROWING IT

In the garden, rosemary does well in full sun, with plenty of space between plants to prevent powdery mildew. It thrives in sandy, well-drained soil with plenty of organic matter.

If you live where winter temperatures dip into the single digits, you can either enjoy rosemary outdoors as an annual or lift it into a pot for overwintering indoors. Rosemary also makes an attractive container plant, by itself or mixed with other herbs, whether or not you wish to bring the pot indoors for the cold months. Pots can be sunk into the ground for easier care.

Overwintering rosemary indoors can be a little tricky, but it's well worth the effort. It seems to work well to prepare the plant early for transition. If it's growing in the garden, scoop it up into a pot six weeks before your first frost and keep it in partial shade. (Choose a pot on the small side. Have gravel or perlite at the bottom for good drainage.) Prune the plant to half its size. During the winter, its spot should be sunny but cool, such as near a drafty window or in an enclosed porch. Water very sparingly. Airflow prevents powdery mildew, a common problem for rosemary indoors. A simple solution of water and baking soda or water and milk works for powdery mildew if the plant does get it. In spring, bring the plant back with warmth, light, and water!

A ROSEMARY TREE!

One fun thing to do with rosemary is to train it into topiary form. (Topiary is the art of training a plant into a fancy shape.) Rosemary is well suited for topiary because it becomes strong and woody with age.

A common topiary shape is a standard—a tree-shaped plant. Begin with a potted plant, 12 to 16 inches tall. It should be vigorous with a straight stem. Strip off the leaves and side shoots, starting at the bottom and upward to about 10 to 12 inches from the soil. Support the trunk with wire or a thin dowel. Let the remaining leaves grow for now.

When your "tree" has reached the height you want, pinch back the tips to form a rounded pom-pom top. Promote growth by giving it an all-purpose fertilizer. Your topiary will grow more bushy with age.

Rosemary standard

ROSEMARY IN USE

Harvest rosemary in midsummer when there's lots of new growth. Pick the leaves from the stems and dry on nonmetallic screen.

In the kitchen, rosemary is often used to flavor meat dishes, especially chicken and lamb. Add some crushed rosemary to olive oil marinades or barbecue sauce. Or use fresh sprigs as a garnish on a meat platter. Use sparingly at first and test taste, because a little bit of rosemary goes a long way!

Rosemary, with its sweet/pungent aroma, is quite useful for making potpourri. It is also a great herb for hair rinses and shampoos.

ROSEMARY HONEY

Ingredients Needed:

1 Tbsp. fresh rosemary leaves, slightly chopped

2 c. honey

Directions:

Stir rosemary leaves into well-warmed honey. Let stand for 5 to 7 days. Rewarm honey and strain. The honey's color may darken, which does not affect the taste.

Common sage

Sage

In almost any herb garden, you will probably see a shrubby plant with grayish-green leaves. (So that is why there is a color known as "sage green"!) You'll notice that the leaves have a soft, pebbly texture and they release a distinct scent—somewhat minty, somewhat camphoraceous. Let me introduce you to sage.

This easy-to-grow perennial is one of the basic, mainstay herbs since it has such a wide variety of uses as a culinary, medicinal, and aromatic plant. The sage plant has long been connected with health, well-being, and longevity. Even its botanical name is from a Latin root, *salvus,* meaning safe and well.

MEETING THE SAGES

Meeting all the sages would be quite an undertaking because there are about 750 of them. Many of them grow in the wild in warm climates, such as in Central and South America. Actually, only a small percentage of the plants in the genus Salvia have been developed for domesticated growing. Nearly all sages do have in common these characteristics: upright flower stalks, narrow scented leaves, and woody stems.

CULINARY SAGE

This group consists of common sage and its color variations. These perennial plants grow from 18 to 24 inches tall and become woody when well established.

Common sage *(Salvia officinalis)* — Common sage, or garden sage, is the most widely grown sage, with narrow, dusty green leaves. In late May, the plant blooms, sending upright lavender flower spikes that are useful in arrangements.

'Berggarten' — This named cultivar of common sage grows only 9 to 12 inches tall and has a well-balanced, compact mound shape. The leaves are large, broad, and rounded. 'Berggarten' is nonflowering, producing lots of leaves that are excellent for cooking. It is one of my favorite plants in the herb garden!

Golden sage *(O. aurea)* — Golden sage is beautifully variegated with splashes of gold around the leaf edges. What a striking plant for herb or rock gardens! 'Icterina' is a named variety.

Purple sage *(O. purpurescens)* — This unusually colored sage has dark purple stems and bluish-purple leaves. Purple sage is a bushy plant suitable for an accent planting.

Golden sage

'Tricolor' — Of all the colored sages, this one is unsurpassed, in my opinion. The foliage is a rainbow of soft pink, creamy white, lavender, and dusty green. Like other variegated plants, 'Tricolor' grows more slowly.

Clary sage

Salvia farinacea

MORE SAGE

Here are several sages that are not used as much for culinary purposes, but are useful in rock gardens, perennial borders, and nature gardens. For many more kinds of sage, explore any perennial catalog.

Clary sage *(Salvia sclarea)* — This tall, dominant sage stands out in an herb garden or perennial bed. The large gray leaves are heavily textured. Its stunning flower spikes, in shades of lavender and pink, attract bees and hummingbirds like magnets. Clary sage readily self-sows when the flowers are allowed to mature to seed.

Pineapple sage *(Salvia elegans)* — A tender sage grown as an annual in Zones 7 and above, this eye-catching plant has scarlet flowers and a sweet pineapple scent. It has culinary use also.

Meadow sage *(Salvia nemorosa)* — This tall, decorative sage is perfect for perennial borders, with profusely long-lasting flower spikes. There are a number of named varieties having blooms of pinks, blues, and lavender.

Also in the sage family are the popular annual bedding plants known as salvias. *Salvia farinacea* 'Victorian Blue' is widely planted for its intensely blue spikes that dry beautifully.

Pineapple sage

SAGE—FROM SEED PACKET OR DIVISION

Sage is an easy plant to propagate, by seed or division. Years ago, when I was discovering the fascinating world of herbs, sage was the very first herb I planted. What a thrill as those new plants emerged!

When starting sage indoors from seed, plant it three to four weeks before the last expected frost date. Sage germinates best in well-lit settings, so cover only lightly with potting mix. Refrain from over-frequent watering to prevent dampening off. Transplant outdoors after danger of frost is past.

Sage can also be started outdoors by seed. Once the soil temperature is at least 50°F (bean and corn planting time), it's okay to plant sage. Sow at a shallow depth of ¼ inch. Keep watered so that the soil stays moist. After the seedlings are an inch or two high, thin them, leaving 18 to 24 inches between plants.

Established sage plants are easily divided by simply pulling apart a root clump or slicing with a shovel. This can be done in early spring or late fall, when the plant is not actively growing.

IN THE GARDEN

Sage thrives in full sun (pouting in the shade) and is both wind and drought resistant. Nearly any soil type is suitable; even acidic soil is tolerable. Sage is also a versatile plant in patio containers.

Though it is tough, sage has a tendency to decline after several years, as far as producing new growth. Suddenly the plant no longer has a lush, bushy look. Instead, it has scraggly, leggy stalks with only sparse new growth at the tips. Trim ruthlessly in early spring to keep the plant looking vibrant. At least one-third of the old plant should be trimmed off. Old woody stems that appear inactive can be removed close to the ground, and softer, newer growth can take over. After flowering time, trim off the spent flower stalks, unless you want to save seeds. The new growth that follows is perfect for drying.

When ready to harvest sage leaves, simply snip fresh, new leaves and hang to dry. For best flavor, strip the leaves from the stem and dry on a nonmetallic screen. If the leaves are thick, pop the screen into an oven that has been turned to warm and turned off again. The leaves should be dried until crispy. Grind by rubbing over a screen, or store leaves whole in glass jars for the best flavor preservation and crumble when needed.

When winter is around the corner, cover your sage with some type of mulch. The variegated types especially benefit from winter protection.

SAGE TO EAT

It has been said that sage has three flavors. When fresh, it tastes light and minty; when dried, its taste is strong and bold; when cooked too long, it's sadly bitter. There's some truth to this saying.

Probably the most popular use for sage is as a meat seasoning. Perhaps it's because the distinct flavor is easily and well absorbed by meat. Another reason could be the fact that sage helps break up the fats and grease in meats, especially pork.

Sage can be incorporated in a variety of ways. Fresh sage rubbed onto chicken prior to barbecuing or other preparation gives a flavorful twist. A dash of sage vinegar in marinade is handy too. Many bologna and sausage recipes call for ground dried sage.

Another traditional use for sage is in the stuffing, or dressing, used to stuff the turkey at Thanksgiving. Sage also complements cheese such as ricotta.

AN ASTRINGENT ANTIBACTERIAL

Although sage is not a widely used supplement, it does have some medicinal value as an astringent. (Astringents contract and reduce body secretions.) Sage is useful for maintaining a clear facial skin by tightening pores and reducing oily sheen when used as a facial steam. Simply rubbing fresh sage leaves on insect bites and itches can provide relief. Using a sage rinse helps reduce scalp oiliness and flakes.

Taken internally, whether as tea, drops, or capsules, sage can help break up mucous congestion from bronchitis. It also reduces excessive sweating from fever. Sage can help clear up diarrhea, but should not be used if there is danger of dehydration. Another effect sage has is inhibiting milk flow for nursing mothers.

Sage tea is also a good antibacterial gargle. Rinsing the mouth several times daily with cooled or lukewarm tea helps get rid of mouth sores or gum inflammation.

SAGE TEA

Ingredients Needed:
1 c. hot water, not boiling
2 tsp. fresh or 1 tsp. dried sage leaves

Directions:
Steep only a short time.
Sweeten to taste and serve.

Summer savory

Savory

For the past two thousand years, savory has been an important herb for cooks. In Germany, savory is known as *Bohnenkraut* (bean herb), which reveals its excellent ability to blend with vegetables, especially green beans. In the garden, too, savory is an ideal companion plant for beans, including string beans and pole beans. Its spicy leaves repel bean beetles.

There are two kinds of savory. The annual form is summer savory, a fast-growing annual plant with a peppery yet pleasant taste. The perennial form, winter savory, has a stronger, more biting taste. This plant is an evergreen herb, hardy in Zones 5 to 9.

SUMMER SAVORY

This annual herb is easily grown from seed. An early beginning is good for extended leaf harvest, so start seeds four to six weeks before the frost-free date. Germination takes about a week. Like dill and some other annual herbs, summer savory doesn't transplant very well. Sow seeds in peat pots or a tray where you can scoop out lots of medium without disturbing the new little roots. Or you can sow seeds outdoors after danger of frost in the spot where you intend it to grow.

Summer savory *(Satureja hortensis)* does best in full sun, in average garden soil. It needs no special care, and pests and diseases are rare. The plant grows 12 to 20 inches tall. Its leggy, pink-brown stems are mostly upright, with loose whorls of narrow green leaves. Mature plants become somewhat top-heavy, and often lean or half recline on the ground. As the plant matures, tiny pale lavender flowers bloom. I like to give the plant a good trimming before the flower buds open to promote another flush of growth.

Summer savory

Harvest fresh leaves as you need them. In early spring you can pluck little seedlings, thinning the row at the same time! Summer savory leaves can be harvested at any time for fresh use and screen dried for winter use.

When frost threatens, and you would like a quick method to preserve summer savory, you can pull the entire plant and make a natural hook by clipping off the main branch, keeping a stub about two inches long. Hang the plant upside down on a string to dry. Its reddish stem color brightens when dried and makes nice edible kitchen decor.

WINTER SAVORY

Winter savory *(Satureja montana)* is an evergreen herb that grows up to 24 inches tall. Its appearance is similar to that of summer savory, but more bushy with stiffer stems. Its glossy, dark green leaves have a shiny, clean appeal. The tiny white flowers scattered among the foliage remind me of twinkling stars in the night sky. Leaves of winter savory can be used fresh or dried.

Creeping or dwarf winter savory *(S. montana 'procumbens')* grows about 6 inches tall. It is a good, small-range ground cover, since its fast-growing branches root wherever they touch the soil. Its branches are stiff and angular. Good trimming will keep the plant looking tidy.

Winter savory seed germinates slowly and can be sown directly outdoors. Or you may prefer buying started plants. Once you have established plants and would like to propagate more, try the spring layering method. In early spring lay a main branch flat and cover with soil. By late summer, the covered part will have roots of its own. Clip from the main plant and resituate with a shovel.

COOKING WITH SAVORY

Many cooks prefer the peppery yet delicate flavor of summer savory for milder vegetables like cabbage and summer squash. Winter savory, with its tongue-tingling zing, is good for rice and chicken. Yet it can also be used interchangeably in any recipe that calls for savory, especially if you prefer a more pronounced herb flavor.

Summer savory is best known for its use as a bean flavoring. Snip it finely and add generously to buttery green beans or stir-fry. It also blends well with peas and lentils.

Many other vegetable dishes, from steamed carrots to tomato juice, are enhanced by a sprinkle of its peppery leaves.

Savory can be added to bouquet garni, a cluster of dried or fresh herbs that is simmered in soups, then removed before serving. For salt-free cooking, try a combination of dried savory, lovage, and morjoram. Other culinary uses for savory include herbal vinegar and herb butters.

Summer savory

Scented Geraniums

OLD-TIME TREASURES

Are there any flowers that give more summery cheer than geraniums? Even though they're the most common of bedding plants, we are always delighted by perky geraniums.

There is another type of geranium that deserves appreciation; not so much with our eyes, but with our noses! These are the scented geraniums, old-fashioned and unique. Because of their tiny single flowers, they have never entered the commercial limelight. Yet these humble plants are among the most rewarding plants to grow—scent-wise.

WHERE DOES THE SCENT COME FROM?

Rose geranium leaf

Usually, thinking of "sweet" plants brings colorful aromatic flowers to mind. After all, to enjoy our fragrant favorites like roses and honeysuckle, we bury our noses into the blossoms, inhaling deeply to experience the perfume. But if scented geraniums have only tiny flower clusters, where does the huge fragrance come from?

The answer is this: the entire plant is scented, even the stems! Every leaf and stem is lined with microscopic scent pockets, and the slightest contact causes these pockets to burst, releasing the scent into the air or onto your hand. You can enjoy the fragrance without picking any leaves; just rub between your thumb and fingers then sniff your fingertips. On a warm, breezy day as the wind rustles the plants, you may smell them yards away.

WHERE DO THEY COME FROM?

Until the early 1600s, scented geraniums were a secret, growing wild in the arid hills of South Africa. Then, after explorers found them and took them back to Europe, scented geraniums became immensely popular. They did not take nearly as much care as the other plants from far away that were appearing in Europe. The French perfume makers also saw opportunity in these scented plants, as did the gardeners, and soon there was great competition to develop new plants with unique scents.

One after the other, new plants appeared, smelling like roses, apples, oranges, nutmeg, or citronella. By the mid 1800s there were more than 200 kinds, many with fanciful names. Many of these old-time cultivars have been dropped, but some are part of modern collections today.

Early pioneers brought scented geraniums to America. No doubt these delightful plants brought cheer and beauty to the primitive homes and gardens! They also added sweet flavors to jellies and cakes before sugar was widely used.

Today the fascination with these long-loved plants remains alive. Even though the colorful flowering geraniums have surpassed them in popularity, scented geraniums are a true delight for gardeners. Most likely, scented geraniums will continue to receive increased attention.

SCENTED GERANIUMS

EXPLORING THE PLANTS

To grow scented geraniums is a continual adventure. First of all, the variety is astounding! From tiny 6-inch mounds to yard-high ramblers and eager creepers, all sizes are available. Textures vary also from fuzzy, woolly, and velvety to smooth, glossy, and waxy. Green is the common color, but it may be variegated with gray, white, and darker green. And the scents—what a medley! From sweet to spicy, fruity to floral, piney to pepperminty, the possibilities are vast. Last of all, the flowers may be pink, rose, scarlet, lavender, or white, or showy combinations of two colors.

Scented geraniums are considered heirloom plants, untouched by the hosts of patents that surround the geraniums in our flower beds. During the 1800s, growers hybridized new varieties, naming them as they pleased, until there were so many similar kinds and intercrossed plants that confusion reigned. Finally, in the 1940s, a group in New England gave some guidelines to classify the plants, first by scent, then by leaf shape and flower color. The categories are general and somewhat flexible. Let's explore the main ones, listing some specific varieties.

ROSE GROUP: SWEET!

The rose group is the largest and most cherished group, with convincingly authentic rose fragrance. In fact, rose geranium oil is a good economical substitute for the expensive true rose oil. Rose-scented geraniums have a vigorous rambling habit and may grow up to 2½ feet tall and 3 feet wide in good soil.

A bit of trimming easily controls size. Most rose-scenteds have deeply cut or lobed leaves, slightly fuzzy. Flowers are pink, lavender, or white, a few with darker throats.

Suggested varieties: **'Attar of Roses'**—sweet, sweet; **'Old-Fashioned Rose'**—large, rambling grower; **'Chicago Rose'**—leaves have dark green centers; **'Grey Lady Plymouth'**—gray edged; **'Cinnamon Rose'**—spicy rose scent; **'Snowflake'**—variegated white/green; **'Skeleton Rose'**—leaves have a bony look, very fragrant.

'Attar of Roses'

FRUIT AND SPICE GROUP: DELICIOUS!

This large group is not only fragrant, but delicious! All scented geraniums are edible and the fruity, spicy ones are especially tempting. Most of these actually do smell like their names.

Compared to the rose group, the fruit and spice plants are smaller, averaging up to 18 to 24 inches. Many have more compact, upright growing habits. Most of the lemon plants have finely crisped leaves like curly parsley, growing along stout stems for a column-like look. Nutmeg and apple have a mounded shape—12-inches tall with round velvety leaves and are suitable for hanging baskets or pots.

Coconut scented geranium

Suggested varieties: **Apple**—green apple scent. Refreshing! **Coconut**—spreading, fuchsia-colored blossoms; **Gooseberry**—tiny variegated plant; **Lime**—good lime scent, crisp and clean; **'Frensham'**, **'Prince Rupert'**, **'Fingerbowl'**—all lemon-scented and good for indoors; **Nutmeg**—spicy sweet scent, velvety gray leaves; **Orange**—good citrusy fragrance; **'Pineapple'**—fruity, tropical aroma; **Strawberry**—tiny pink flowers, delicious berry scent.

MINT AND PUNGENT GROUP: AROMATIC!

This group veers a bit from the sweet air of scented geraniums to give us a variety of tantalizing piney, minty, and camphoraceous scents, some more pungent than pleasant! These grow tall and rambling like rose geraniums, becoming large plants. Full sun is generally craved, except for mint geraniums. These do best in partial shade. Many in this group have attractive pink or rose flowers and a number are light lavender or pink with maroon or purple centers, which are beautiful for pressing.

Suggested varieties: **'Citronella'**—lemony, citronella scent; mosquito repellent; **'Clorinda'**—large rosy-pink flowers, eucalyptus scent; **Fernleaf**—lacy-look leaves, pink flowers; **'Mrs. Taylor'**—bright red flowers, pungent; **Peppermint**—strong mint smell; **Pine**—finely cut leaves with rich piney aroma; **'Sweet Miriam'**—very fragrant, spicy, pungent.

'Mrs. Taylor'

OAKLEAF GROUP: ATTRACTIVE!

As their name indicates, these plants have leaves that resemble the lobed leaves of oaks. They grow tall and have a vigorous habit, with brisk, pungent scents. The attractive symmetrical leaves are pretty for pressing. A few varieties are variegated.

Suggested varieties: **Oakleaf**—tall, with rich, pungent scent; **Variegated**

SCENTED GERANIUMS |149|

Oak—splashed with white; **'Fair Ellen'**—showy pink flowers; leaf has dark midsection.

GROWING SCENTED GERANIUMS

The growing needs for scented geraniums are close to common geraniums. Start with plants, either from a greenhouse or mail-order source. (Seeds are hard to find and a bit difficult to germinate.) Plant in a sunny spot, with well-drained soil. Make sure you know how big the plants will become and give them plenty of space to grow. Fertilizer is not a must. Well-fertilized plants are apt to produce more leaves and not as many flowers.

Geraniums are not too fond of wet leaves, so water with a soaker hose, or part the leaves and give a good soak right to the roots with watering can or hose. Having the plants a bit on the dry side is okay.

Insects and diseases are usually not a problem outdoors. Indoor pots may attract some aphids or mites. Use insecticidal soap to get rid of them. Like common bedding geraniums, scenteds are tender perennials and will not survive frost and snow unless overwintered indoors. To do this, trim the plant down and lift it out of the garden into a pot. A sunny basement or garage window is a good spot. Keep soil moist but not wet. Or you can take cuttings from established plants and have new young plants for the next spring.

A BEAUTY IN THE GARDEN OR BOUQUET

Scented geraniums are a beauty in the garden, with good growth and form. The largest kinds grow in billowing mounds, while smaller kinds are perfect for rock gardens and smaller corners. Scented geraniums are also good potted plants, indoors or out. Wherever they are, I like to have each plant labeled clearly (a flat wooden stake lettered by a permanent marker) for ready comparing and enjoying. After all, the simplest, best way to enjoy these plants is simply touching, nibbling, and sniffing.

Some varieties bloom continuously, others now and then, and some but rarely. Flowers usually develop at the extreme tips of the plants, so skip trimming if you desire flowers. Bloom time is usually late summer.

PRESERVING THE PLEASURES

There are many ways to preserve the entrancing scents and flavors of scented geraniums. Drying is one excellent method. Snip leaves (after dew has

Scented geranium in bloom

dried) and lay on screens, out of direct light, or pop into a slightly warm oven. Some varieties have large fleshy leaves; cut them into smaller pieces. Dry until you can crumble with your fingers. The texture may be somewhat leathery, and color may fade to a yellow green, but the scent is still there!

Sachets, small cloth bags filled with dried leaves, give a refreshing sweet scent to drawers and closets or chests. Scented geraniums are perfect potpourri ingredients, mixed or alone.

Press-drying is another rewarding project. Select perfect leaves or barely open flowers and place between acid-free paper, weighted by heavy books until dry. These make pretty cards, bookmarks, and mottoes.

A TASTEFUL TOUCH

The sweet fruity leaves and flowers of rose, fruit, and spice geraniums add a dainty colorful touch to various foods. Here are several suggestions:

SWEET HONEY

Directions:

Mince several fresh leaves of fruit-flavored geraniums. Place in a small jar of honey. After 12 hours, remove and taste. Repeat if desired. Serve on bread or biscuits for something different.

JELLY DECOR

Directions:

Just before pouring a clear jelly into jars, place several deeply colored flowers in bottom of jar. They will give a touch of color and a slightly sweet twist.

CAKE CREATION

Directions:

Line a cake pan with waxed paper, then cover the bottom of pan with scented geranium leaves, single layer. Pour in cake batter (yellow, or spice, or carrot). Bake as usual. When finished, invert pan, peel off wax paper, and you have an edible floral topper!

BEAUTIFUL BUTTER

Directions:

Mince rose geranium leaves finely and mix into softened butter. Shape into a patty and chill. Garnish with flowers; serve with biscuits or toast.

Sweet Bay

The flat, smooth leaves of sweet bay *(Laurus nobilis)* are readily found in spice racks and bits of its light green leaves are a key part of pickling spice. But do you know its attractive, green, leafy form?

A number of names including bay laurel, bay leaf, sweet laurel, and true bay are used for sweet bay. There is also an ornamental shrub simply known as bay, so being familiar with the botanical name will avoid confusion.

A TENDER, SLOW-GROWING TREE

Sweet bay grows in warm climates like southern Europe or Zones 8 to 10 in the United States. It cannot withstand snow. In its native Turkey, this evergreen tree may eventually grow to a height of 50 feet. Container-grown plants, even when planted in a large barrel, hardly grow taller than 60 inches and often have a bush-like form. It takes several years for a sweet bay to grow from 12 to 24 inches tall.

Sweet bay's leathery, symmetrical leaves are all glossy and dark green, with sharp edges. Rotate a leaf and find a lighter sage green color on its underside. These lovely leaves are referred to in the phrase, "Don't rest on your laurels." This saying harkens back to ancient Rome when bay leaves were formed into wreaths and worn like crowns by honored athletes and scholars.

Since container-grown bay is unlikely to flower, I was surprised to read in an herbal encyclopedia that small, creamy white flowers appear in spring. A dark berry-like seed then forms.

A beautiful but hard-to-find strain known as 'Golden' or 'Aurea' has new growth with a vivid golden tinge. I could find it in only one catalog and even that with a note: call for availability. Another specialty sweet bay is a variegated green and white form named "Variegata".

GROWING IT

Unless you reside in Zone 8 or warmer, grow sweet bay in a container that can be moved indoors to your basement or garage when it gets cold. Although it does not require greenhouse environment, it should be kept above 40°F at all times. Frost will damage the tender tips.

Sweet bay leaves

Young plants can be grown in a quart or gallon pot at first then transferred to a 3- or 5-gallon tub as it grows. Bay does well with plenty of light, but does not tolerate becoming sunbaked. Keep well watered, and on very warm days place the plant where it gets only a half day of sun. In winter, keep it in a bright spot, but do not water often. In spring, move outdoors and feed with a 10-10-10 fertilizer or similar.

Diseases are rarely a problem, but scale insects have a special liking for bay. A swipe of horticultural oil or sudsy Ivory soap water on leaf underside will eradicate them.

Sweet bay can be trained to grow in a treelike form. Keep lower branches clipped to have a clean trunk topped with a leafy ball. The plant can also be shaped as a cone or rounded bush. Pinching the leaf tips will promote fuller, bushier growth. To harvest leaves, clip, then air dry in a single layer. For leaves to be completely flat when dried, they must be pressed.

A PROPAGATION CHALLENGE

Sweet bay can be grown by seed or propagated by cuttings, but both methods require lots of patience. The best option is to purchase a potted plant. When sowing seeds, germination can take place in ten to twenty days but can be prolonged up to six months. Seeds should be fresh and not too dehydrated from long storage. The most common commercial propagation is by cuttings, but that, too, is a slow process.

You may, however, want to take up the challenge to start a few more bay plants from an established plant. All you need is a good sharp pruners, and a tray or pots with sterile rooting medium like perlite. In midsummer snip off several branches, about 6 to 8 inches long, that are woody but still have greenish bark. Strip the leaves from the bottom portion of the branches and stick them into the pots. Because heat speeds rooting, placing the tray or pots on a bottom heat mat works well. Or you can enclose pots like little greenhouses, using a clear plastic bag held up with three or four long sticks. Mist with water regularly; never allow the soil to dry out. Resist the temptation to tug on the cuttings to check for new roots. Instead, watch first for new buds at the top.

An alternate method of propagation can be used if you're fortunate enough to have a root sucker come up alongside the main plant. Let it grow until 4 to 5 inches tall, then dig down and clip the side shoot from the larger root, keeping as much soil and fine new roots intact as possible while lifting it into a new pot.

A HEARTY SPICE

Sweet bay's hearty flavor is complex, mostly spicy with a hint of bitterness.

It has been called the foundation of French cooking, but I am most familiar with its usefulness as a pickling spice. Along with two compatible flavors, vinegar and black pepper, sweet bay is an essential spice for pickling cucumbers, beans, or relish, and meat specialties like pickled beef heart.

Sweet bay leaves

Unlike some other herbs that need to be added shortly before serving, sweet bay releases flavor best when simmered for a long time. Alone or as a bouquet garnish, bay imparts a full, hearty flavor to beef-based stews and roasts. Many recipes call for simmering the leaf then removing it because, if eaten, the sharp edges of dried bay leaf could irritate or cut the stomach.

Both fresh or dried bay leaves can be used to make a water-based concentrate. Mince or break up leaves and simmer until your bay "tea" is well flavored. Strain, then return bay water to heat in an open saucepan. Through continued evaporation, the mixture becomes more and more concentrated, and somewhat darker in color. Simmer until it meets your taste. If it's too strong, just add clear water. Refrigerate the bay concentrate if not used all at once. This is convenient for adding to meat marinades and soups.

If you are buying bay leaf, look for undamaged, light green leaves. Faded, broken leaves lack flavor.

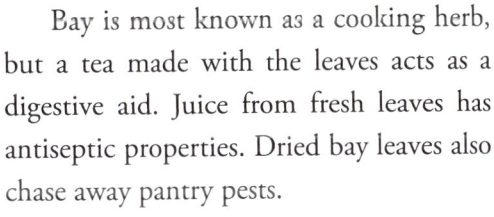

Bay is most known as a cooking herb, but a tea made with the leaves acts as a digestive aid. Juice from fresh leaves has antiseptic properties. Dried bay leaves also chase away pantry pests.

Dried bay leaves

SWEET BAY

Sweet Marjoram

Sweet marjoram *(Origanum marjorana)* is a dainty aromatic herb related to oregano. It is also known as garden or knotted marjoram (pronounced MAR-juh-rum) due to its popularity in formal knot gardens.

The ancient Greeks and Egyptians adored the herb, which symbolized honor and joy. They grew it abundantly for culinary purposes as well as household use. In colonial times, sweet marjoram was often used as a strewing herb. Fresh leaves were scattered on the floor and crushed by walking to release aroma. Soon the room was filled with the captivating, slightly musky scent.

As oregano's "cousin," sweet marjoram shares somewhat similar growing habits and uses. Its fuzzy gray-green leaves line upright stems that reach on to 2 feet high. In late summer, tiny white flowers appear in clusters at the plant's outer tips and finally produce seed heads with a stacked-up appearance that beg to be touched.

GROW IT BY SEED

Gardeners in growing Zones 7 to 9 can grow sweet marjoram as a perennial. However, since it does not tolerate frost, I grow it as an annual here in the North. Plant seeds indoors six to eight weeks before last frost date for a head start. Transplant outdoors after all danger of frost. Sweet marjoram can also be propagated by division.

A home in full sun is practically a must for sweet marjoram. Fertile soil is also important. The herb is drought-sensitive, so water regularly and apply mulch to prevent droopy, thirsty leaves. Insect pests and diseases rarely pose a problem.

In late summer, just before flowering, the plant is ready for harvest. Snip off sections and hang to dry, or strip leaves from the stems and dry on nonmetallic screen. To grind, rub over screen.

MAKING USE OF SWEET MARJORAM

Sweet marjoram lends a distinctive touch to sachets and potpourris. The dried leaves have a long-lasting scent, and look beautiful in wreaths.

In the kitchen, sweet marjoram can be used like oregano, although its flavor is less intense and more sweet. Fresh leaves rubbed over raw beef roasts impart its rich flavor. Egg dishes such as omelets and scrambled eggs are delicious with the addition of sweet marjoram. It also caters well to white sauces and soups with a creamy base, potato soup for example. Like all other herbs, use sparingly at first and increase amount as you grow more accustomed to its flavor.

Sweet marjoram tea is know for aiding digestion, so consider it when making herbal tea blends. It is also versatile for making herbal vinegars.

French thyme

What a Thyme!

The herb thyme *(Thymus spp.)* is a short, aromatic plant that's been around for a long time. Cooks have prized it for centuries, and even today, in France, bunches of thyme (pronounced TIME) are as readily available as bunches of parsley.

Long a symbol of strength and courage, thyme grows resolutely in its native area, the arid scrublands of Italy and Spain. No wonder it thrives in rock gardens and dry, uneven nooks and crannies.

THYME FOR VARIETY

Thyme comes in a tremendous number of types—possibly four hundred or more. All of them are edible, although some are more tasty than others. These hundreds of kinds belong to two groups, upright and creeping. Upright thymes grow 10 to 18 inches tall and include culinary and lemon varieties. Creeping thymes form a soft mat up to 6 inches tall with tiny, decorative flowers. A delight for bees!

The upright culinary types have narrow dark green leaves growing in clusters along thin stems. English thyme is the standard choice for cooking, along with French thyme, which is nearly identical, but just a bit milder and sweeter. Lemon thymes have more rounded leaves and come in a plain green or in attractive variegations such as 'Golden Lemon' and 'Silver Queen'. And when it's "thyme" for adventure, try 'Caraway', 'Coconut', or 'Nutmeg'.

Most creeping thymes have tiny, intriguing leaves and long-lasting flowers ranging from white or light pink to scarlet. Some bloom early in summer and others later. By careful selection, you can have a carpet of color through most of the growing season. Creeping thyme very nicely fills the racks between stepping stones and pavers. An old saying says, "The more it is trodden upon, the more it grows."

Among the hardiest, most resilient are red creeping and pink creeping thymes. Mother-of-thyme is also a useful ground cover. Another of my favorites is fast-growing 'Pink Chintz' with cheery pink blossoms and smooth, bright green leaves. Woolly thyme has wee, irresistibly fuzzy gray-green leaves that hug the ground.

THYME FOR THE GARDEN

Seed propagation is often inconsistent and difficult, so if I want a new thyme, I'll choose a potted plant from an herb nursery. Or if I see an attractive plant in a friend's garden, I'll bring home a few sprigs and press them into fine soil after dipping the ends with rooting hormone. Or dig up a start in early spring.

As a shorter plant, thyme looks best along the edge of a garden or container. It can even be trimmed to a neat little hedge that is just as green in winter as in summer.

Thyme will survive nearly anywhere—even in problem areas. In rich soil, stems may be more prone to rotting. Be sure to plant in full sun. During the growing season, avoid thick layers of mulch or bark chips around the plant and keep plants well-manicured for airflow. Both upright and creeping thymes are usually very hardy, but a cover of mulch in winter minimizes freeze-back. Lemon thymes are less hardy, and simply need to be replaced.

Mature thyme eventually has gnarled, woody stems. It helps to trim upright thymes soon after flowering to encourage a fresh flush of growth. Thyme leaves can be harvested at any time by pinching or shearing. I once saw a time-saving tip—use only an inch or so of the newest growth, and mince, stems and all. Otherwise, you'll need to strip the leaves from twig-like stems. In winter, you can even retrieve a snippet from under the snow!

THYME FOR COOKING

Some herbs assert their own flavor in dishes. Thyme with its pungent sharpness is no exception. Used sparingly, though, it supports and highlights other flavors. Combined with basil, chives, and parsley, fresh thyme is part of the famous bouquet garni combination. Some cooks like to pair it with garlic and lemon.

Thyme can be used fresh or dried in soups, from creamy oyster chowder to broth-based chicken vegetable soup. As for meats, it is traditionally associated with chicken and seafood, but I also like it for beef roasts and sausage. Now and then I add a dash of dried thyme flakes to cooked beets or carrots as a change of pace in wintertime fare. Thyme gives distinct appeal to herbed butter or cheese spread, and a sprig or two for garnish looks great, too.

Thyme vinegar is good for both salad dressings and medicinal uses. To make flavored honey, put clean, dry thyme sprigs, slightly bruised, into honey for two to three weeks, then strain.

THYME FOR HOME REMEDIES

Thyme is a natural antiseptic due to thymol, an acidic compound. A strong infusion of English thyme can be used as an antiseptic gargle for sore throats, or as a hair rinse for treating dandruff and adding shine. Thyme also helps loosen a croup. A dab of thyme vinegar helps soothe minor insect bites and scratches.

THYME BUTTER

Ingredients needed:
½ c. butter, softened
1½ tsp. thyme (dried and ground)
Directions:

Mix well and chill. It takes several days for the butter to absorb the flavor. Delicious on whole wheat or rye bread.

THYME WREATH

Materials needed:
lots of thyme in full bunches 4 to 5 inches long
cardboard
string

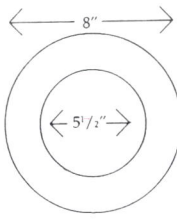

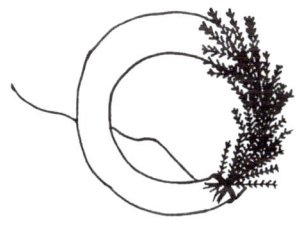

Directions:

Cut cardboard into circle, outside diameter 8 inches, inside 5½ inches. Cut a piece of string 24 inches long. Tie on end around one bunch of thyme and fasten to cardboard by wrapping and knotting string around cardboard and thyme. Position second bunch to overlap with first bunch, covering the string of first bunch. Wrap string around this and repeat this positioning and wrapping process until cardboard is covered. If string grows short, knot on an additional length. Insert your last bunch of thyme under the first bunch. To fasten string at the end, tie it to the tail of the beginning string. With string end you can make a loop to hang wreath on nail.

Dried thyme may be brittle. Moisten lightly with spray bottle to make it more pliable.

Hang your thyme wreath in your kitchen and snip off a bit when cooking.

THYME

All thy garments smell of myrrh, and aloes, and cassia, out of the ivory palaces, whereby they have made thee glad.

PSALM 45:8

SECTION III
Harvesting Time

"Herbs are versatile, both fresh and dried. Since summer doesn't always last, we preserve its bounty for future benefit. In this section, you'll learn the basics of harvest: what to pick, and when and how."

—*Gracia*

L-R: Dill, lettuce

Lemon basil

Prime for Picking

An herb gardener can begin enjoying the rewards of her efforts soon after sowing seeds or planting new plants into her garden.

Unlike fruits or vegetables that are ripe for picking at a certain stage, herb leaves and flowers can be harvested throughout the growing season. Certain herbs produce useful seeds or roots. Isn't it marvelous how plants are so beneficial to man? These green, growing creations are a gift from God.

CLIP, CLIP, CLIP: THREE REASONS

For me, herbal harvest occurs frequently, here a snippet, there a snippet, all summer long. Usually my decision to grab a clippers and cut some herbs

Gracia's Herbs

is based on one of three reasons. First, a specific herb may be needed for a recipe, a salve, or a poultice. Such a harvest may be quick, dashing to the kitchen garden just outside our north door for a fresh sprig of oregano, or deliberate, placing a variety of leaves and blossoms into a gathering basket for making a batch of potpourri.

Second, in midsummer plants are in the ideal stage to collect and store for winter use. Perhaps it's chocolate mint just before flowering, when the leaves are plentiful, smooth, and unblemished. Or it may be sunny calendula blossoms, just opened. Drying is often a preferred method for preservation.

Third, leafy plants need periodic clipping for the best appearance and flavor, or to prevent reseeding. Take basil, for example. Regular pinching keeps the plant compact, with fresh new growth. I don't necessarily utilize every such trimming. Sometimes they're added to the compost bin.

The three reasons for harvesting often overlap. The sweet basils need a trimming, but I also need lots for the salsa we're canning. The extra sprigs are laid on a screen to dry.

Sometimes, upon noticing a plant in its midsummer prime, I'm spurred to find a use for it, especially culinary herbs. How could I use this lemon verbena (or salad burnet or tarragon)? It's fun to experiment. An herbal guidebook can provide ideas, open to adaptation depending on your tastes.

HARVESTING LEAVES

L-R: Greek oregano, spearmint, rosemary, 'Berggarten' sage, curly parsley

Needle-like rosemary, fuzzy marjoram, tall lovage: how does one know what to cut, how much, and when? One key to success is to become familiar with the plants' growing habits. Are they annuals or perennials? Soft-stemmed or woody? Is the plant a prolific leaf maker or does it grow slowly? Do I need to sow successively for a continuous crop? A good reference book with pictures can provide detailed information.

When harvesting leaves, it may seem like you're cutting off most of the plant. But that's okay! Even a very young plant will tolerate having a leaf or two pinched off for test tasting.

Fast-growing annuals will rebound after a trimming. Perennials like oregano and thyme also benefit from a midsummer top removal.

Many herbs bloom at least once in a summer. By cutting at least a third of the plant just before the flowers appear, you'll get the leaves when their essential oil level is high and the flavor is best. Harvesting leaves at this stage also prevents messy self-sowing and scraggly-looking flower stalks later on. Aggressive plants like lemon balm are well controlled with a good manicure.

Pick clean, dry leaves after the dew has dried in the morning. Clipping on a sunny, breezy day minimizes disease. A sharp pruners makes a clean cut, not chewing up stems. I avoid clipping just before a rain since fresh stem wounds are prone to mildew and rot. Of course, common sense says not to clip right after a rain either, when the leaves are spattered and tousled. Leaves can be rinsed, but that's an extra step. I rarely find it necessary to rinse leaves, since I don't use any sprays and only mulch for fertilizer.

Thin, smooth leaves like those of basil, mint, and flat leaf parsley dry quickly. Pick them individually from the stem and spread on screens to dry.

HARVESTING SEEDS

Dill, coriander, anise, caraway, fennel, cumin, and more: these plants are grown for their flavorful seeds. Seed-producing plants grow to maturity, then bloom, and finally develop seeds that ripen. If left too long, the seeds will drop to the soil, nature's way of ensuring a repeat cycle. Seeds must be collected before they're all brown and dry and falling from the stems. Dill is often cut in its green stage, too.

Dill seed heads

The seed-producing herbs mentioned here all have similar flower clusters borne on long stems, spreading to form a sort of umbrella-like head at the top. This makes seed collection relatively easy. Once the seeds have their mature color (often a shade of brown) but are still intact, the entire stem is clipped and hung to dry. Or you can pop it into a brown paper bag, keeping it open to allow airflow, and lay it on a counter to dry. Some of the seeds may loosen as they dry, but they're inside the bag.

Another aspect of seed saving is collecting seeds for next year's planting. Allow a plant to flower, then collect seeds when the seed heads are mature. This may be a fun project for young gardeners, and seeds make fine, inexpensive gifts when presented in a handmade packet. Some good choices are anise, hyssop, basil, parsley, calendula, borage, oregano, lovage, and more.

HARVESTING FLOWERS

Purple lavender, yellow calendula, blue borage, pink chives, white feverfew, rosy echinacea… Flowering herbs come in an amazing palette of colors and forms. Fresh flowers can be used for herbal vinegars or edible garnish. Another option is bouquets, either herbs alone or mixed with other cut flowers. Many herb blossoms are ideal for drying, whether for teas or dried arrangements.

Cut the flowers soon after opening, when the petals still have a fresh, new look. Flowers with florets and multiple parts, like lavender and basil, should be clipped when the topmost buds are still tight, unopened.

Long-stemmed flowers like lavender are best clipped individually, then bunched to dry. Short-stemmed blossoms like feverfew can be shorn from the plant. Screen drying works well for such blossoms.

Chamomile blossoms

HARVESTING ROOTS

Certain herbs, especially medicinal plants, have roots that contain useful healing properties. Two examples are comfrey and echinacea. Horseradish is a root known for its sharp flavor. Most

Rooted parsley

PRIME FOR PICKING |167|

herbs grown for their roots are perennials.

It takes at least a year, maybe two, until the roots are large enough for digging. Ideally, roots are dug in late summer or fall, when the top of the plant is no longer actively growing. In the fall you can also salvage part of the root clump, perhaps an outer portion to replant, because removing a root usually means the end of a plant. I prefer not to wash roots that will be used in a salve or tincture, but to scrub them clean with a vegetable brush. This often removes the thin outer skin to reveal a clean interior.

Herb	Part(s) Used
Anise	Seeds
Anise Hyssop	Leaves
Basil	Leaves, Flowers
Bay Laurel	Leaves
Borage	Flowers, Leaves
Burnet, Salad	Leaves
Calendula	Flowers
Caraway	Seeds
Catnip	Leaves
Chamomile	Flowers
Chives	Leaves, Flowers
Cilantro	Leaves
Comfrey	Leaves, Roots
Coriander	Seeds
Cumin	Seeds
Dill	Seeds, Leaves
Echinacea	Roots, Leaves, Flowers
Fennel	Seeds, Leaves
Feverfew	Leaves, Flowers
Horehound	Leaves
Horseradish	Roots
Hyssop	Leaves
Lavender	Flowers, Leaves
Lemon Balm	Leaves
Lemon Verbena	Leaves
Lovage	Leaves, Stems
Marjoram	Leaves
Mint	Leaves
Oregano	Leaves
Parsley	Leaves
Rosemary	Leaves, Flowers
Sage	Leaves, Flowers
Savory	Leaves
Scented Geranium	Leaves, Flowers
Tarragon	Leaves
Thyme	Leaves

Gracia's Herbs

L-R: Chamomile, oregano, yarrow

Home-Dried Herbs

For any gardener, summer is the ultimate season — full of warmth and garden-fresh goodness. No, summer does not always last, but it's possible—easily possible—to preserve a bit of this beloved season by drying herbs, and so, even in the middle of winter, we can enjoy a steaming cup of mint tea or a hearty pot of chili complete with basil and oregano.

The principle of drying is simple, whether you wish to dry herbs or flowers, beneficial weeds, or any other plant. Simply cut, bring indoors, and expose to airflow until the plant's moisture is evaporated. Removing the moisture prevents spoilage, so a fully dried, crispy-to-touch plant can easily be stored in a glass jar or other tight container with its flavors intact for up to a year or more.

Equipment Checklist for Drying Herbs

- ☐ Plant Shears
- ☐ Screens
- ☐ String
- ☐ Small Rubber Bands
- ☐ Paper Clips
- ☐ Jars to Store Dried Herbs

Drying herbs requires little equipment. A few everyday supplies like rubber bands and paper clips simplify the process. The end product—home-dried herbs—gives us economical, tasty options for cooking, canning, or baking. Home-dried herbs also reward us with fresher, tastier products that have never been parked on a supermarket shelf.

Besides the edible uses of dried herbs, you may wish to take advantage of their natural beauty as a decorative touch. Dried herbs can be paired with other dried everlastings such as strawflowers and gomphrena for beautiful bunches or bouquets. Some of my favorite arrangements have been made using only culinary herbs (woolly sage, green rosemary, fragrant thyme, golden seeds of fennel, and nigella) placed in a basket. What a pretty addition to the kitchen!

WHICH ONE FOR DRYING?

Nearly any herb can be dried, with the exception of a few like chives and cilantro which turn bland and colorless when dry. (These are easier used fresh or frozen instead of dried.) See the list for a selection of easy-to-dry herbs that are widely used.

If you grow some herbs, but the idea of drying and using them is new to you, let your field of interest guide your choices. Do you enjoy adding flavors to foods? Open your spice rack. Does it contain some seasonings you could dry yourself? Are soups your specialty? Perhaps you'd find lovage or parsley useful. Is pizza a favorite

Herbs That Dry Well

- Basil (all kinds)
- Catnip
- Dill Leaf
- Lavender
- Lemon Balm
- Lemon Verbena
- Lovage
- Marjoram
- Mint (all kinds)
- Oregano
- Parsley
- Rosemary
- Sage
- Savory
- Scented Geraniums
- Stevia
- Tarragon
- Thyme

dish? Oregano and basil definitely would come handy for you! Are meats your specialty? The robust flavors of sage and tarragon fit perfectly with a meaty main dish.

Perhaps your interest is more health related, so catnip for stomachache, thyme for insect bites, or horehound for a cough are ideal selections. And don't forget the favorite—mint for tea, and lots of it!

Have you enjoyed working with dried flowers and other everlastings? The fragrant floral herbs like lavender, rosemary, hyssop, or scented geraniums add a vast variety for bouquets, decorative bunches, or other homemade creations. Many herbs also have intriguing seed heads or unusual leaves.

THE WHEN AND WHAT OF HARVEST

For fast, efficient harvest of herbs and flowers, a good plant shears is a valuable tool. (A kitchen shears works for softer stems.) Not only is a plant shears handy in the garden, but also when getting your herbs ready for screens and bunches. It's much better for the plant to have a nice clean cut than a ragged, torn tip.

Another handy item is a gathering basket which is wide and shallow with a tall handle, perfect for trucking in loads of leaves and mounds of flowers. A shallow box or even bowls also work. Keeping the different plants separated makes it easier to prepare for drying once you get indoors.

LEAVES—When is a good time to harvest leafy green plants like mint, basil, or stevia? Really, anytime the plant is green and growing! You can pinch off a snippet from even the most tender young plant, but for a sizable amount for drying, mid to late summer is a good time. The plant is well established and can regrow a bunch of new leaves.

Many herbs have a time of flowering in summer. I like to take off the material for drying before the flowering time when the plant is in a lush, leafy stage. Sometimes a plant is flowering before I know it, so snip, snip, it gets a good trimming, which promotes a flush of new growth, perfect for drying.

Most plants, whether a tall bush like lovage

Spearmint

or a spriggy creeper like oregano, can tolerate having half or two-thirds of their foliage clipped off. Of course, in drought or other stressful growing conditions, only smaller amounts should be removed to prevent plant shock.

Leaves can be harvested from annual plants right up to frost, but perennials need a bit of time to wind down for winter, so don't harvest closer to the expected frost date than four to six weeks. Otherwise there's a lot of tender growth that is liable for freeze-back.

When cutting leaves, choose the topmost, clean leaves to minimize sorting. If you have a number of plants or, for example, a huge patch of mint, you can afford to be very choosy and snip off only the choice young tips. If the leaves are dusty or muddy, you can rinse them in clear water, but I avoid wetting the leaves if at all possible. Sort out any yellowed leaves or other plant debris.

FLOWERS AND SEEDS—When collecting single blossoms such as feverfew, chamomile, or calendula, pick them just on the verge of being fully opened. They should have a fresh, young look. Early picking prevents shattering and disintegration when dried.

Other flowers come in cluster and wand shapes; for example, lavender or tansy. Observe them closely and clip when the bottom or inner flowers are opened and the top, outer flowers are still closed buds.

Clip seeds (fennel, caraway, dill, and others) when brown and "ripe" looking, but still attached to the stalks and not readily dropping. Herb seeds will shatter and scatter quite voluntarily if left too long.

The minute a leaf or flower is removed from the plant, the drying process begins. You can aid this natural process by putting the plant material in a dry airy spot where the drying is quick and thorough. Here are a few pointers.

SCREENS FOR LEAVES

For the quickest drying time and the best-tasting product, I prefer to clip the leaves off the stems and spread them single layer on screens. This works especially well for plants with broad, flat leaves such as mints, basil, sage, or stevia. Screen drying is also the best method for drying individual blossoms like feverfew or chamomile because it allows air to flow all around the part. Every leaf and flower can dry on its own with no stem to draw out the sap.

Old window screens are fine. I also use some homemade ones which are merely a 16-inch-square piece of screen stapled to a perimeter of thin, wooden slats. One advantage of a smaller screen like this is that you can pop them into the oven (unheated) for speedier drying. Screens also allow you to move your drying matter quickly from place to place.

L-R: Basil, rosemary, thyme, oregano, sweet marjoram, prostrate rosemary

If you have no screens, the next best option is to lay them flat, single layer, on a clean surface such as a table. Even though it's plentiful and absorbent, I never lay leaves onto newspaper. Why? Well, have you seen your hands covered with dark smudges after handling a newspaper? I don't want that on my food!

A STRING FOR BUNCHES AND BRANCHES

Not all plants have broad, flat leaves. Some, like thyme and oregano, have short woody stems lined with tiny leaves. Lavender and rosemary are upright with longer stems. An efficient way to dry these is to tie in bunches and hang to dry. Bunching can be used for leafy plants too if you don't have time to dry individual leaves.

Bunched herbs and flowers can be hung to dry anywhere in an airy spot out of direct sunlight. It's also handy to have them where you can observe the drying process, not in an out-of-the-way corner. Besides, the bunches look pretty too, especially along a beam or other rustic structure.

I've found it convenient to have a heavy string or twine stretched up all summer, which allows a constant on and off with lots of bunches. Mine is a burlap twine 15 feet long. Plan ahead and secure your string or wire well if you anticipate a lot of weight hanging on it. What a disappointment to have a downed string, and a mess too!

Bunches can be tied with string, but as the branches dry and shrink, the bunch loosens and pieces may drop out. Using rubber bands prevents this problem. The tiny rubbers for little girls' hair are a perfect size, holding ten or twelve stems. Have plenty on hand and cut loose when the drying is done.

A quick and easy way to hang bunches from the string is done with a paper clip bent to an S shape. Hook one part of the S into the bunch at the rubber band, and hang the other over the string. So simple!

Dried mint leaves

Another way to dry big branchy plants, such as tarragon or seed stalks, with little effort is to hold the stalk upside down and clip off a strong, topmost side branch to form a little hook which can be hooked over the string. Then when the plant is dried, you can remove it with little crumbling. The clipped-off side branches can be bunched and rubber banded, if you wish.

This natural hook method works well to rapidly manage large amounts of plant material. I use it especially when desperately salvaging annuals from frost—scented geraniums, basils, summer savory. Just clip and hang and the drying process begins. Later I might clip off individual leaves or form smaller bunches.

The natural hook also is perfect for dried flowers like statice, artemisia, gomphrena, or even roses.

WHEN IS IT DONE?

Many factors affect the length of drying time—the humidity in the air, the thickness of the leaves, or the size of a bunch. Generally a week is plenty of time for drying. A warm area, like a gas oven slightly heated by the pilot, makes for faster drying. A dried leaf should be crispy and should crumble when rubbed between your fingers.

I like to gather up dried culinary and medicinal herbs and put them into jars as soon as possible so they don't get dusty. Clear glass jars are my favorite. They're sanitary and allow you to see what's inside. Label and date each jar.

The flavor of a plant is preserved better in a whole leaf, since crumbling releases the fragrant oil, so I stuff the leaves into jars whole and crush them as I use them. It's also better to use several smaller jars than one big jar if you have a large amount. The leaves in unopened jars will retain their flavor longer.

Bunched herbs, especially those with woody stems, are better stored after stripping the leaves from the stems. If you wish, you can "grind" herbs ready for a shaker by rubbing over a screen, with a pan or bowl beneath to catch the flakes.

Flowers can be arranged as soon as dried or you can collect them in a box and keep them out of sunlight until you are ready to use them.

Putting Weeds to Work

THE ART OF WILDCRAFTING

Have you ever heard the saying, "A weed is a plant whose virtues are not yet discovered?" It's true. Many of the weeds which we eagerly uproot or whack down can be put to good use. Perhaps weeds like dandelions and plantain are so common that we hardly think of them as safe sources for vitamins, minerals, and healing properties.

Gathering and using weeds (known as wildcrafting) is a rewarding art. It frees you to use plants for food, medicine, ointments, and salves, and even bouquets, without having to grow them. Ramble into your backyard and collect! What a wonderful way to employ God's wonderful provision of plants!

A FEW POINTERS

First of all, know what you are collecting. Are you familiar with the wild plants in your area? Avoid any poisonous plants! Also, let rare or endangered plants grow undisturbed in their native habitat.

Knowing your plants keeps your wildcrafting safe, plus it makes pulling weeds a bit less drudgery. Instead of this-light-green-plant-with-white-star-flowers-that's-creeping-all-over, you know you're dealing with chickweed.

Often when traveling locally by buggy or bike, or hiking on the back forty, I like to observe the weeds I encounter, playing a sort of game with myself—Name that Weed. When an unfamiliar one appears, I check my Peterson wildflower guide, or if I don't have the guide along, a bit of the plant goes into my pocket for identifying later. This is an excellent way to build a broad familiarity with local plants.

When wildcrafting, gather plants that are untrampled, and free from dirt and vehicle exhaust. Meadows, fencerows, and creek edges are good, clean sites. It helps to keep a sort of mental inventory of where certain plants abound, like plantain along the north edge of the raspberry patch, jewelweed along Johnson Creek, or yarrow near a neighbor's ditch. Undisturbed, these plants will flourish in the same spot year after year.

After gathering plants, you can use them fresh or dry them for later use. Old window screens are handy for drying sizable amounts of leaves. Out of direct sunlight, but with good air circulation is best. Once the leaves are dry (usually a week or two), I pack them in wide-mouth glass jars with tight-fitting lids and label them with name of plant and date collected.

When using wild plants for food or medicine, follow recommendations of a professional. Use proven, well-documented books and follow their guidelines for usage carefully.

A WILDCRAFTING STORY

In the fall my family works together to keep a wildcrafting tradition alive by making an herbal salve. This salve has an interesting history. We make it using a recipe passed down from my great-great-grandfather. This tradition began sometime during the 1890s when a German tramp appeared one day on the Raber homestead in Holmes County, Ohio. He was looking for a buyer for his exceptional herbal salve recipe.

"For one dollar, I will sell you this recipe for a salve that can heal every wound in your body. And I will help you make your first batch." Great-great-grandfather John agreed to the terms and handed over a dollar—quite a sum in those days for a mere recipe. Then the tramp threatened to break every bone in his body if the recipe was ever given to anyone else!

That very day John and the tramp set out with shovel and clippers to collect the necessary roots and leaves—plantain from the yard, marshmallow root from along the creek, celandine and comfrey from the orchard, and other healing plants from the woods and pastures on the Raber farm.

They returned from foraging and cooked up a batch of salve in the iron kettle, using beeswax, butter, and mutton tallow as a base and screening out the chopped roots and leaves once they were cooked limp. When the finished salve was poured into earthen crocks and cooling in the cellar, the tramp continued on his way. He was never seen again.

The salve-making was carried on by John's daughter Emma, who later married Amos Mast. For years it was known as Amos Emmy salve or simply drawing salve. Emma's daughter Iva, my grandmother, passed on the art to her children, and today we use the same time-tested recipe. The original paper with German script, now yellowed with age, has been placed with the family heirlooms.

We don't know how many years before the tramp's appearance this salve was first made. Possibly it had its origin in early colonial days or the old country! We do know this blend of infection-fighting herbs heals cuts, scrapes, and wounds and draws out pain. Grandma used to say that no one ever got blood poisoning or gangrene while using this salve.

SIX VALUABLE WEEDS

The following six plants may seem like just plain weeds, but a closer look reveals some good value for healing and nutrition. These grow widely in most areas of the United States and are very plentiful, so gather all you need.

BURDOCK

This tall plant *(Arctium lappa)* with broad leaves is best known for its cocklebur seeds that cling to any passerby. It grows in fields and wastelands and can form big patches. It has a biennial growing habit, growing only leaves the first year then producing seeds in the next. When it reaches maturity in the second year the plant is at least 4 feet tall with huge leaves.

Burdock

Burdock is highly useful for dressing burns, even severe ones. Together with a special salve, burdock protects and soothes the burned area, keeping it sterile, and the dressing can be changed without pain. Leaves from the first-year plant, collected in June, are the best. Second-year leaves will also work, but the more pronounced spiny ribs may press into a tender wound and should be removed. Dry and store the leaves, then soak in hot water before using. Allow to cool a bit before placing on a burn. More details can be found in the book *Comfort for the Burned and Wounded* by John W. Keim.

Burdock leaves and root can be made into tea. A cup a day will help cleanse the blood and tone the liver. It also promotes sweating and acts as a diuretic. Cooled tea (infusion) helps clear acne when dabbed on the face.

A fun use for burdock cockleburs is forming little baskets. Each cockbur is a ball with tiny, tiny hooks. If you observe closely, you will see why the inventors of Velcro got their idea from these clinging seeds. Press them together in a basket shape. You can even make a handle!

RED CLOVER

This familiar plant *(Trifolium pratense)* with rounded pink flowers grows liberally along roadsides and in fields. It prefers moist habitat, grows to about fifteen inches, and blooms all summer. The flowers are the useful part of this weed, so pluck them and dry on screens single layer. When dry, their color changes to a deep purple.

Red clover blossoms

Red clover tea (1 tablespoon dried to a cup of water) boosts the immune system to fight off winter illnesses, plus guards against bronchial and respiratory complaints. It is mild and safe for children.

DANDELION

Is this despised plant with sunshiny yellow blooms actually useful? Yes! Some people declare, "If you can't beat 'em, eat 'em," and that is exactly the thing to do. In fact, dandelion *(Taraxacum officinale)* was brought overseas by early settlers who grew it in their gardens. All parts are edible, including the roots, and are an excellent source of many vitamins.

One favorite dish is dandelion gravy served with toast or salt water potatoes. To make the gravy, start with a basic white sauce. You can add bits of bacon or ham, and sliced

Dandelion

hard-boiled eggs if desired, and salt and pepper. Last add tender young dandelion leaves and serve immediately. This is a good dish for early spring before garden vegetables are ready for harvest.

The leaves are at their mildest before flowering. Cut finely with a kitchen shears and add to salad. Or serve along with a vinegar dressing as a side dish for roasts and other meats. Fried dandelion flowers is another dish. Dip in egg and roll in flour, then fry with butter. It tastes somewhat like mushrooms.

Dandelion also has some medicinal value. Tea made from the root promotes appetite and good digestion.

JEWELWEED

This plant *(Impatiens capensis)* is a moisture lover found along creeks and ditches. It grows up to 24 inches tall with bright orange blossoms hanging like jewels amidst smooth green leaves. It's in the impatiens family, having the same juicy stem. In summer and fall, the flowers mature to hanging green seedpods that burst dramatically when touched, shooting the seed away from the plant. My brothers search out

Jewelweed flower

PUTTING WEEDS TO WORK

patches of jewelweed just to pop seeds!

Jewelweed is a skin care plant, anti-itch and anti-hives, and one of the best natural poison ivy remedies. It's easy to use. Take a handful of leaves, rustle them up to bruise and release the juices, then rub on affected areas. If I'm treating a case of hives or poison ivy and need a bunch of leaves, I break off several entire stalks and place them in a pail of water at home. The leaves are effective parts, but recent studies show that the red knoblike growth near the bottom of the stem may be even more so. Break open these knobs and rub the juice directly on the itch.

Another method of applying jewelweed is a compress. Make a tea with 2 teaspoons fresh or 1 teaspoon dried leaves and boil for 10 minutes. Cool the brew, then soak an absorbent cloth in the liquid until sopping and place onto the irritated area. Resoak and reapply if needed.

More Useful Wild Plants

- Boneset
- Celandine
- Chickweed
- Chicory
- Comfrey
- Goldenrod
- Marshmallow
- Milkweed
- Mullein
- St. John's Wort
- Shepherd's Purse
- Yarrow
- Yellow Dock

PLANTAIN

Plantain *(Plantago sp.)* is a common lawn weed with broad, glossy leaves, 4 to 6 inches tall, and has a taller flower stalk. There is also a narrow-leaved variety. Both can be used. The best time to pick these leaves is in summer when they are shiny and fresh looking.

Mash fresh leaves and apply the pulp for a soothing remedy for sunburn and rashes, and healing application for cuts and burns. Plantain also helps relieve the itch of poison ivy and insect bites. The smooth glossy leaves can be dried for a healing, painless burn dressing as described for burdock. Because they are much smaller than burdock, it's more time-consuming to gather a large amount.

Broad leaved plantain

STINGING NETTLE

Stinging nettle *(Urtica diocia)* is not usually a plant we want to get close to. But did you know that stinging nettles are a popular vegetable in India? Heat will disarm the plant's trichomes or stinging hairs, leaving only nutrient-rich green leaves that can be used like spinach. Once leaves are cooked, steamed, or dried, the stinging is gone.

Nettles grow in patches, spreading by underground rhizomes. They are quite plentiful in our back forty, so I have a limitless supply of tender young leaves for nettle trial dishes. I'll be sure to wear gloves, too. Once, while weeding, I accidentally touched a mature plant, one with real hairs on the underside of the leaves. It wasn't until later in the day, while washing dishes, that my hands really began to burn. Was it the warm water? The burning, stinging sensations went on for several hours. Still, nettles are only a local mechanical skin irritant, not an allergen. Only where you touch will be affected.

Stinging nettles

Some people who suffer from arthritis even find a certain relief by touching nettle and allowing one discomfort to counteract another. Mostly, though, nettle is used dried, as a tea, to relieve hay fever and cough, and to boost the immune system. Nettle is often taken in combination with other tonic herbs.

So slip into your gloves and gather a bunch to dry. Use in a tea, 2 teaspoons dried per cup of water, and steep till cool.

In case you do get in contact, do you know what can take away the unpleasant sensation? Another wild plant—of course! Use a handful of jewelweed.

Capturing the Fun of Fragrance

MAKING GARDEN POTPOURRI

In summer, the herb garden hosts an array of delightful fragrance. For example, lavender's sweet refined perfume, the refreshing piney hints of rosemary, and the sharp citrusy zing of lemon verbena. How can these lovely aromas be captured for later, indoor enjoyment?

The answer is potpourri! Potpourri, a word borrowed from French, is any mixture of dried fragrant herbs and flowers, pretty to look at and delightful to smell. Putting together potpourri (pronounced poh-por-EE) doesn't require a lot of exotic ingredients, but you can utilize blossoms and foliage from your very own garden.

Potpourri was brought to fame in recent years by the interior decorators who dyed wood chips, added nose-tickling artificial oils, and sold the mix in fancy packaging that furthered the hoax. Authentic garden potpourri is made from dried plants rather than color-coordinated shavings that could be used to start a campfire!

Making your own potpourri provides a lot of opportunity for creativity. There are no hard, set recipes to follow. The basic parts of potpourri are the base, bulk, oils, and fixative. Fragrant petals and leaves form the base. Additional leaves and flowers for color and volume are known as bulk. Essential oils can enhance and empower the natural scents, while fixatives are certain roots and plants that absorb and lock in the fragrance.

To make your own potpourri from scratch, you must be a sort of botanical pack rat, keeping a summer-long vigil for things to dry. Several old window screens in an undisturbed location can be constantly filled with petals, blossoms, and leaves. Spread out a single layer for quick drying. Once the things are crispy dry, place into glass jars and reload the screens. For things that dry well by hanging (bunches of lavender, for example), a permanent string in an airy but out of direct sunlight area is perfect. Put rubber bands around the bunches, fasten to the string with a paper clip bent into an S-hook, and taking on and off is quite easy.

MATERIALS FOR THE BASE

Good base materials are highly scented and not too crumbly when dried. Roses are one of the best. The most richly scented are the old-fashioned cabbage and damask types. Certain tea roses are also quite fragrant. Climbing roses, especially the deep red ones, though not as fragrant, provide a lot of attractive bulk. Rose leaves, clipped and dried whole on a screen, add a nice touch of green. Delicate, half-opened buds are another beautiful rose product.

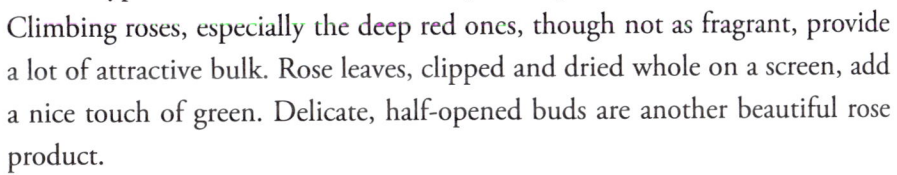

Lavender, both leaves and flowers, is another fragrant potpourri base. It is suitable to use alone, although lavender must be squeezed or handled to release the scent, unless lots of oils are added.

Scented geranium leaves are another good base. They seem to be a little overlooked; I think they deserve more recognition! True, these leaves are not as pretty as rose petals, but the range of vivid scents they possess overrides their looks. There are roughly six groups—rose scented, lemon, fruit and spice pungent, mint, and oak leaf.

Lemony herbs, verbena, thyme, balm, and basil are also useful base materials. Although basils and mints are richly fragrant, the dried leaves tend to be somewhat crumbly in a mixture. For this reason, I prefer using the dried flower spikes of basil leaves. Some mints such as woolly spearmint and variegated pineapple mint are more fleshy and stronger.

MATERIALS FOR BULK

Bulk materials should enhance and complement the base, both by color and scent. Sometimes the two overlap. If you plan to display the potpourri in a clear container, color is fairly important.

Flowers of all kinds, anything that dries well, make good bulk. Statice, strawflowers, globe amaranth, artemisia, and others especially for drying are perfect. Many other flowers, from snapdragons to hollyhocks, peonies to larkspur, are also valuable. Some blossoms can be dried whole, including calendula, chamomile, bee balm, black-eyed Susan, and Queen Anne's lace.

Little extras, such as bark, rose hips, cones, and seed heads, add a special visual interest, as well as enhancing the theme of the potpourri.

ESSENTIAL OILS FOR SCENT POWER

Essential and fragrant oils are the quickest, easiest way to add scent power to a mixture. Refreshing an aged mixture is also as easy as adding a few drops.

For good potpourri, oils are not an absolute must; they do tend to be somewhat expensive. Essential oils are the most expensive, being pure plant extracts. Fragrant oils are often synthetic and have a greater range of "flavors," from peaches n' cream to sea breeze. These can also be used in many other projects, such as candles, soaps, and salves.

Some catalogs offer oils in dropper cans. This is convenient, but I prefer no dropper. Prolonged contact with oil can cause a rubber dropper to disintegrate and you then have an unusable black syrup!

FIXATIVES FOR SCENT KEEPING

After choosing the base and bulk of a potpourri, there's another important element: the fixative. Fixatives are certain roots or other matter that absorb the fragile perfumes of a potpourri, and "lock" it in for a longer lasting effect. Back in the olden days of spice caravans and whaling ships, the most widely used fixatives were gum resins, derived from rare trees in the Middle East, and costly animal oils such as ambergris and musk oil. Here are several practical plant fixatives you can grow or collect on your own.

Orris Root *(Iris germanica* x *florentina)*: This is one of the best home-grown fixatives, so it's no wonder orris root keeps popping up in many potpourri recipes. Orris in itself has a faintly sweet odor, making it suitable for any sweet potpourri. The root of this delicate white flowering iris is the part used. After digging, wash and slice thinly (a Salad Master works well, creating thin, petal-like pieces that dry easily). It can also be dried whole, then ground into powder.

Calamus Root *(Acorus calamus)*: Long ago, calamus leaves were often strewn on the floors of castles and cathedrals, where foot traffic released its pungent, spicy-musk aroma. This plant, also known as sweet flag, closely resembles cattails, but produces no brown spikes. Instead, a yellow catkin grows out the side of a leaf stalk about 12 to 18 inches above the ground. The leaves also have a more yellow-green hue compared to cattails. Calamus prefers rich, low-lying areas, such as a creek bottom that floods frequently. After digging and scrubbing, the root should be dried whole, and pieces cut off as needed with a sharp shears.

Corncob—Believe it or not, dried corncob is a fixative. Its highly porous nature causes it to readily absorb scents and oils. Corncob is sold commercially as cellulose fiber. The red of the corncob complements most any sort of potpourri. Our hand meat grinder, set at its coarsest setting, makes nice sized bits, about ½ inch in diameter.

Calamus root

CAPTURING THE FUN OF FRAGRANCE |185|

PUTTING IT TOGETHER

Once you have a goodly array of dried materials to work with, perhaps one fall day, it's time to assemble your potpourri. Several large old bowls and measuring cups are handy. Batch size can vary, from a cup or two to a gallon or two, depending on the amount of goods you have. Refer to the recipes for a basic idea on amounts. Any potpourri mixture tends to settle once it's in a jar; if the quart jar is to be full, prepare an ample amount and add more within a few weeks.

I've found it works well to mix the base and bulk items together, and mix the oils and fixatives separately in a smaller container. Some recommend letting the oils and fixatives mellow together in a covered jar for several days or even a week or two, then adding it to the main mix. Stirring it well is important, so that all parts of the mix come into contact with each other, ensuring a complete blend. Several weeks after being mixed, the scents become well blended for potpourri at its best.

THE FINISHED PRODUCT

Displaying and using your potpourri is the most rewarding part! The best containers are those with lids, to trap the fragrance, and release it when the lid is lifted. My favorites are old-fashioned canning jars with glass caps and wire closure, for quick on and off with the lid. Decorative tins are also attractive, but essential oils can somewhat react with the metal. I prefer ceramic and glass instead. Another idea is using a globe-like glass jar and stretching a lace or fabric topper on top, fastened with a broad ribbon. This allows the scent to permeate a room or drawer. An open bowl with potpourri, especially if it has a lot of interesting berries and such in it, makes a nice centerpiece. A shallow bowl might even have space for a pillar candle situated in the middle.

It isn't difficult to collect a lot of attractive containers when you keep your eyes open. Old crocks or jugs, tall glass jars with cork stoppers, unusual short, fat jars—you may find them at yard sales or even in junk piles.

SACHETS

Potpourris are also excellent drawer and closet fresheners when packaged as sachets. A sachet (pronounced sash-AY) is a fabric bag filled with dried materials.

Mesh filled with potpourri and tied with lace or ribbon makes a quick and easy sachet. To make a basic sachet bag, take a piece of loosely woven cotton fabric, 5x12 inches, and fold it in half, right sides together. Sew a seam on the two sides, leaving a ⅜-inch seam allowance. Turn right side out and finish top edge either by folding under and top stitching or edging with lace. (In making sachet bags, there's a lot of room for creativity.) Stuff the bag with potpourri or your favorite dried herb. Tie with a piece of lace or cotton cord. Tuck your newly made sachet into a drawer to "make scents!" Opening a drawer and experiencing a rich, fragrant whiff seems to transport you to summer, recapturing the pleasant scents of field and flower.

Perhaps you'd like to spend more time making sachets of fascinating shapes. Simply cut two identical fabrics in any shape—heart, oval, star, shell, blossom. About 4x4 inches is a nice size. Sew together with a ½-inch seam allowance, leaving an opening to stuff in the potpourri, then stitch shut by hand. These are nice gifts.

You can also make a bath sachet, placing a handful of dried lavender blossoms onto a square of muslin and tying up the corners. Float the bag under the running tap water, squeezing it once in a while to release more oils. You can almost hear the bees buzz as you inhale the rich lavender!

RECIPES FOR POTPOURRI

FOLLOW THESE RATIOS FOR A QUART OF POTPOURRI

Base: 3 c.
Bulk: 1 c.
Oils: 5 to 10 drops (optional)
Fixative: ¼ to ½ c. (¾ c. when using corncob)

CITRUS POTPOURRI

Base: Lemon verbena leaves; lemon basil flower spikes; lemon thyme sprigs; lemon balm; scented geranium, lemon type.
Bulk: Orange, lemon, or tangerine peel, spiral cut; calendula blossoms; bee balm blossoms.
Oils: Citrus oil.
Fixatives: Orris root; calamus root; corncob.

FRUITY POTPOURRI

Base: Lemon verbena leaves; pineapple sage leaves; scented geranium leaves; fruit or coconut type anise hyssop flower spikes; jarrah; fennel seed heads.
Bulk: Chamomile blossoms; rose hips or petals; dried apple slices, with peel intact; grape tendrils; mints, fruity kinds: leaves, dried.
Oils: Citrus oil, apple, or other fruit scents.
Fixatives: Calamus root; corncob.

LAVENDER POTPOURRI

Base: Lavender flowers, leaves.
Bulk: Blue flowers: larkspur, delphinium, *Salvia farinacea*; other dried flowers for color, if you want to display in glass.
Oils: Lavender oil; rose oil.
Fixatives: Corncob; orris root.

PINEY POTPOURRI

Base: Rosemary; sage leaves; scented geraniums, leaves, pungent types.
Bulk: Hemlock cones; white paper birch bark curls; pine needles; rose hips; dried seed heads; teasel; money plant.
Oils: Citrus oil.
Fixatives: Orris root; calamus root; corncob.

SPICY MUSK POTPOURRI

Base: Marjoram; sage leaves; lemon verbena; Sweet Annie, can also be used by itself; opal basil flower spikes.
Bulk: Clary sage leaves; cinnamon sticks; whole cloves; coriander seeds; catnip leaves.
Oils: Sandalwood oil; musk fragrance oil; spice oils.
Fixatives: Corncobs; calamus root; clary sage also acts as fixative.

SUMMER BEAUTY BLEND

Base: Red rose petals.
Bulk: Blue delphinium, Black-eyed Susan blossoms.
Oils: Rose oil.
Fixatives: None. This showy mixture is definitely to be displayed!

SWEET ROSE POTPOURRI

Base: Rose petals—red, pink, or other colors; scented geranium leaves, rose-scented type.
Bulk: Rose leaves; rosebuds; peony petals, red or pink; peony buds; carnation petals, red or pink; other dried flowers; artemisia.
Oils: Rose oil; rose geranium oil; lavender oil.
Fixatives: Corncob; orris root.

Whether therefore ye eat, or drink, or whatsoever ye do, do all to the glory of God.

I CORINTHIANS 10:31

SECTION IV

HERBS IN THE
Kitchen

Clockwise from top: Mint, oregano, cilantro, basil, thyme, rosemary

"Mmmm. Where but in the kitchen do we realize the full-bodied zest of herbs? Whether for cooking or canning, baking or bruising, herbs add natural flavor and color to our favorite dishes. This section highlights my favorite culinary herbs. You'll discover flavors that complement each other and tips to enhance your cooking the herbal way."

—Gracia

Cooking with Herbs

To flavor main dishes with herbs doesn't require a course in culinary school. However, because of their varying tastes, whether sweet and spicy, or strong and peppery, certain herbs taste right with certain foods. Of course, your preferred tastes supersede any charts.

One secret of herbal-flavored cooking, especially for main dishes, lies in using a quantity that enhances rather than overpowers. A pinch of rosemary in chicken noodle soup will keep partakers wondering, "What makes this so good?" while a tablespoon might have them reaching for water between bites.

First of all, have herbs close and convenient to use. A kitchen garden (readily accessible from the kitchen) is ideal since fresh herb flavors surpass dried forms. If fresh sprigs are nearby, you will much more easily incorporate them in cooking. Store dried herbs in shakers and within easy reach. A dark or covered location will preserve dried flavor better than an open spice rack.

Experiment with new tastes in dishes you already make. Try only one unfamiliar herb at a time. You can test-taste by adding a bit of seasoning to a small portion of the dish before affecting the entire batch. Once you have developed a taste for one certain herb, combine with other compatible flavors. Some herbs have a loud, overbearing taste, while others are more subdued. Experiment!

Fresh herbs have a higher moisture content than dried. Therefore, it takes about three times the amount of fresh leaves to equal the strength of dried.

Make sure dried herbs are finely ground before adding to food. This allows the taste to be evenly distributed and not clumped. Snip fresh herbs directly into pot, or mince larger amounts on a cutting board with a knife. You can also bruise a large bunch between your hands, throw into the pot, and allow the essential oils to simmer out. Remove before serving.

By cooking with herbs you can reduce salt while adding a burst of vitamins and minerals. Most green, leafy herbs are high in vitamin A and C. You can also avoid the preservatives found in many seasoning mixes. Following is a chart to get you started.

Herb	What to Use	Taste	Common Usage	Other Possibilities
Basil, Sweet	fresh or dried leaves	spicy with hints of clove	anything tomato	Soups, especially tomato-based; a must for tomato sauces, pizza, pasta, pesto; blends well with vegetables, fish, and poultry; large fresh leaves with hamburger sandwiches. A sweet complement to oregano and rosemary.
Chives	fresh or frozen leaves, fresh flowers	mild onion	baked potatoes	This unsurpassed mild, oniony herb is perfect for soups, esp. chicken noodle and potato. Chop finely for adding to meat loaf, chicken, fish, creamy sauces.
Cilantro	fresh leaves, dried seed (coriander)	parsley with citrus	Mexican food	Use fresh leaves abundantly for perfect flavor in tacos, salsa, guacamole, enchiladas, burritos, and other Mexican dishes, such as casseroles, roll-ups, wraps, rice, and beans.
Dill	fresh or dried seeds and leaves (dillweed)	fresh, delicate	pickling cucumbers	Use with sour cream for vegetable dip; chopped leaves with stuffed eggs, or add a dash of dill vinegar for stuffing; potato salad; leaves with creamy soups or tomato soups; chicken, shrimp, fish; seeds with vegetables like carrots, cabbage, beans, tomato soup.
Lovage	fresh or dried leaves and stems	celery-like	celery substitute	Adds a hearty celery taste in vegetables and chicken, soups, potato salad, tomato juice, dressing. A good salt substitute.
Parsley	fresh or frozen leaves	refreshing, green	potatoes or as garnish	Use in tomato and vegetable soups; noodles. Flat leaf is preferred for cooking; curly varieties add attractive touch to meat platters.

|194| *Gracia's Herbs*

Herb	What to Use	Taste	Common Usage	Other Possibilities
Rosemary	fresh or dried leaves	resinous, piney	with basil and oregano for Italian seasoning	Add a pinch of this distinctive herb to chicken noodle soup; use with roasts, chicken, fish, pizza, pasta; especially spaghetti and lasagna; tomato sauces.
Oregano	fresh or dried leaves	sharp, aromatic	pizza	An extremely versatile herb that enhances anything with tomatoes, meaty stews, vegetable soups. An ideal partner for basil.
Sage	fresh or dried leaves	camphoraceous, musky	meats	A key ingredient in sausage and other pork dishes; also poultry. Helps neutralize the fats in meats, tomato soups. Fresh leaves have a slightly sweeter taste—ideal for vegetables like beans, eggplant.
Savory	fresh or dried leaves	peppery, spicy	vegetables as a salt substitute	Peppery flavor accompanies vegetables; especially beans, lentils, peas, string beans, cabbage, turnips, alone or in soups; also vinegar in salad dressings, meat marinade.
Thyme	fresh or dried leaves	strong, pungent	meats, esp. chicken	Any kind of soups and sauces, whether creamy, brothy, or tomato-based; herb butters. Use somewhat sparingly—its best function is to blend flavors.
Tarragon	fresh or dried leaves	licorice, sharp	creamy sauces	Best known for its distinctive taste in French cooking. An accent for chicken, fish, green vegetables.

COOKING WITH HERBS

Herbal Mixes

FOR COLORFUL COOKING

Any single herb added to a dish can provide pleasing flavor, but have you explored a blend of herbs? Combining compatible herbs brings out the best of all of them and creates a well-rounded but pleasantly complex effect. Certain herbs impart a vital, basic taste, while others act as colorful accents.

Some herbal mixes, like fines herbes, have been used for centuries and have come to represent a regional flavor. Other blends such as poultry seasoning lend a distinctive touch that we connect with certain foods.

Both fresh or dried herbs can be used for mixes. Just use a bit more for fresh herbs. Recipes for herbal mixes often consist of three to five (sometimes more) selected culinary herbs but are readily adaptable to your tastes and items you have on hand.

If you don't have herbs of your own, the spice shelf of a bulk food store or even your local grocery is an excellent resource. By using bulk herbs you can put together your own blends. Scan the ingredient list of prepared mixes. Sometimes you can glean ideas.

Dried herb mixes should be stored in a tight container. A shaker with large holes accommodates flaked and minced leaves and makes adding a dash while cooking quick and easy. Ground mixes can be spooned out of a container. Store at room temperature.

Not only are herbal mixes useful for cooking, but they provide low salt or no salt flavorings. Try an herbal popcorn seasoning—oregano and basil with a dab of garlic powder is good.

USEFUL HERBS FOR MIXES

Basil—spicy, sweet, refreshing
Chervil—delicate, complex, anise-like
Cilantro—onion, parsley
Chives—mild onion
Dill—flavorful but subtle
Fennel—sweet licorice
Lovage—strong celery
Marjoram—like oregano but sweeter
Mint—refreshing, green
Oregano—dominant, spicy, pungent
Parsley—pleasant, fresh
Rosemary—rich evergreen
Sage—earthy, bold
Savory—green, grassy
Tarragon—strong licorice
Thyme—sharp and robust

SEEDS FOR MIXES

Anise—clear licorice
Celery—warm and satisfying
Cumin—hot, rustic
Caraway—slightly sweeter than cumin
Dill—punch of flavor
Fennel—sweet licorice

BOUQUET GARNI

A traditional blend inspired by the French that adds a hearty goodness to soups, stews, and other long-simmering dishes. Tie fresh herbs into a little bunch, 4 to 5 inches long, rustle between your palms, and toss into the pot while simmering. Dried herbs can be crumbled and placed in a tea ball or cheesecloth. Remove before serving.

Ingredients Needed:

3 sprigs parsley	4 to 5 leaves chives
2 sprigs thyme	Optional: A sprig or two of lovage, marjoram, basil, or bay leaf

FINES HERBES

Fresh herbs must be used for this delicate blend. The subtle hints of anise and onion go well with mild dairy and egg-based recipes such as white sauce and omelet. Other good combinations are with fish, potatoes, and rice. Add within the last minutes of cooking.

Ingredients Needed:

Equal amounts of fresh minced leaves of the following:

parsley	tarragon
chives	chervil

ITALIAN MIX

This extremely versatile mix is indispensable when making pizza, meatballs, pasta, and other tomato-based dishes. For larger amounts, use cup or pound instead of tablespoon.

Ingredients Needed:

1 Tbsp. parsley flakes	½ Tbsp. oregano flakes
1 Tbsp. sweet basil flakes	½ Tbsp. minced dried onion, optional

Gracia's Herbs

ZESTY HERB MIX

Perfect for soups or breads. Herbs can be fresh or dried.

Ingredients Needed:

1 part thyme   3 parts summer savory

2 parts parsley

POULTRY SEASONING

Just a pinch of this finely ground powder spices up chicken broth for soup or gravy. It's also useful in dressing (stuffing) and sprinkled on croutons.

Ingredients Needed:

2 Tbsp. ground sage   1 Tbsp. ground rosemary

1 Tbsp. ground thyme

HERBAL BUTTER BLEND

Perfect for summer when fresh herbs are plentiful!

Ingredients Needed:

½ c. butter   1 tsp. oregano

8 oz. cream cheese   1 Tbsp. dill

1 Tbsp. chives

Directions:

To prepare, allow butter and cream cheese to soften. Cream together along with chopped herbs. Pat into a small dish. (Clear glass looks pretty.) Chill for several hours or overnight. Garnish with a few sprigs of thyme and an opal basil leaf.

HERB BREAD MIX

This mix works well fresh or dried. Add to bread dough before mixing in flour, or sprinkle on top of bread sticks. Use for one loaf.

Ingredients Needed:

1 tsp. basil   1 tsp. thyme

1 tsp. oregano

BREAD TOPPER

Ingredients Needed:

1 Tbsp. Italian herb mix   4 Tbsp. melted butter

Directions:

Brush top of loaves after baking, while still warm.

Herbs in the Bakery

When herbs and dough are combined, it's a winning combination! You can improvise your regular bread recipe by adding a single herb for a more dominant flavor or a blend for variation. Perhaps you want to create an herbal mix that suits your taste. There are no "rules" to break! Generally use at least one tablespoon dried herbs per loaf or per dozen of buns.

Then there are also other herb-flavored breads and rolls. Many of these are tasty appetizers which highlight the excellent combination—herbs, butter, and grains.

Gracia's Herbs

TOPPING YOUR BREAD

After the loaves or buns are formed, add the finishing touch by sprinkling with herb seeds. First, brush with melted butter or beaten egg to make the seeds stick to the dough. Here are some options:

SESAME - Sesame's golden brown seeds are readily seen atop breads, buns, and croissants. Grown in semi-tropical climates, this seed is not readily grown in gardens. Most seeds, available in stores and bulk food outlets, are lightly toasted, giving a full-bodied flavor.

CARAWAY - These narrow, dark brown seeds are an essential for rye bread, giving the distinctive "rye bread" taste. Caraway is a biennial plant, producing seeds in its second year, and is quite easy to grow.

NIGELLA (Love in a Mist) - This carefree plant is fun to grow, developing papery seedpods in late summer. Open the pods to reveal black seeds—lots of them! These seeds have a neutral flavor and are highly visible on top of breads or biscuits.

DILL - Sprinkle these flat, chewy seeds onto breads for a subtle dill flavor. My favorite variety of dill, 'Dukat', is especially known for its richly flavored seeds.

BUTTERY GARLIC BREAD

Here's a quick and easy garlic bread.

Ingredients:

½ c. butter, softened
¼ c. cream cheese, softened
2 Tbsp. garlic powder
1 Tbsp. sour cream and onion powder
1 tsp. chopped fresh oregano
1 tsp. chopped fresh parsley
1 tsp. chopped fresh basil

Directions:

Cream together butter and cream cheese. Add other ingredients (herbs can be adjusted to taste) and mix well. Spread onto bread slices, both sides. Put loaf together again, wrap in aluminum foil, and warm in oven at 350°F for 10 to 15 minutes. Serve while warm.

DILLY BREAD IN A CASSEROLE

This delicious bread can be formed into a round loaf or individual buns. Cottage cheese gives it a unique flavor and texture. Serve the buns with herb butter for a sensational appetizer!

Ingredients Needed:

1 pkg. active dry yeast	1 tsp. salt
¼ c. warm water	¼ tsp. baking soda
1 c. small curd cottage cheese, creamed	1 egg, beaten
2 Tbsp. sugar	2¼–2½ c. flour
1 Tbsp. minced onion	dill seed for garnish
1 Tbsp. softened butter	
⅓ c. chopped fresh dill weed or 2 Tbsp. dried dill	

Directions:

Dissolve yeast in warm water. Heat cottage cheese to lukewarm and combine with yeast mixture. Add rest of ingredients, except flour, and blend together. Add flour, a small amount at a time, mixing well after each addition, until a stiff dough forms. Cover and let rise until double in size, about 50 to 60 minutes. Knead dough and form into a well-greased 8-inch round glass or ceramic casserole dish (1½ to 2 qt. size). Cover and let rise again until light, about 30 to 40 minutes. Bake at 350°F for 40 to 50 minutes, until golden. Brush with melted butter and sprinkle lightly with salt and dill seed. Serve warm. Delicious with soup and cheddar cheese.

DILLY BREAD BUNS

Use Dilly Bread in a Casserole recipe for dough. After dough has risen, knead well and divide into two parts. Form 12 buns with each part. Place in well-greased cake pan and let rise. Bake at 350°F for 12 to 15 minutes, or until golden. Brush with melted butter and sprinkle lightly with salt and dill seed. Serve warm. Yield: 2 dozen buns.

CREAMY CHIVE RINGS

These attractive rings are sure to become a favorite!

Ingredients:

1 pkg. dry yeast
¼ c. warm water
1 c. milk
6 Tbsp. butter
¼ c. instant potato flakes
⅓ c. sugar
1¼ tsp. salt
1 egg, beaten
3¾–4¼ c. flour

Directions:

Dissolve yeast in water. Heat milk, butter, potato flakes, sugar, and salt. (Do not boil.) Cool to room temperature and add yeast mixture. Mix well, then add egg and flour. Let dough rise until double; punch. Divide dough into two parts. Roll each part into a 12x16-inch rectangle. Divide filling and spread onto rectangles. Starting along wide end, roll dough jellyroll style and seal edges. Place onto greased cookie sheets, seam side down, forming the roll into a wreath-like ring. Cut slices into ring, 1 inch apart, almost through, but leave connected at bottom. Lay slices flat, overlapping each other slightly. Brush with melted butter and sprinkle with sesame seeds. Bake at 350°F for 20 to 25 minutes or until golden brown. Makes two rings.

Chopped chives

Filling:

1 egg, beaten
¾ c. cream or rich milk
⅓ c. chopped fresh chives
½ tsp. salt

Directions:

Carefully heat in double boiler until thick; cool. (Note: dried chives can be substituted for fresh chives.)

HERBS IN THE BAKERY |203|

OREGANO BREAD

Ingredients:

2 envelopes active dry yeast
2 c. warm water
1 tsp. sugar
¼ c. vegetable oil
2 Tbsp. honey
½ c. wheat germ

2 Tbsp. dried oregano leaves, ground
1 Tbsp. dried parsley leaves, ground
1 Tbsp. dried basil leaves, ground
4 tsp. salt
6½ c. flour (approx.)

Directions:

Sprinkle yeast over warm water in a large bowl. Stir to dissolve. Add sugar and let set until the mixture bubbles. Add oil, honey, wheat germ, seasonings, and 2 cups of the flour. (Note: whole wheat flour can be used for a portion of the flour.) Beat until smooth and shiny, then beat in remaining flour to make a stiff dough. Let set in a warm place until dough rises double in bulk, about an hour. Shape into four long, skinny loaves on greased cookie sheets. Brush the tops lightly with oil. Cover and let rise until almost double in bulk, about 45 minutes. Cut three diagonal slashes on top of each loaf. Bake at 400°F for about 30 minutes. Do not wrap the loaves until they are completely cool. Yield: 4 loaves.

SWEET FLAVORS

The sweet lemon-flavored herbs—lemon verbena, lemon balm, and lemon thyme—lend themselves well as additions to cakes and other sweet pastries. In the following recipes, most of the taste is given by infusion, rather than using a lot of ground herbs. Make infusions by steeping the herbs in liquid, which in these recipes is milk. While heating the milk over medium heat, place the sprigs into the saucepan and bruise with a spoon to release the juices. As soon as milk begins to bubble, remove from heat; strain and cool to room temperature. Do NOT allow to boil. This can be prepared ahead and refrigerated.

MOIST LEMON LOAF

Ingredients:

¾ c. milk
1 Tbsp. finely chopped lemon thyme
2 c. all-purpose flour
1½ tsp. baking powder
¼ tsp. salt
2 Tbsp. lemon juice
6 Tbsp. butter, room temperature
1 c. sugar
2 eggs

Directions:

Preheat the oven to 325°F. Heat the milk (do not boil) with the chopped thyme and let steep, strain, and cool. Mix the flour, baking powder, and salt in a large bowl. In another bowl, cream the butter and add the sugar. Beat until the mixture is light and fluffy. Beat in the eggs, one at a time. Add the lemon juice. Add the flour mixture alternately with the herbed milk. Mix until just blended. Bake for 50 minutes in a buttered loaf pan. Glaze while loaf is still warm.

SPICE N' THYME CAKE

Ingredients:

2½ c. unbleached flour
1¼ tsp. baking powder
1 tsp. baking soda
1 tsp. nutmeg
1 tsp. cinnamon
¼ tsp. ground cloves
¼ tsp. ginger
¾ tsp. salt
12 Tbsp. butter, softened
1½ c. sugar
3 extra-large eggs, separated
½ c. milk, steeped with 15 to 20 sprigs lemon thyme
¾ c. nonfat buttermilk
2 Tbsp. minced fresh lemon thyme leaves
⅓ c. chopped English walnuts

Directions:

Preheat oven to 350°F. Lightly grease a 9x13-inch baking pan and dust it lightly with flour. Sift flour with the baking powder, baking soda, spices, and salt, and set aside. In a large bowl, whip the butter and sugar, and beat until fluffy. Add the egg yolks one at a time and buttermilk, beating well after each addition. Slowly stir in milk mixture, alternating with the flour mixture. Beat egg whites separately and fold into the batter, adding thyme and walnuts last. Bake for 35 minutes, or until cake springs back to touch. Frost with cream cheese icing and garnish with thyme sprigs.

LEMON VERBENA ANGEL FOOD CAKE

This angel food cake with a twist is among our favorites. The natural lemon flavor is delightfully delicate, not overpowering. Yes, you'll see little green flakes in your cake!

Ingredients:

1¼ c. cake flour
1½ c. sugar, divided
1½ c. egg whites
　(about 12 to 14 extra large)
1¼ tsp. cream of tartar
¼ tsp. salt
¼ tsp. vanilla
2 Tbsp. lemon juice
¾ c. packed finely minced fresh lemon verbena or lemon balm leaves, or as desired (⅔ c. dried)

Directions:

Preheat oven to 375°F. Sift flour and ¾ cup of the sugar together. Sift twice and set aside. Beat egg whites, cream of tartar, and salt until foamy. Add rest of sugar, several tablespoons at a time, beating until peaks form. Fold in flour mixture. Add vanilla, lemon juice, and lemon verbena or lemon balm leaves. Bake in a tube pan at 350°F for 45 to 60 minutes or until cake is golden brown on top. Invert to cool. Glaze or frost, if desired. Garnish with fresh lemon verbena sprigs to serve.

LEMON GLAZE

Ingredients Needed:

2 handfuls lemon verbena leaves
lemon basil or lemon geraniums for more intense flavor, optional
　(may be used as a substitute for lemon verbena)
½ c. water
dash of vanilla
2 c. powdered sugar

Directions:

Mince leaves finely and cover with water and vanilla. Allow to stand at least one hour. Strain out leaves. Add powdered sugar until a syrupy consistency forms. Drizzle over angel food cake. For a yellow tinge, add a drop or two of yellow food coloring before mixing in sugar.

Herbal Vinegars

Herbal vinegars are fun and easy to make! The idea is basic: putting together vinegar and herb parts for some time, usually a few weeks, until the vinegar is thoroughly infused with the good herby flavors. Finally, the vinegar is strained. Now you've conveniently captured the essence of an herb—or blend of herbs—in liquid form! You can add a dash of whatever flavor you have on hand simply by popping a cork.

Not only are herbal vinegars very versatile for cooking, they're also very pretty when stored in tall, decorative jars or dainty cruets. A sprig or two of thyme leaves or a nasturtium blossom suspended in the vinegar creates a work of art worthy for display.

A bottle of herbal vinegar is a creative gift idea. Dress up the jar with a fabric bow and a personalized label.

CHOOSING THE VINEGAR

The best choices for making herbal vinegars are apple cider vinegar and wine vinegars, both white and red. These have smooth, mild flavors which blend well with other tastes. Distilled white vinegar is almost too harsh and too acidic, and balsamic vinegar already has plenty of flavor.

Color may be a factor in your choice as well. I like the transparency of apple cider and white wine vinegar even though the color turns darker after adding herbs. In other applications, rosy red wine vinegar is pretty, too. Deeply colored leaves like those of opal basil will change lighter vinegar to a medium pink, and darker to a much deeper shade.

Have you heard of herbal oils? Try using light oils like a high quality extra virgin olive oil instead of vinegar, but follow the same steps. They don't have quite as long shelf life, so use within three or four months.

Herbs for Vinegars
Basil (all kinds)
Bay
Chervil
Chives
Dill Leaves
Garlic
Marjoram
Mint
Nasturtium
Oregano
Rosemary
Sage
Savory
Tarragon
Thyme

CHOOSING THE HERBS

Your choice of herbs depends mainly on your tastes! Do you have a favorite herb that you'd like all by itself? Or do you prefer a complex blend of this and that? Think of the end uses. Salad dressings? Then try basil, or dill, or chives for mild dressings, and nasturtiums and tarragon for bolder ones. For marinades, select more sturdy flavors like garlic, rosemary, and sage. Use chervil, fennel, or mint for a bit of sweetness.

The most commonly used plant part is the leaves, but any stems, flowers, and seed heads can also work. Some flowers, such as chives, are beautiful as a garnish in finished vinegar. Blossoms will determine the vinegar color.

MAKING THE VINEGAR

A BASIC RECIPE

1 part herb leaves or flowers

2 parts vinegar

One cup loosely packed herbs with two cups of vinegar is a good amount to start.

First, collect clean, unblemished leaves in the morning after dew has dried. Keep in mind the size of your batch, and collect accordingly. Wash if necessary and pat completely dry. Moisture will cloud the vinegar. Also keep your eyes open for any insect guests!

Vinegar reacts chemically to metal, so avoid any copper or aluminum utensils. Select a glass jar and sterilize it with hot water. Choose a jar that allows only a little airspace between vinegar and lid. Measure the herb leaves and stuff them into the jar. Do not cut or mince them. Measure the vinegar and pour over herbs. With a wooden spoon, poke into the jar and bruise the leaves. This releases oils into the vinegar. Remove any air bubbles and cover jar with a plastic lid.

Label and date each jar. This is important! Once I improvised an herbal blend vinegar recipe that turned out to be particularly pleasing, but the recipe was lost because of incomplete labeling.

Some vinegar makers use the heated method, heating the vinegar to just below boiling point before pouring over the herbs. This shortens the aging period to ten to fourteen days, but it also destroys some of the vinegar's acidity.

Place the jar in an area with indirect lighting. Sunshine will speed up the brewing process, but it will also cloud the vinegar. Give the jar a shake every few days. After about four weeks, open jar and taste. If you'd like it a bit stronger, let it age an

Equipment Checklist for Making Vinegar

- ❑ Glass Jar, Pint or Quart
- ❑ Plastic Lid
- ❑ Decorative Glass Jar or Cruet
- ❑ Straining Cloth or Coffee Filter
- ❑ Plastic Funnel
- ❑ Wooden or Plastic Spoon

L-R: Thyme, rosemary, thyme, savory vinegars

HERBAL VINEGARS

additional two weeks. (If even then it's too mild for you, strain out the old herbs and repeat the process with fresh leaves.) If the vinegar is too pungent for your taste, dilute with unflavored vinegar.

Once it is done to your satisfaction, strain the vinegar twice to remove any and all particles. Bottle in an attractive glass jar (one with a cork closure is nice). Insert a fresh sprig of herb for looks. You can pull this sprig out upon occasion and snip off a piece to use, but after it is no longer covered with vinegar, toss to avoid mold problems. Store the vinegar in a dark cool place. If you want to keep it within handy reach when cooking, a darker spot on your countertop will do.

Herbal vinegars will keep eighteen months or longer, if properly prepared and stored.

Rosemary vinegar

HOW DO I USE VINEGAR?

Because they are liquid, herbal vinegars are convenient to add to soups, salad dressings, barbecue sauces, and marinades. They can also be used for pickling. Don't fear to experiment with new uses!

Sweet basil vinegar is good for salad dressing. Add a dash to tomato juice or salsa. Chives' light onion flavor makes it a perfect option for marinades and salad dressings. I like to add dill vinegar to egg yolks before mashing for pickled eggs. Three-bean salad, potato salad, and cucumber salad will have a delicious tanginess with the addition of dill vinegar. Nasturtium has a peppery flavor. It's a good choice for salad dressings and appetizers. Sage is one of my favorites! Drizzle some onto meats and use in barbecue sauce.

Thyme with vinegars

TOMATOES + HERBS = *Delicious*

Tomatoes are red treasures of the garden, abundant, tasty, and useful in many, many ways. Thick slices make quick, delicious sandwiches or a fat-free snack. Bright red juice forms the base for hearty soups, while a smooth puree is the first step of spaghetti and pizza sauce. Salsa, ketchup, hot sauce—all these show the great variety of tomatoes.

After exploring tomato possibilities, let's look at the best natural flavorings for tomato-based foods. Did you guess herbs? Good for you! Various herbs enhance the complex flavor of the tomato to bring out a sweetness or a spicy effect. Although tomatoes serve as the base, it is often the herbs that form the flavors we crave—oregano on pizza, for example.

BASIL—A GREEN BLESSING

In midsummer, basil and fresh tomatoes overlap for a winning combination. Sweet basil's smooth green leaves are packed with summer's sweetness and a hint of spice. Many cooks prefer the Genovese strains of sweet basil that originate from Genoa, Italy, home of delicious pastas and pizzas. Other basils like Thai, cinnamon, or lemon add the right touch to spicy tomato-based sauces like ketchup or barbecue sauce.

Basil can be used fresh or dried. Fresh is definitely the most flavorful. Another way to preserve basil is to chop finely, adding a bit of water, and freeze in an ice cube tray. Simply add a basil cube to soup or spaghetti.

Basil is a heat-loving annual. Sow directly in the garden after danger of frost is past. For an earlier harvest, sow indoors and transplant as early as possible. One secret to lush, bushy basil is to keep the tips pinched. The plant will respond by becoming more leafy.

BAY—HEARTY LEAF

Making hearty soups? Cooking a pot of spaghetti sauce? The subtle sweet, earthy flavor of bay leaf adds a full-bodied touch. Bay leaves are broad and fleshy; shiny dark green when fresh, stiff light green when dried. Ground dried bay leaf is often used. Whole dried leaves can be simmered with the dish until limp, but remove them before serving. Bay's sharp edges are not good for a stomach.

Bay grows to be an attractive little bush. It is a native to warm climates. In northern areas grow bay in a planter and place near a north window to overwinter. It prefers dry soil, but a frequent misting keeps the leaves shiny and attractive.

CILANTRO—TEX-MEX DELIGHT

To add a distinct south-of-the-border twist to salsa or chili, cilantro is the perfect choice. The cilantro plant grows a profusion of bright green leaves somewhat like parsley, but with a more pronounced, piquant zest. Its best form is fresh, finely chopped, and added at the last minute in liberal amounts. What a burst of adventure for the taste buds!

Freshly chopped cilantro with vinegar and tomato chunks is a quick condiment for rice or tacos. For those who like hot foods, mince and add a chili pepper or even a habanero.

When the cilantro plant matures, it forms seeds known under another name—coriander. These dried round seeds also are a spice that's compatible with tomato, but are sweeter and more concentrated than the leafy part of the plant.

To grow cilantro, sow seeds in the garden in early spring. For a continuous supply of tender young plants sow every four weeks. Several varieties such as 'Santo' and 'Delfino' are slower to go to seed.

CUMIN—SEEDS WITH A PUNCH

Are you familiar with caraway? The taste of cumin resembles caraway's, but has more richness, more punch. These dark brown seeds liven up salsa and other tomato dishes that need intensity. Many taco and chili seasonings have cumin as a prominent ingredient. Crush the seeds slightly for full benefit of the inner flavor.

Cumin is grown from seed and needs a long growing season for maturity. Sow indoors about six weeks before the last frost date, then transplant.

LOVAGE—CELERY SUBSTITUTE

Lovage is a mainstay in my herb garden. First, it is so dependable, returning year after year despite cold winters and dry summers. Second, lovage is the perfect substitute for celery, a vegetable that takes the right conditions and a bit of effort to grow. This handsome perennial rises grandly to 5 feet or taller in early spring.

All parts of the plant are edible, with true celery flavor. The smooth leaves are fine fresh or dried. I like to add a sprinkling of dried lovage and a dash of lemon to a glass of tomato juice. Lovage stems chopped into small bits perform just like celery in vegetable soups.

OREGANO—THE PIZZA HERB

A crust topped with meat, cheese, or vegetables forms the food that is widely popular across the globe. In America, pizza is such a favorite food that if all the pizza consumed in one day were put together it would cover 85 acres!

What is the most essential part of a delicious pizza? To me it is the sauce, seasoned to perfection with oregano, basil, and more. Of all herbs, none is so special to pizza as oregano, and of all oreganos none is so important as the Greek strain. What true pizza goodness!

When making pizza sauce add minced Greek oregano abundantly. For an unsurpassable savor, sprinkle dried oregano flakes onto the pizza before layering on the cheese.

Oregano is a fairly hardy perennial, sun-loving with a spreading habit. Start by seed, or for best success, select a plant.

PARSLEY—TRUE GARDEN GOODNESS

This familiar frilly favorite is not only good in many tomato-based dishes, but it's also good for you! Green parsley is packed with many vitamins and minerals and a healthy amount of chlorophyll. You may pick between showy curly parsley and dark green Italian (flat leaf) parsley. Is there really a difference in flavor between the two? Yes, slightly. Whenever possible I use the Italian variety for cooking, mincing a liberal amount into nearly any tomato soup, sauce, or salsa.

Parsley is a biennial. It remains leafy the first year then sends up a seed-bearing stalk the next year. For the best leaf harvest, plant each year. Starting from seed is moderately easy. Germination is speeded by soaking the seeds in very warm water before sowing.

AND MORE...

Various other herbs also combine well with tomatoes. Chives lends an oniony taste, mild but delicious. Its slender bright green leaves are a pretty garnish floating on top of soups. Another herb, fennel, has a delicate licorice flavor. Sage has a bolder effect. Use it sparingly to infuse a robust, musky undertone to barbecue sauce. Thyme brings out the acidic side of tomatoes with its sharp, distinct tone, useful in marinades or pasta sauce. Simmer a fresh sprig briefly then remove, or flavor to taste with tiny pinches of dried ground powder.

Beyond Lettuce—

USING HERBS AS GREENS

Crinkly lettuce, crispy cabbage, and smooth basil: what do they have in common? Perhaps we should first study the differences. They're different shades of garden-fresh emerald and each has its own distinctive flavor and texture. But all three are greens, plants grown for their leafy parts, usually eaten raw.

Greens is a somewhat broad term, and includes our favorite lettuce, cabbage, spinach, and other leafy plants often prepared as salads or sandwiches. But another good source (though often overlooked) for healthy, delicious greens is the herb garden.

To be considered a good green, a plant should meet several characteristics. First, its texture should be crisp or smooth, not woolly, prickly, or too fleshy, and suitable for fresh eating. It should also have a mild taste that blends well with other salad or sandwich ingredients. The plant should be quick-growing and prolific, with easy-to-harvest leaves.

A number of leafy herbs have the traits of good greens and provide some interesting variety for salads and other foods. Of course, the most common greens such as lettuce will always be the mainstays, but adding herbs will enhance and enrich our selection.

Using herbs in their just-picked-from-the-garden stage is the most nutritious way to serve them. All the flavor and vitamins stay intact and are not lost by heating. It's also the most effortless way to use them. Just pick, rinse, pat dry, and chop. Sometimes it is not even necessary to rinse.

HERBS AS GREENS—A LIST

Mild/Salad Flavors
Sweet Basil
Cilantro
Dill
Italian Parsley

Sorta Sweet Flavors
Fennel
Mint
Tarragon

Vegetable Flavors
Chives (onion)
Lovage (celery)
Salad Burnet (cucumber)

Spicy, Tangy Flavors
Basils (Spicy or Thai types)
Garlic Greens
Marjoram
Oregano
Savory
Sorrel
Thyme

FROM PICKING TO PREPARING

When harvesting leaves, choose tender, young leaves and tips that are free from blemishes. Rinse if necessary, and prepare for serving by stripping leaves from stems (for salad burnet, oregano, thyme, tarragon, or mint) or cutting into fine pieces with kitchen shears. Discard big stems, except for lovage, which can be chopped like celery. Putting herbs in a moistened bag and placing into the refrigerator will crisp them just like lettuce, and give them up to a week of storage life. Or if you will not be using herbs for several hours and do not want them wilted, simply place them in water like a bouquet until ready to use.

SALADS

As there are many kinds of salads, so there are also many kinds of herbs and many possibilities for tasty combinations. Here are some ideas, plus you may discover some of your own preferred salad additions. You can also add herb greens to haystacks, tortilla roll-ups, and other dishes that use greens.

GARDEN—An abundance of lettuce or spinach with radishes, tomatoes, or cucumbers plus grated cheese or bacon crumbles can make a meal in itself! Here's some more variety: basils (especially sweet), chives, Italian parsley (a healthy, dark green addition), salad burnet, tarragon, and sorrel.

PASTA—For this type of salad, cool, light, and sweet vegetable flavors are desired to add a special touch that does not dominate. Chop finely and add to dressing one or more of these herbs: basil, chives, dill, lovage.

TACO—A spicy, zesty, Tex-Mex touch is what you need with this salad. These herbs help achieve that effect: cilantro, basil, chives, oregano, garlic greens, and marjoram.

BEAN SALADS—Sweet and sour, with vinegar and these herbs: chives, dill, savory, sorrel, and tarragon.

COLESLAW—A variety of herbs can be added, depending on the type of dressing: lovage, fennel, and dill.

POTATO SALAD—A favorite salad for picnics or anytime. These herbs add the perfect flavors: chives (mild onion), dill, and lovage (can be substituted for celery).

CUCUMBER SALAD Cool, mild, refreshing. Here are some herbs that blend right in: dill, salad burnet, borage flowers (for garnish).

SANDWICHES

Here's another interesting way to use herb greens. Herbs, along with lettuce, spinach, and sprouts, are excellent sandwich materials. Make sure the herbs are well rinsed and trimmed and free of thick stem parts. It's best to use somewhat large-leaved herbs for eating ease. Chives and thyme are a bit hard to use on a sandwich with their fine leaves, unless in a spread, like meat or egg salad.

Mild/Salad flavored greens (see list) are perfect for eating with lettuce and cheese sandwiches, as are vegetable flavors. Spicy flavors go well with grilled chicken or burgers. Dill is good with fish. A large, smooth leaf of sweet basil is a great complement to a barbecued hamburger.

APPETIZERS

Fresh herb greens are a delicious way to flavor cheese balls, butters, or spreads as appetizers. Chives and dill make a pretty, finishing touch when minced, then pressed onto the outside of a cheese ball.

CREAMY SPREAD

Ingredients Needed:

½ c. butter
⅔ c. sour cream
8 oz. cream cheese
2 Tbsp. sour cream
onion powder
1 Tbsp. chopped chives or 3 Tbsp. chopped dill weed

Directions:

Soften, then blend. Garnish with dill or parsley and serve with bread. It is very yummy with garlic or cheese bread. Or dab onto wheat crackers and top with bits of dill, or chives, or meat tidbits such as ham and pepperoni. This is also a tasty pretzel or chip dip.

Viola flowers

Please Eat the Petals

Where can you harvest tasty edibles? From the vegetable garden come many nutritious leafy and crunchy vegetables; from the orchard, juicy fruits; from the herb garden, flavorful sprigs, but did you know it is also a source of edible blossoms? And flower beds, too, are places of harvest!

Many herbs bloom throughout the summer, fitting into both herb and flower categories. Though we mostly use the leaves of culinary herbs, their blossoms are edible and impart the flavor of the plant in a milder form. Common flowers like nasturtium, bachelor's button, and calendula, and some wildflowers, including dandelion and violet, have been long-time favorites in foods—salads, for example. Others like hollyhock, petunia, gladiolus, and fuchsia are widely grown for their beauty, but are also edible. Have you nibbled these yet?

For several reasons I love to gather the blossoms of herbs and flowers for eating. One is the sense of homemade adventure with minimal effort. The flowers are growing anyhow, so why not enjoy them in as many ways as possible? They charm us with bright, cheery colors, but they also provide texture, color, and flavor no other food group can offer. Another reason is the season-long variety. From early spring to fall (or winter, with indoor plants), the question, "What can we eat now?" always reveals a delicious answer.

Does the idea of eating petals seem strange to you? The velvetlike texture of flower petals is actually similar to that of lettuce and other greens. And the flavors range from mild (again, like lettuce) to sweet and fruity, or zingy and peppery. Some flowers like salvias, snapdragons, and tulips are safe to eat, but have a bitter taste.

Many flowers are safe and tasty, yet like other plant families, there are poisonous kinds, too. Even the common iris, daffodil, and lily-of-the-valley are toxic, so make sure you know what you are eating! Unless you are certain of its identity and safeness, don't pop just any flower into your mouth. If in doubt, avoid!

Also, any blossoms for eating must be clean and chemical free. Those perfect red roses from the florist are laden with sprays. Admire them only with your eyes! Of course when you pick from your own garden you don't need to worry about chemicals. Commercially grown herbs and flowers are okay if labeled organic.

Edible flowers are simple to pick and prepare for eating. Blossoms are in their best crisp, fresh state in the morning, but harvest is okay anytime. Rinse if necessary and blot dry with a dish towel. Snip off any stems or sepals (little green leaf-like parts just beneath the flowers). If a day or two will elapse before you want to serve them, place the stems in a vase with water, just like a bouquet.

IDEAS FOR FUN, FLOWERY FOODS

A mixture of food and flowers offers healthy variety and a simple but special touch to any meal. Which flower is best used where? There are no hard, fast rules, but here are some suggestions. No doubt you may come up with some of your own intriguing combinations.

MAIN DISHES

Flowers are delicate, so you will not really cook them, but they are useful in stir-fry or added at the last minute to soups. Daylily buds or okra buds both have a vegetable-like appeal. Try them steamed or stir-fried with other vegetables. The bright yellow blossoms of squash and pumpkins can be dipped in eggs and flour and sautéed briefly. They have a nutty flavor similar to grown squash. Be sure to pick the male blossoms, which are in long, slender stems. The female blossoms will have a tiny squash already forming at the base.

Here's an idea for fondue lovers. Dip the flower spikes of basil or garden sage into a thin batter, then into oil for a crispy, flavorful experience.

A sprinkling of basil flowers, especially the lavender from the purple varieties, adds a mild basil taste and appealing color atop tomato soups, pasta, or pizza. Chive blossoms with the individual florets snipped apart are also good with chicken noodle soup or baked potatoes. Dandelion leaves and flowers are favorites for gravy. Snip the petals from the bitter stem.

Calendula petals give a rich, golden color to rice or pasta. Because of this, it is known as "poor man's saffron." Simply toss a tablespoon or two of petals, plucked from the stem, to simmer with water before adding the rice.

SALADS

Create a masterpiece salad by combining lettuce, spinach, and other garden-fresh vegetables with a topping of edible flowers! In salads, the texture and flavor of fresh flowers can be savored to the fullest. They can be mixed right into the salad, placed on a platter as a colorful bed for lettuce and other greens, or tossed on top for the finishing touch.

Nasturtiums with salad

Mild flowers that blend well with lettuce salad include garden peas, bachelor's buttons, rose petals, violets, borage, and gladiolus (remove anthers). Avoid sweet peas; parts of the plant are toxic.

For contrasting flavors, select flowers like oniony chives, spicy basil, tangy calendula, or peppery nasturtiums. Here's an interesting tidbit on the vividly colored nasturtium: the lighter colors like yellow and orange are mildest. The dark scarlet will truly awaken your taste buds!

Edible flowers enhance other salads besides lettuce salad. Some options for a showy pasta or potato salad are pink chives, lavender basil, bright blue borage, or light green dill. Borage, with its mild cuke flavor, is a great addition to cucumber salad.

APPETIZERS

Edible flowers are the perfect ingredient for creating dainty, healthy snacks for teatime or anytime. Bright red bee balm and purple anise hyssop add delight to a cup of tea. Drop a few blossoms to float in a glass teapot or in individual cups. Cold drinks with floral ice are so pretty. You can freeze blossoms in ice cubes or use a 9x13-inch pan to make chunks. Violets, bee balm, anise hyssop, and borage are attractive and colorful in punch and other cold beverages.

Ice cubes with fruit and flowers

Cheese and flowers with a peppery, zingy flavor are a tasty combination. Decorate a cheese ball by pressing chive florets, borage, or basil flowers onto the outside. The wide-open blossoms of nasturtiums are perfect for serving dabs of cheese ball.

Stuffed cherry tomatoes are another quick appetizer. Slice off the top and scoop out the pulp. Fill with softened cream cheese or ricotta and top with chive florets or borage blossoms.

DESSERTS

Sweet, fruity flowers make an attractive garnish for fruit salad and gelatin molds. Blooms with honey sweetness are rose petals, lavender, rosemary, scented geraniums, and the fruity tender sages—pineapple, tangerine, and honeydew.

Violets and pansies can be candied with an egg white coating. Make sure the blossoms are clean and dry. Whip an egg white with a teaspoon of fine granulated sugar until soft peaks form, then dip the blossoms. Lay onto wax paper to dry. These can be stored in a tight container for several days. These make a sweet treat by themselves or an enchanting topper for cakes or cupcakes.

You can also use fresh edible flowers for all-natural cake decorating. By topping the cake with sweet, colorful blooms, an elegant but inexpensive look is possible without an excess of frosting. Select bright-colored, mild-flavored flowers that do not wilt easily. Press them onto a frosted cake in an artful arrangement. Pansies and Johnny-jump-ups are lovely. Others, like rose petals, lavender, chamomile, or fuchsia, provide a broad color selection.

Pansy blossom

A Dash of Warmth

FIVE HERBS AND SPICES FOR WINTERTIME

During the cold season, we're tempted to retreat into survival mode, waiting for spring. Winter's waning light slows our system and even the hardiest souls are touched with a bit of lethargy. We try to evade the snow and icicles by sticking to our warm indoor haven as much as possible. One-pot meals and steaming hot beverages become our comfort food.

You don't necessarily need a ticket to the Bahamas to escape winter's chill. A dash of warmth awaits you in the kitchen! Various herbs and spices have warming properties that rouse our hibernating taste buds and urge our heart to pump more blood to our shivering toes and fingers. Here are five of my cold-weather favorites.

BAY

Making hearty beef stew? Cooking a pot of spaghetti? Sweet, earthy bay leaf adds a full-bodied touch to tummy-warming concoctions. Because bay's flavor is not easily diminished by cooking, it is ideal for dishes that simmer for a long time. Bay leaves are broad and fleshy; glossy dark green when fresh, brittle light green when dried. They do have a distinctive taste, so use bay sparingly. A mere pinch of dried ground bay is plenty for a pot of tomato-based soup. Or you can simmer whole leaves, dried or fresh, until limp. Remove them before serving, since ingesting the sharp-edged leaves is not a good idea.

Parsley and bay leaf

Bay grows to be an attractive little bush in its native warm climates. In northern areas it can be grown in a pot and overwintered indoors near a north window. It prefers dry soil, but a frequent misting keeps the leaves shiny and beautiful, ready to enhance that pot of beefy vegetable soup.

CINNAMON

Here's a spice that creates an atmosphere. Cinnamon's sweet, intense aroma invokes warmth and caring, love and home and happiness, harvest goodness and holiday cheer. Secretly, I also detect the aroma of perpetual summer, considering the tropical lands in which this favorite spice is grown. You can enjoy its mildly stimulating, warming effects in your favorite foods.

Cinnamon's spicy sweetness pairs well with fruits. Would an apple pie be complete without a sprinkling of cinnamon? Nearly any apple cakes, breads, muffins, and crisps call for a dab of the tasty, reddish-brown powder. Apple butter and apple jelly, as well as mulled cider, are evidence of the cinnamon/apple

A DASH OF WARMTH

affinity. And, mmm, spicy pumpkin pie and pumpkin bread tantalize us with their goodness. Winter squash and sweet potatoes in various forms are also enhanced by cinnamon.

Although it is most commonly used as a baking spice (warm rolls, anyone?) cinnamon provides surprising versatility. Mix it with three parts sugar for a toast topping or a roll-in for cookies. Stick cinnamon presents a whole set of additional possibilities, including festive beverages hot or cold. I love to prop a stick into a mug of cappuccino, or if you please, coffee. Or try cinnamon tea, steeping one stick in one cup of water for 15 minutes. A stick of cinnamon makes a pretty garnish for a fruity punch.

GARLIC

Powerful, pungent garlic is among the best wintertime foods. This living bulb enriches meats and main dishes while deterring seasonal viruses. I love the convenient premeasured cloves which are easily minced and used raw in salads, condiments, and sandwich spread. When cooked for a long time, garlic's flavor will nearly disappear, so add toward the last of cooking time when making a hot dish. Garlic is great with stir-fry or meats like chicken and beef. It also enhances beans, potatoes, and rice.

Garlic and chili pepper

Roasting garlic brings out a smooth, nutty flavor. Select small- or medium-sized bulbs. Slice off a small top portion to expose the cloves and drizzle with olive oil. Wrap each bulb tightly in tinfoil and bake until tender. In our wood-fired cookstove, it takes about 30 minutes roughly at 350°F. Squeeze out the roasted pulp and serve with meats or vegetables. Or make a delicious garlic bread by spreading onto toast. A wonderful side dish.

GINGER

Will eating this golden root give you the reckless confidence of the legendary Gingerbread Man? Hardly. Yet ginger does have pleasantly stimulating properties. It promotes circulation to chilled toes and fingers and helps relieve arthritis, which is often worse in cold weather.

Tangy ginger adds a warm, satisfying touch to many foods, from chewy gingersnaps to fruity syrups. The delicious fresh root, which can be found in

Ginger root

the produce section of your local grocery, is easily chopped or grated and added to fruit salads, or sprinkled atop yogurt. Dried ground ginger is widely used for baking in breads and cookies.

For maximum benefit with the simplest preparation, make ginger tea. Tea made from fresh ginger root has the best flavor. Grate one ounce of root and simmer for ten minutes in a pint of water. Whole dried ginger is the second-best option. Pour boiling water over and let steep for five minutes, then mash the softened root with a mortar and pestle, and strain. If you don't mind a cup of tea with sediment you can simply stir ½ teaspoon of ground ginger into a cup of hot water.

PEPPER

A dash of this feisty spice will encourage circulation, aid digestion, and help control high blood pressure, warming you from the inside out. In fact, cayenne pepper, made from the tiny, red-hot chili pepper, is practically heat in a can. Add a fraction of a teaspoon to a pot of tomato-based soup or pasta sauce and increase the amount according to your taste. Cayenne (with a dash of basil flakes to moderate the heat) will dress up winter squash, beans or rice, adding welcome BTUs. Ground jalapeño is another high-temperature spice, although not quite so scorching as cayenne. Chipotle pepper, red-ripened jalapeños dried in smoke then ground, has an interesting, robust taste.

Not everyone is fond of spicy hot pepper. Milder options include paprika, which adds a pretty red color to foods and a touch of mild heat to Mexican dishes and chicken wings. Red pepper is made from larger hot peppers, not the tiny searing cayenne. Black pepper is not a true pepper, but the peppercorn fruit of a tropical vine. It is used much like other ground peppers and gives a zippy taste to meats and casseroles.

Still chilly? Try these additional warming herbs and spices: basil, cardamom, cloves, fenugreek, mustard, nutmeg, thyme, and turmeric.

Cayenne pepper

A DASH OF WARMTH

He that goeth forth and weepeth, bearing precious seed, shall doubtless come again with rejoicing, bringing his sheaves with him.

PSALM 126:6

SECTION V

A Season for Herbs

"'While the earth remaineth, seedtime and harvest, and cold and heat, and summer and winter, and day and night shall not cease'. As seasons revolve from one to the next, the herb garden continually enters phases of growth and dormancy, renewal and rest. In my own garden, each season has its own beauties and opportunities."

—*Gracia*

Herbal Harbingers of Spring

Gardeners in the North anticipate spring as soon as day length begins to increase in midwinter. At first, a few more minutes daily of the sun's feeble rays hardly seem to make a difference. Yet gradually the increasing warmth ushers in a new season. God's promise of seedtime always remains.

But wait, there's a brisk chill in the air, frost may strike for several more weeks, and most of the woody plants appear to be sleeping yet. Is spring really here? Look to various herbal harbingers—or messengers—for proof of spring. I've selected five hardy perennials that bravely emerge very early. Long before you expect to see tender green leaves, their roots absorb all available warmth. Even when the initial sprouts encounter a touch of frost, this underground energy enables these plants to thrive. If you wish to move, divide, or share root clumps of these plants, early spring is the right time.

CHIVES

Chives *(Allium schoenoprasum)* may be an oh-so-common herb, but every spring I'm thrilled to see its spiky leaves poking upward. They signal that spring is truly here! This is one of the very first plants that I can snip for kitchen use. The roots—like slim little onions—are also edible.

Soon it will also provide the earliest bursts of color in the herb garden. Both common chives and garlic chives are great ornamental plants, common chives with its round, pink globe-like flowers and the later-blooming garlic chives with neat, long-stemmed white blossoms.

HORSERADISH

Horseradish *(Amoracia rusticana)* is famous for its spicy roots. If it's not among the plants you know, consider planting some this spring. The ground or grated roots, mixed with vinegar and kept refrigerated, make a zippy spread for sandwiches, meats, and more.

Besides its popularity as a condiment, horseradish is also a common ingredient in health tonics. The penetrating fumes will open sinuses and its "heat" increases blood circulation.

Country lore recommends to dig horseradish roots in any month that has an *r* in its name. March and April are ideal for digging, and you can keep this aggressive plant in check by removing a good deal of root material. Anything left in the ground will soon send out light green leaves, ready for another growing season.

LOVAGE

Always dependable, lovage provides early spring greens that taste like celery. The first sprouts are dark green, almost purple, suitable fresh for salads or steamed as a vegetable. Lovage *(Levisticum officinalis)* rapidly grows upward into its tall, symmetrical form. A well-established clump will yield quite an amount of tender leaves and stems for spring eating, as well as plenty of leaves for summer cooking and drying.

MINT

The hardiest mints *(Mentha sp.)* also begin to grow very early, before all the frost leaves the ground. If you're impatient for the taste of fresh mint, you can hurry mint beds along by covering with cold frames. Or you can dig up a root section 4 to 6 inches long (notice the series of buds, ready to take off?) and plant it indoors in a gallon pot with potting soil. Keep evenly moist, but not wet, and you'll soon be rewarded with lush green growth. Mints such as peppermint, spearmint, chocolate, and Swiss mint grow with amazing speed in a protected environment.

FRENCH SORREL

Hardy and reliable, French sorrel *(Rumex scutatus),* sometimes called garden sorrel, is one of the best herbs to grow if you want early greens for salads and soups. It's among the very first to wake from winter dormancy. This leafy plant can be eaten all summer, but the bright green growth of early spring is most people's favorite. These first leaflets contain a toned-down form of sorrel's tart, lemony flavor, and are more tender than the mature stalks.

A Summer Agenda

When it's time to turn the calender page to June, I remark with pleasure, "Summer begins! Soon!" Warm days with a maximum of sunshine, bursting thundershowers, and every plant in the herb garden at its green growing best. Summer is busy and beautiful.

HARVEST

My favorite thing about the warmest season is the joy of harvest, which for herb gardeners means an abundance of fresh, leafy herbs and edible flowers. Try fresh, torn basil leaves on pizza, and iced chocolate mint tea in tall glasses. I can't wait to bake a loaf of herb bread with garlic bits and 'Za'atar' oregano.

Having an ample amount of garden-grown seasonings like oregano is also valuable when you're doing summer canning projects like tomato sauces, salsa, or pickles.

What combines the distinctive tastes of summer better than a picnic meal? Use fresh herbs to enrich the menu and broaden your eating horizons. Barbecue is often a key part of a picnic meal, so don't overlook sage and rosemary, which go well with a variety of meats. You can even use them as a disposable brush for the sauce. Sandwiches can be topped off with tomatoes and basil leaves, and chopped chives go well with roasted hot dogs. Don't forget to use parsley for garnish, then nibble it, too!

Next is salad. I love taco salad with lots of cilantro or lettuce salad with nasturtiums and opal basil sprigs. An herbal dip is perfect with carrot sticks and other relishes. Sour cream or plain yogurt can be flavored with dill and tarragon, or chives and thyme. Minty iced tea is always a satisfying drink for any summer meal, but if you seek a bit of adventure try combinations of lemon verbena, anise hyssop, or the spicy basils.

The tastes of summer can be preserved by drying herbs for future use. Pick herbs such as mint, savory, and basil before they produce seed heads and screen-dry the leaves. To avoid shattering seed heads such as those of dill, caraway, and cumin, it is best to pick them before they are overly ripe. Lavender flowers also keep their color best when cut just before fully opened.

Summer is also the time to think ahead and collect items for pantry and medicine cabinet. Teas including mint, catnip, and horehound will be dried, then packed into jars and clean plastic pails with tight lids. Smaller amounts of oregano, basil, and rosemary will go into shakers for seasonings. In late summer, the time will come to make our time-tested Amos Emmy salve. It's always a task to collect and prepare all the leaves and roots, but I'll enjoy the satisfaction of a tableful of tins cooling in the evening air, first a liquid amber color, then finally a tan with a tint of green and a rich medicinal herb smell.

I'll also tuck leaves and flowers into a thick, old phone book for pressing: lavender scented geraniums, rosemary tips, basil flower stalks. Next on my list is snipping dill seed heads as they turn brown, long stems intact, to make a harvest bouquet or bunch, along with Chinese lanterns and bittersweet

Gracia's Herbs

boughs—a combination I saw recently at our neighbor's house on top of an antique buffet table. Simple, but impressive.

If you're planning projects such as soap or potpourri, you might want to collect a stash of dried botanical materials. An assortment of pressed herb leaves and flowers is nice to have on hand if wintertime projects such as making cards appeal to you.

Finally, one of the simplest ways to enjoy the bounty of summer is bringing in a bouquet. A varied selection of herbs and flowers, from lacy fennel to fuzzy marjoram, blesses the eye with rich textures and colors.

MAINTAIN

With a bit of maintenance, an herb garden can have an attractive appearance all summer long. A good layer of mulch (composted leaves or other organic matter) in spring will simplify summer weed control and conserve moisture, while adding nutrients to the soil. Mulch also keeps edible plants clean, not spattered with mud after a rain shower.

A sharp pruning shears is my favorite garden maintenance tool. Clipping off old blossoms and seed stalks keeps plants looking tidy and encourages new growth. The resulting second flush of new leaves in late summer is ideal for drying, too. And by removing the fading blossoms of chives and other notorious self-growing herbs, you'll prevent unwanted reseeding.

PROPAGATE

Most times we think of spring as the proper season for starting plants. But summer, when the plants are actively growing, is the ideal time for certain techniques, like softwood cuttings and stem layering. With little more than a pruning shears or a trowel, you can enlarge your collection of semi-woody plants such as lavender and scented geraniums. For complete details consult a good propagation handbook.

Late summer is the time to sow cilantro, calendula, and other cool-weather herbs for fall gardens. You may also decide to sow perennial herbs in summer when the sun's steady warmth enhances germination in an outdoor area. Another possibility is starting a few of the most common culinary herbs in pots for an indoor windowsill garden in winter.

A SUMMER AGENDA

Fall Transitions

For the gardener, fall is a time of transition, with frost as the focal point. I'm glad the transition is gentle and gradual, because it's rather sad to see summer ebbing. Yet there's a sense of accomplishment to finish up the gardening year and tuck in for winter. Both the garden and the gardener welcome a season of rest.

COOL-WEATHER HERBS

As summer wanes and the days become shorter and nights more brisk, most perennial plants slow down their growth to harden off and conserve their energy for winter survival. Other herbs actually thrive at this time of year. Annuals such as parsley, calendula, and cilantro prefer cool spring and autumn weather. They appear lush and prime when not stressed by summer's heat. You can take advantage of the fall growing window by sowing seeds in midsummer for nice plants by fall. Or grow them in a cold frame for herbs until the snow flies and beyond.

A tender perennial like pineapple sage is well suited for long growing seasons. In our northern area, it may just be coming into bloom as frost nears. I always regret that the hummingbirds are no longer around to sip from its nectar-laden drooping red blossoms. But then I love to pluck the blossoms myself and capture the sweetness on an October day!

NEW BEGINNINGS

It seems contradictory, but fall is an ideal time for new beginnings for certain herbs. Seeds of dill and cilantro, borage and calendula can be sown wherever you want them to grow the following year. Simply toss seeds onto prepared soil prior to frost and tamp in gently. In very early spring, at the first hint of warmth and often before you can work the rest of your garden, you'll see promising little seedlings!

If you wish to have plants like thyme and mint indoors during the winter, whether in windowsill pots or larger planters, early fall is the time to lift out a section, and place it in the new container. Fall is also the time for taking cuttings of scented geraniums if you wish to keep them over for next year.

GROWING SEASON'S END

Frost is inevitable, but it usually comes with a warning. This sends me into a hurry-scurry last-chance mode. I dash around the garden at dusk, plucking leaves from basil, stevia, and other tender plants for immediate use in the kitchen. Supposedly they aren't as flavorful now as in midsummer, but I don't mind. After a frost, they'll be limp, and blackened, and done.

When frost threatens, I throw old blankets over the scented geraniums. These are sturdier and will stay green until really cold weather hits. A mild frost will not harm tender perennials such as bay or rosemary in pots, but they should soon be situated in a more protected area.

Frost is actually beneficial to perennials, since it helps harden them for winter. I like to cover lavender and thyme with a thick layer of leaf mulch for winter protection, but not until after several hard frosts. It's good for them to acclimate.

PUTTING THE GARDEN TO BED

What a satisfying feeling to clean up the garden in preparation for winter. Weeds that had been hiding among the annuals prior to frost are pulled. Old flower stalks and gangly stems get clipped and discarded. Snow, once it falls, will have a snug, blanketing effect.

L-R: Rosemary, lemon balm

Winter Herbs

Do gardeners in the North enjoy winter as much as any other season? I suspect so! Winter gives us opportunity to reflect on the past growing season, while looking forward in anticipation for the next. It's part of the rhythm of life. The perennials are asleep, covered with snowdrifts. But eventually they'll be roused out of their dormancy to face a new growing season—a fresh start. How can you, the gardener, utilize winter productively?

DREAM AND REFLECT

Experience is the best teacher, they say. Use the lessons and experiences from last summer as a springboard to plan for the future. What worked well?

Gracia's Herbs

What didn't? What do you need more of? Do you need to rearrange or perhaps eradicate certain plants? Were there weed or pest or disease issues that need prevention? You might even want to jot down your gardening successes and mistakes for future reference.

Winter is the time to dream. New plants, new things to try, new designs for the garden. Stick with familiar plants, then move on to new ones as time and space allow, constantly expanding your herbal horizons. One fun way to expand your plant collection is to build around a theme. This could be according to taste, color, shape, size, or usage. Themes can be narrow (collections of mints, basils, or lavenders) or wide (lemon-flavored plants or herbs mentioned in the Bible). Some other options are silver plants, variegated plants, butterfly and hummingbird plants, bitter herbs, pizza herbs, salve and tincture plants, night-blooming plants, colonial herbs, poetic herbs, and many more.

BROWSE THE CATALOGS

The timing is always unique, I think. Just as the coldest grip of winter descends upon us, colorful gardening catalogs arrive with their promise of next summer's bounty.

Seed and plant catalogs offer not only lots of choices, but also useful information about different plants. Many descriptions give a general idea of an herb's common uses, along with growing requirements. Although I get a number of herb catalogs, I usually order only from one or two companies. The rest are mainly for reference: pictures, charts, descriptions. I also like to stay abreast of any new varieties.

Pencil and scrap paper are a must as I check what's still in my seed box from previous years, then browse current catalogs. I jot down anything of interest for possible ordering, but usually end up crossing out an item or two (or more) from my wish list before actually filling out an order blank. After determining which seeds and plants I'll order, it's possible to make a sketch of the garden for planning purposes. Graph paper is nice, but not a must.

READ A BOOK

Long winter evenings are perfect for reading. You may read or reread a book you already have, or decide to add a profitable title to your shelf. From many herb and gardening titles I've gleaned a wealth of basic information for both culinary and medicinal uses. Plant history and lore is interesting as well.

Herb seed and plant catalogs often list herb-related books. Another catalog with lots of herb titles is Farm and Garden Bookstore.

SUBSCRIBE

Over the years, a subscription to *Herb Companion,* a colorful bimonthly magazine, has broadened my herbal horizons tremendously. This magazine is now *Mother Earth Living*. I also like the *Herb Quarterly*. Both periodicals feature a wide range of herb-related culinary and medicinal subjects by professional and amateur gardeners. Another bonus is the advertising. I've been led to good sources for dried herbs, salves, and soap-making supplies, and more. (The occasional article may have questionable healing methods or New Age philosophy. Discernment is needed.)

WINDOWSILL HERBS

Gardeners love to see green growing leaves, and this is possible in winter, too. If you have a sunny windowsill, you might grow herbs in small pots for convenient picking as you cook. Annuals such as basil and cilantro are easily started from seed. Keep uniformly warm for best germination. The plants will never grow as vigorously as they would outdoors or in a greenhouse, but even tiny leaves are worth it. Garlic greens do well.

For slower-growing perennials, like thyme, oregano, or sage, it's better to plan in advance, and start with small potted plants. This could be from a root cutting of your larger plant outdoors, or a small, new plant from an herb nursery, or seeds you sowed in midsummer.

OVERWINTERING POTTED HERBS

If you have tender herbs like rosemary, lemongrass, or bay laurel growing in pots, you will bring them indoors for winter protection. A nice side benefit is more time to observe and enjoy them, since all the other herbs lie buried beneath mulch and snow. With the proper care, these herbs often thrive indoors. Other plants like scented geraniums simply endure winter. They are merely kept alive with just enough water and kept moderately cool until spring comes once again.

Resources

BOOKS

This is the best, most inclusive place to buy books on any herb-related subject. Their catalog includes titles by all major horticultural publishers including Acres, Chelsea Green, and Storey Books.

Farm & Garden Books
0090 W 300 S, LaGrange, IN 46761
(800) 728-8860

MAGAZINES

Contact these publishers for current subscription prices.

Mother Earth Living
1503 SW 42nd Street, Topeka, KS 66609-1265
(800) 456-6018

The Herb Quarterly
PO Box 433099, Palm Coast, FL 32143-9824
(510) 668-0268

GARLIC

Filaree Farm's catalog is chock full of garlic info—an excellent reference.

A membership in the Garlic Seed Foundation includes their "regular, and not-so-regular" newsletter, *The Garlic Press*, with garlic-growing info, current research, recipes, and anecdotes.

Filaree Farm
182 Conconully Highway, Okanogan, WA 98840
(509) 422-6940
Catalog $2

Garlic Seed Foundation
Rose Valley Farm, Rose, NY 14542-0149
Membership $15

HERB SEEDS AND PLANTS

My first choice for potted herbs is Backyard Herbs and Flowers, by Leroy and Susan Yoder and family. They have many plants, seeds, and garlic available by mail or at their retail store. They'll be happy to send you a catalog!

I like the informative catalogs for Horizon Herbs and Richters. They offer both common and uncommon culinary and medicinal plants. Well-Sweep Herb Farm also has a very complete listing, including some plants available in quart-sized pots.

Harris Seeds is a great source for herb seeds and plugs for commercial growers. Johnny's Selected Seeds offers organic herb plugs and an extensive selection of herb seeds.

Backyard Herbs and Flowers

8128 Maurer Road, Apple Creek, OH 44606

Harris Seeds

355 Paul Road, Rochester, NY 14624
(800) 544-7938

Horizon Herbs LLC

PO Box 69, Williams, OR 97544
(541) 846-6704

Johnny's Selected Seeds

955 Benton Avenue, Winslow, ME 04901
(877) 564-6697

Richters

357 Highway 47, Goodwood, ON, Canada   L0C 1A0
(800) 668-4372
(905) 640-6677

Well-Sweep Herb Farm

205 Mount Bethel Road, Port Murray, NJ 07865-4147
(908) 852-5390
Catalog $3

HERBS FOR HEALTH

For a great selection of bulk herbs, salve-making supplies, essential oils, teas, and more, contact Backyard Herbs. High-quality herbal tinctures by Natural Answers may be available at your local store, or from their own catalog, NewLight Health. Mountain Rose Herbs is a source for the finest organic herbs, teas, and spices. Want to make your own herbal tinctures? Contact Walnut Creek Botanicals for a brochure listing their convenient tincture kits.

Backyard Herbs and Flowers
8128 Maurer Road, Apple Creek, OH 44606

Mountain Rose Herbs
PO Box 50220, Eugene, OR 97405
(800) 879-3337

Natural Answers/NewLight Health
670 Phillips Road, Millersburg, PA 17061
(717) 692-5100

Walnut Creek Botanicals
2325 Township Road 444, Sugarcreek, OH 44681
(330) 893-1095

For Further Reading

My favorite herb-growing references include these books:

- **The Beginner's Guide to Edible Herbs:**
  26 Herbs Everyone Should Grow & Enjoy
  (Charles W.G. Smith; Storey Publishing, 2010)
- **Growing & Using Herbs Successfully**
  (Betty E.M. Jacobs; Storey Publishing, 1976, 1981)
- **The Herb Gardener**
  (Susan McClure; Storey Publishing, 1996)
- **The Herb Book**
  (John Lust; reprinted by Dover Books, 2014)

For passionate writing on herbal cooking, plus lots of recipes, read these books:

- **Herb Mixtures & Spicy Blends**
  (Deborah L. Balmuth, ed.; Storey Publishing, 1996)
- **Herbal Vinegars**
  (Maggie Oster; Storey Publishing, 1994)

For practical medicinal how-to, I refer often to these excellent books:

- **Back Yard Pharmacy:** Weeds That Heal
  (Rachel Weaver; Share-A-Care Publications, 2013)
- **Be Your Child's Pediatrician**
  (Rachel Weaver; Share-A-Care Publications, 2013)
- **Be Your Own Doctor**
  (Rachel Weaver; Share-A-Care Publications, 2010)
- **The Green Pharmacy**
  (James A. Duke; Rodale Press, 1997)

Some of the best garlic-growing advice is found in this book:

- **Growing Great Garlic:**
  The Definitive Guide for Organic Gardeners and Small Farmers
  (R.L. Engeland; Filaree Productions, 1991)

Index

A

Allergies 55, 60, 102, 124
Aloe Vera 14
Amos Emmy Salve 177, 234
Amos Mast 177
Anise Hyssop 5, 6, 13, 19, 20, 23, 35, 40, 41, 42, 71, 168, 188, 222, 234
Anti-Inflammatory 53
Apple 7, 8, 13, 26, 37, 58, 65, 97, 98, 107, 122, 123, 126, 147, 149, 188, 208, 225
Astringent 53, 142

B

Bachelor's Buttons 219, 221
Basil 3, 5, 6, 8, 10, 17, 18, 19, 20, 23, 25, 28, 29, 30, 31, 33, 36, 37, 43, 44, 45, 46, 47, 94, 111, 113, 120, 129, 160, 164, 165, 166, 167, 168, 169, 170, 171, 172, 173, 174, 184, 188, 189, 191, 194, 195, 197, 198, 199, 201, 204, 206, 208, 210, 212, 214, 215, 216, 217, 218, 221, 222, 227, 233, 234, 237, 239, 240
Bay 152, 153, 154, 155, 168, 198, 208, 212, 225, 237, 240
Bee Balm 5, 8, 30, 36, 41, 184, 188, 222
Beeswax 177
Borage 6, 8, 12, 23, 35, 47, 48, 49, 67, 167, 168, 217, 221, 222, 237
Bouquet 31, 41, 45, 65, 77, 118, 129, 133, 145, 150, 155, 160, 167, 170, 171, 175, 198, 217, 220, 234, 235
Bread 11, 13, 30, 46, 49, 53, 66, 80, 87, 96, 126, 129, 130, 151, 161, 199, 200, 201, 202, 204, 218, 225, 226, 227, 233
Bronchitis 97, 142
Bugs 37
Burdock 69, 178, 180
Burnet 8, 12, 23, 35, 165, 168, 216, 217
Butter 46, 49, 53, 66, 80, 96, 102, 126, 133, 145, 151, 160, 161, 177, 179, 195, 199, 200, 201, 202, 203, 205, 218, 225

C

Calamus Root 185, 188, 189
Calcium 49, 65, 70, 134
Calendula 5, 14, 18, 20, 23, 35, 36, 50, 51, 52, 53, 165, 167, 168, 172, 184, 188, 219, 221, 222, 235, 236, 237
Caraway 11, 23, 30, 159, 166, 168, 172, 198, 201, 213, 234
Catnip 7, 13, 19, 20, 23, 41, 54, 55, 56, 57, 61, 168, 170, 171, 189, 234
Celery 8, 12, 73, 77, 87, 117, 118, 119, 131, 194, 197, 198, 213, 216, 217, 231
Chamomile 6, 13, 20, 23, 30, 32, 36, 41, 57, 58, 59, 60, 61, 167, 168, 169, 172, 173, 184, 188, 223
Chervil 23, 36, 197, 198, 208
Chives 6, 10, 17, 19, 20, 23, 30, 33, 36, 62, 63, 64, 65, 66, 94, 96, 160, 167, 168, 170, 194, 197, 198, 199, 203, 208, 210, 214, 216, 217, 218, 222, 231, 234, 235
Chlorophyll 44, 67, 72, 75, 134, 214
Cholesterol 15, 98
Cilantro 21, 23, 30, 35, 36, 37, 72, 74, 75, 168, 170, 191, 194, 197, 212, 213, 216, 217, 234, 235, 236, 237, 240
Cinnamon 38, 45, 148, 189, 205, 212, 225, 226
Citronella 7, 147, 149
Clogged Sinus 60, 98, 102, 124, 231
Coconut 7, 149, 159, 188
Colic 55, 87
Comfrey 14, 67, 68, 69, 70, 71, 167, 168, 177, 180
Coriander 72, 73, 74, 75, 166, 168, 189, 194, 213
Corncob 109, 185, 188, 189
Cough 14, 55, 60, 87, 88, 97, 123, 171, 181
Cucumber 6, 8, 12, 30, 47, 49, 80, 87, 155, 194, 210, 216, 217, 222
Cumin 76, 166, 168, 198, 213, 234

D

Dandelion 175, 179, 219, 221
Daylily 221
Dill 5, 6, 7, 10, 11, 17, 18, 19, 21, 23, 30, 35, 36, 37, 47, 76, 77, 78, 79, 80, 85, 86, 95, 144, 163, 166, 168, 170, 172, 194, 197, 198, 199, 201, 202, 208, 210, 216, 217, 218, 222, 234, 237
Drainage 17, 27, 28, 118, 128, 136

E

Ear Infection 60, 97
Echinacea 6, 14, 31, 81, 82, 83, 84, 87, 167, 168
Epazote 35
Essential Oil 60, 107, 109, 116, 166, 183, 184, 186, 193, 243

F

Fall 21, 42, 52, 68, 73, 74, 83, 86, 91, 92, 93, 94, 100, 103, 111, 118, 119, 128, 132, 141, 168, 176, 179, 186, 220, 235, 236, 237
Fennel 5, 6, 11, 17, 19, 20, 23, 42, 77, 78, 85, 86, 87, 166, 168, 170, 172, 188, 197, 198, 208, 214, 216, 217, 235
Feverfew 6, 23, 31, 36, 167, 168, 172, 173
Flax 6, 15
French 90, 94, 96, 104, 147, 155, 182, 195, 198
Frost 22, 23, 41, 42, 45, 48, 50, 52, 56, 63, 74, 78, 79, 83, 104, 105, 106, 111, 128, 132, 136, 140, 144, 150, 153, 157, 172, 174, 212, 213, 230, 232, 236, 237
Fuchsia 220, 223

G

Garlic 14, 46, 63, 65, 75, 80, 88, 89, 90, 91, 92, 94, 95, 96, 97, 98, 120, 129, 160, 197, 201, 208, 216, 217, 218, 226, 231, 233, 240, 241, 242, 244
Geraniums 7, 25, 35, 114, 146, 147, 148, 149, 150, 151, 168, 170, 171, 174, 184, 188, 189, 206, 223, 234, 235, 237, 240
Germination 22, 23, 30, 37, 56, 63, 78, 83, 104, 111, 132, 144, 154, 214, 235, 240
Ginger 6, 8, 61, 122, 205, 226, 227
Gingivitis 60
Gladiolus 219, 221
Goldenseal 14
Grass 2, 25, 26, 32, 62, 64, 68
Greek 10, 127, 128, 214

H

Hanging Baskets 28, 32, 33, 149
Heartburn 60
Herbal Vinegar 37, 129, 145, 207, 208, 210
Herb Garden 3, 4, 5, 6, 8, 9, 11, 12, 15, 16, 17, 18, 25, 27, 28, 30, 35, 37, 40, 41, 54, 59, 62, 64, 67, 86, 103, 111, 117, 118, 138, 139, 140, 182, 213, 216, 219, 229, 231, 233, 235
Hollyhock 184, 219
Honey 13, 30, 52, 55, 57, 60, 61, 82, 108, 110, 113, 116, 137, 151, 160, 204, 223
Horehound 41, 168, 171, 234
Horseradish 99, 100, 101, 102, 167, 168, 231
Hot Sauce 211

I

Insect Bites 108, 116, 142, 160, 171, 180
Insomnia 60
Intestinal Cramps 53

J

Jellies 44, 45, 46, 60, 113, 126, 147, 151, 225
Jewelweed 176, 179, 180, 181
John W. Keim 178

K

Ketchup 10, 94, 101, 102, 211, 212

L

Lavender 5, 6, 7, 15, 17, 20, 26, 29, 30, 31, 35, 37, 41, 44, 45, 56, 57, 62, 82, 83, 90, 103, 104, 105, 106, 107, 108, 109, 115, 127, 139, 140, 144, 148, 149, 167, 168, 170, 171, 172, 173, 182, 183, 187, 188, 189, 221, 222, 223, 234, 235, 237, 239
Lemon 7, 8, 45, 46, 56, 61, 102, 108, 109, 110, 111, 112, 113, 114, 115, 116, 133, 149, 159, 160, 184, 188, 204, 205, 206, 212, 213, 232, 239
Lemon Balm 8, 36, 111, 112, 113, 116, 166, 188, 204, 206, 238
Lemon Verbena 33, 115, 116, 165, 182, 188, 189, 204, 206, 234
Lettuce 44, 74, 87, 163, 215, 216, 217, 218, 220, 221, 222, 234
Lovage 5, 8, 11, 12, 19, 20, 23, 26, 35, 37, 117, 118, 119, 120, 145, 165, 167, 168, 170, 171, 194, 197, 198, 213, 216, 217, 231

M

Marinades 46, 65, 79, 97, 137, 142, 155, 195, 208, 210, 214
Marjoram 5, 11, 12, 20, 23, 30, 33, 129, 156, 157, 165, 168, 170, 173, 189, 197, 198, 208, 216, 217, 235
Marshmallow 87, 177, 180
Menthol 123, 124
Migraine 116, 124
Mint 5, 6, 8, 13, 17, 19, 20, 36, 41, 42, 49, 56, 61, 71, 76, 111, 112, 113, 118, 121, 122, 123, 124, 125, 126, 138, 149, 165, 166, 168, 169, 170, 171, 172, 174, 184, 188, 191, 197, 208, 216, 232, 233, 234, 237, 239
Monarda 19, 20
Mulch 5, 24, 25, 26, 27, 28, 35, 37, 68, 74, 83, 84, 91, 92, 100, 112, 115, 119, 123, 129, 132, 141, 157, 160, 166, 235, 237, 240
Mutton Tallow 177

N

Nasturtium 18, 207, 208, 219, 222, 234
Nettle 28, 181
Nigella 12, 30, 36, 170, 201

O

Okra 221
Omega-3 49

Gracia's Herbs

Onions 10, 14, 62, 65, 66, 73, 75, 80, 91, 92, 94, 96, 101, 120, 194, 197, 198, 201, 202, 210, 216, 217, 218, 231
Oregano 5, 6, 10, 11, 12, 19, 20, 23, 27, 31, 36, 41, 46, 127, 128, 129, 156, 157, 165, 166, 167, 168, 169, 170, 171, 172, 173, 191, 194, 195, 197, 198, 199, 201, 204, 208, 211, 214, 216, 217, 233, 234, 240
Orris Root 185, 188, 189

P

Pansies 52, 223
Parsley 7, 10, 11, 17, 19, 20, 23, 28, 30, 72, 73, 77, 97, 114, 120, 129, 130, 131, 132, 133, 134, 149, 158, 160, 165, 166, 167, 168, 170, 194, 197, 198, 199, 201, 204, 212, 214, 216, 217, 218, 225, 234, 236
Pennyroyal 13
Pepper 12, 13, 29, 75, 143, 145, 155, 179, 192, 195, 210, 213, 220, 222, 226, 227
Peppermint 8, 13, 19, 57, 122, 123, 124, 125, 126, 149, 232
Phosphorus 17, 53
Pizza Sauce 10, 46, 94, 211, 214
Plantain 175, 176, 177, 180
Potassium 49, 70
Potpourri 15, 45, 75, 109, 114, 116, 137, 151, 157, 165, 182, 183, 184, 185, 186, 187, 188, 235
Pregnant 87, 120, 124
Pumpkin 35, 53, 221, 226

R

Rachel Weaver 107, 244
Raised Beds 17, 27, 59
Red Clover 178, 179
Rose 7, 57, 82, 92, 106, 109, 147, 148, 149, 151, 174, 183, 184, 188, 189, 220, 221, 223
Rosemary 6, 7, 11, 12, 13, 19, 20, 24, 25, 26, 33, 35, 37, 39, 46, 129, 135, 136, 165, 168, 170, 171, 173, 182, 189, 191, 192, 194, 195, 197, 199, 208, 209, 210, 223, 234, 237, 238, 240

S

Sachets 15, 37, 75, 107, 114, 116, 157, 187
Sage 6, 7, 8, 11, 12, 15, 17, 18, 19, 20, 23, 29, 30, 31, 33, 35, 41, 61, 129, 138, 139, 140, 141, 142, 153, 165, 168, 170, 171, 172, 188, 189, 195, 197, 199, 208, 210, 214, 221, 234, 237, 240
Salsa 10, 46, 74, 75, 94, 129, 133, 165, 194, 210, 211, 212, 213, 214, 234
Salve 14, 53, 68, 69, 70, 71, 108, 165, 168, 175, 176, 177, 178, 184, 234, 239, 240, 243
Salvias 140, 220
Savory 12, 13, 23, 30, 42, 129, 143, 144, 145, 168, 170, 174, 195, 197, 199, 208, 209, 216, 217, 234
Skin Care 53, 180
Snapdragons 184, 220

Soil pH 17, 105
Sorrel 216, 217, 232
Spaghetti 46, 94, 96, 130, 195, 211, 212, 225
Spearmint 8, 13, 19, 28, 42, 113, 122, 123, 124, 125, 126, 165, 171, 184, 232
Spice 7, 36, 38, 44, 50, 51, 73, 148, 149, 151, 152, 154, 155, 170, 184, 185, 189, 193, 197, 199, 205, 212, 213, 224, 225, 226, 227, 243
Squash 52, 145, 221, 226, 227
Stevia 8, 35, 57, 116, 170, 171, 172, 237
Stress 60, 108
Summer 189, 233, 234
Sweet Annie 15, 189
Sweet Woodruff 15, 32

T

Tansy 5, 23, 26, 31, 35, 172
Tarragon 5, 8, 12, 13, 20, 26, 35, 37, 42, 113, 165, 168, 170, 171, 174, 195, 197, 198, 208, 216, 217, 234
Tea 5, 6, 8, 9, 13, 17, 19, 25, 33, 40, 41, 42, 45, 49, 53, 54, 55, 56, 57, 58, 59, 60, 61, 70, 71, 75, 84, 87, 98, 110, 113, 115, 116, 120, 121, 123, 124, 125, 126, 142, 155, 157, 167, 169, 171, 178, 179, 180, 181, 183, 198, 222, 226, 227, 233, 234, 243
Thyme 3, 5, 6, 7, 10, 11, 17, 18, 19, 20, 23, 25, 26, 27, 28, 31, 32, 33, 35, 36, 37, 46, 56, 111, 114, 115, 129, 158, 159, 160, 161, 166, 168, 170, 171, 173, 184, 188, 191, 195, 197, 198, 199, 204, 205, 207, 208, 209, 210, 214, 216, 218, 227, 234, 237, 240
Tincture 14, 53, 60, 69, 70, 71, 84, 168, 239, 243
Tomatoes 4, 10, 11, 30, 35, 46, 49, 74, 75, 78, 92, 94, 118, 120, 129, 133, 145, 194, 195, 198, 210, 211, 212, 213, 214, 217, 221, 222, 225, 227, 234
Tulips 91, 220

U

Ulcers 53, 60

V

Violet 219, 221, 222, 223

W

Wildcrafting 175, 176
Window Boxes 17, 28, 32
Winter 7, 33, 37, 42, 65, 66, 68, 74, 84, 86, 88, 89, 90, 91, 94, 95, 100, 101, 105, 106, 111, 112, 114, 115, 118, 119, 129, 130, 131, 132, 136, 141, 144, 153, 159, 160, 165, 169, 172, 179, 212, 213, 220, 224, 226, 229, 232, 235, 236, 237, 238, 239, 240
Wormwood 23, 31

Y

Yogurt 80, 102, 227, 234